Daughters Arise!

Daughters Arise!

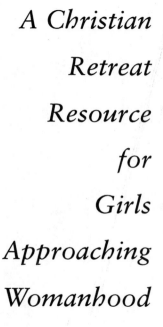

A Christian Retreat Resource for Girls Approaching Womanhood

GLORIA KOLL
DONNA HUMPHREYS
AND
SALLY WINDECKER

The Pilgrim Press
CLEVELAND

Dedication to Young Women

That night I had a dream. In the dream, my mother, eighty years old, thin bones, round body, five feet tall, stood behind me. She bent over from the waist, grabbed me by the ankles, and lifted me straight up. She placed my feet on her shoulders. I stood there above her, erect and tall, five feet off the ground.

I woke up suddenly and knew what the dream meant. We cannot model or even understand the future of a woman in the next generation. But we have it in our power to lift each young woman up, so that she can reach as high as her abilities and talents will take her.

The Pilgrim Press, 700 Prospect Avenue East, Cleveland, Ohio 44115-1100
pilgrimpress.com

Grateful acknowledgement for permission to reprint or use extensive excerpts and adaptations from the following: Laurie Y. J. Aleona, "Lifegiver, Lover of Us All," scribe Marita McDonough; copyright © 1988 Laurie Y. J. Aleona. ■ Angeles Arrien, *The Four-fold Way™: Walking the Paths of the Warrior Teacher, Healer, and Visionary*; copyright © 1993 Angeles Arrien. Used by permission of Twainhart Hill, permissions editor for the author. ■ Christina Baldwin, *Calling the Circle: The First and Future Culture*; copyright © 1994, 1998 Christina Baldwin and Bantam Books. ■ Gaielle Fleming, "Let Your Beauty Sing"; copyright © 1995 Gaielle Fleming. ■ Ralph Metzner, "Four Elements Medicine Wheel Prayer: Turtle Island West Coast"; copyright © 1987 Ralph Metzner and the Green Earth Foundation. ■ Susan Osborn, "Reunion"; copyright ©1997 SUSANSONGS ASCAP. ■ Miriam Therese Winter, "Anointing Psalm"; copyright © 1990 Medical Mission Sisters; "Circle of Love—First Spiral"; copyright © 1982 Medical Mission Sisters; and "Word-Made-Flesh"; copyright © 1982 Medical Mission Sisters. Copyright information for music reproduced in the Journey Pouch appears with each selection.

Library of Congress Cataloging-in-Publication Data

Humphreys, Donna, 1943–
    Daughters arise! : a Christian retreat resource for girls approaching womanhood / Donna Humphreys, Gloria Koll, Sally Windecker.
        p. cm.
    Includes bibliographical references.
    ISBN 0-8298-1469-8 (pbk. : alk. paper)
    1. Spiritual retreats for teenager girls—Methodist Church.   I. Koll, Gloria, 1941- II. Windecker, Sally, 1941- III. Title.

BV5068.R4 H85   2002
269'.633—dc21

2002066253

Contents

Preface

IN MEMORY OF KAREN CHRISTENSON

As new clergy are ordained, the congregation shouts the affirmation, "Worthy! Yes, worthy! Thanks be to God. . . ." But what of all those women of spirit who have died surrounded by silence or contempt? What of every daughter of God who is denied this human sound of affirmation and this roar of Holy respect?—Heather Murray Elkins, *Worshiping Women*

We consecrate *Daughters Arise! A Christian Retreat Resource for Girls Approaching Womanhood* to the life and memory of Karen Christenson, chair of the Pacific Northwest Annual Conference Commission on the Role and Status of Women, June 1998–March 2002. Karen had not yet completed her ordination before her untimely death and thus was denied this sound of holy, human affirmation for her calling. Karen was passionate in her belief that we are each called and that it is the privilege of the church to honor and nurture that call in each daughter and son. We pray that this book and its fruits will be the shout of acclamation to Karen's life, faith, and work. "Worthy! Yes, Worthy!"

HOW IT ALL STARTED

In writing *Daughters Arise!,* based on our retreats (which through the years have had several names, including "Becoming Women" and "Daughters' Journey"), we acknowledge that we are standing on the shoulders of the women and men who came before us. These have worked in a prophetic role to restore the partnership of women with men. They envisioned each fully accepted and honored, giving their gifts of leadership in equal measure, both made in God's image. We owe special tribute to a commission formed in the United Methodist Church in 1972.

Every four years, elected lay representatives from local churches, together with the clergy, gather for "holy conferencing" (as John Wesley described it) to review the structure of the church and to deliberate how to modify it so that it speaks more faithfully to the gospel and to the times in which we live. A Structure Study Commission, established to inform the 1972 General Conference, documented the "strong roles which women played in limited arenas of the local church and the appallingly low levels of participation in significant decision-making places beyond the local church."[1]

Believing that this did not speak faithfully to the gospel, the General Conference voted to create a Commission on the Status and Role of Women (COSROW) to be "advocate, catalyst, and monitor in order to encourage all structures of the church to be proactive in the inclusiveness of women at all levels of decision-making in program and policy."

Further, each regional Annual Conference was charged to form its own Commission on the Status and Role of Women, "to develop ways to foster awareness of issues, problems, and concerns of women throughout the church and to develop programs and strategies to empower women to claim responsibility for and to take leadership in the mission and ministry of the church."

The Pacific Northwest Annual Conference COSROW realized that because of the historical absence of women in leadership roles and opportunities, women had not been encouraged nor mentored in leadership. Thus, they also lacked the confidence and self-esteem necessary to prepare for and claim leadership. The members of COSROW saw this as a mandate to move beyond the foundational work of redressing inequalities of the past, to become proactive in preparing our daughters to claim their inheritance, and to work beside their brothers in Christ. COSROW members envisioned a Christian "rite of passage" as portal of blessing and anointing of young girls by the church "to encourage women to use their spirituality creatively in the total life of the church."

While the content and the design of the Daughters Arise! retreat was created by women from various churches and from each woman's own spiritual center, the impetus and articulation of need came from that visionary group of women and men (lay and clergy) serving on COSROW. We are grateful to them and we hope that we have been faithful to their vision.

PINK FLAMINGOS

It must have been the pink plastic flamingos marching across Flora's lawn, dressed that dark January evening in their winter stocking caps. It must have been then that our hunch was confirmed: This was going to be fun. For most of us, it had been decades since we'd been to a slumber party, and, teased by the flamingos, the girl inside each of us giggled out of hiding.

Joanne and Flora—both United Methodist pastors—thought that a slumber party would be a perfect way to begin planning (not your typical pastoral approach). Joanne, a mother with maturing daughters, wanted to honor—in the community of faith—their passage into womanhood. So this evening, a mutual dream of Joanne, Flora, and others serving on COSROW, had begun to create a rite of passage, a ceremony of becoming.

Snuggled in our pajamas and sleeping bags, comforted by pizza and chocolate, we began to dream together about a rite of passage retreat for our daughters and ourselves. As the talking began, we remembered the journeys we had each made, the joys and hilarities of our own passages, and the places within us not honored and unhealed, the ancient demons of insecurity and loss. Often our own passages had gone unmarked. Even if a wise woman had supported us through these times, our church had been mute, unseeing. We realized these were still tender soul wounds. Could they be blessed by this work of reclamation and celebration?

We learned in our late-night conversation that it would be a joy to conceive and birth this baby, as Joanne put it. But its gestation would be long and not without accompanying labor and birthing pains. We had our own wisdom to reclaim before we could reach out and welcome the young ones.

Donna, Suzanne, and Sally, who attended that first slumber party, belong to "Circle of Stones," a group of women writers. While our writing group named itself before learning of Judith Duerk's *Circle of Stones: Woman's Journey to Herself* (Philadelphia: Innisfree Press, 1999), the book became a dear resource for us. We named ourselves a "Circle of Stones," honoring the tradition of our faith that marks an experience with the Divine by placing a stone. We were also drawn to the biblical image that in the face of injustice, even the stones shall speak.

When it became clear as to the depth and scope this ceremony of passage would need, it came to Flora that Circle of Stones might be willing to become midwives for the ceremony. We few, who had begun among the pink flamingos, were joined by others and the first retreat was born August, 1995, on Whidbey Island, Washington.

You will learn of the continuing process as you read the rest of our story. But in all we have learned, through all of our struggles, failures, and successes, it is a joy to remember our girl-selves, slumber parties, and a few pink flamingos.

PURPOSE

With the vision of the women and men of the Commission on the Status and Role of Women (COSROW) came our increasing awareness of the plight of young women in our society. We knew of our own sense of alienation in church, in culture, in school, in the workplace and of opportunities denied or not even envisioned. But our daughters' lives were complicated by society's difficulties, by exposure to danger, violence, and complexity of choice we couldn't imagine. As two of the retreat mothers put it, "We took a long look at our creative, God-filled, exuberant nine-year-old daughters. We saw them riding the river that flows from childhood to adulthood with an alarming speed. We looked ahead and were afraid. What could we do to deflect a world that can leave our girls hollow-eyed and betrayed? *We decided we would find a way to alter the flow of the river-path our daughters traveled*, even if it meant standing in the way of the current."[2]

Of course, adolescence has never been easy. The Christian church has always tried to equip young people to resist the siren call of the world's destructive temptations. But, as clinical psychologist Mary Pipher has pointed out, girls today face a much more media-saturated, dangerously sexualized culture.[3]

A Brief History

As we women of faith began this task, we acknowledged with sadness that the Christian church has given women and girls mixed messages. The liberating news of the life and teachings of Jesus has been shrouded by millennia of hierarchy and temple patriarchy. But the welcome that *Jesus* offered

Something dramatic happens to girls in early adolescence. Just as planes and ships disappear mysteriously into the Bermuda Triangle, so do the selves of girls . . . crash and burn in a social and developmental Bermuda Triangle.

—Mary Pipher [4]

*I wanted her to experi-
ence with me how im-
portant and fun it can
be to share in and learn
about women's spiritu-
ality.*

—B.J., grandmother

women defied the cultural assumptions of his time. Women such as Mary of Magdala were his friends, supported his ministry, and were the first witnesses of his resurrection. Paul records the importance of women in the early church. Consider Phoebe, a minister of the church at Cenchreae (Rom. 16:1–2) or Luke's story of Lydia, a prosperous Macedonian woman who opened her home to Paul and Silas (Acts 16:13–15).

From the apparent full participation and authority in the earliest churches, women were soon relegated to a secondary role. It is unclear why the churches retreated from Jesus' model of equality between the sexes, but it is certain that after several centuries, women who chose a life of religious expression had few options but life in a convent. While some were sent there for lack of a dowry, perhaps others saw the walls of the convent as a bulwark against the greater confines of married life. The few voices of women's faith preserved for us, including Hildegard of Bingen and Mechthild of Magdeburg, came from the protection and relative freedom of the convent.

Even in the twentieth century, women have gained rights and recognition more slowly in the church than in the secular world, winning the right to vote in political elections earlier than in church matters. Some churches still ban women from becoming ordained or from leading worship.

In addition, much of Christianity adopted a philosophy that split asunder the wholeness of spirit and body. It saw the body as impediment to the soaring of the human spirit. Further, it distorted the message by identifying women's bodies with the "weakness of the flesh."

We yearn to hear Jesus anew and to hear the church speak clearly liberating words to our daughters and to us in our time and culture. Though inequalities within the church still persist, the message of Christ is breaking through. We hear it in the inclusion of more Bible stories about women in the lectionary. We hear it in songs, writings, and sermons of women. We hear it in the new respect many men in the church now give to the ideas and leadership of women and in the response of women who are learning to respect their own abilities and witness.

We knew we needed to reintroduce our daughters and ourselves to the authentic gospel of Jesus' accepting love. Could our work welcome and support our daughters' journeys and also reach the women who long to remain in the church or to return to it—those who find the tradition still sweet? *Within our vision for this work is the desire for the church to be present to the work of redeeming and blessing our soul wounds.*

It soon became clear that more than writing a ceremony of passage for girls-becoming-women, we wanted to create a journeying community for them and, consequently, for ourselves. We wanted space to teach, encourage, support, affirm, and celebrate these young women. We also yearned to reclaim women's ways of working and storytelling in circle—as women had always done—around a quilt, around the village well, at the birth of a child, sharing their work, stories, and wisdom. We wanted to recover our faith's feminine voice, unearthing its message, not only for our own and our daughters' blessing, but for the church's own redemption and rebirth.

Reflecting on our lives, we became convinced that the choices a woman makes out of respect for her inner knowing could be both wise and liberating. Rather than being an object for someone else's demands, women— younger or older—can become the subject of their own stories,[6] certain of Jesus' welcome and confident that the Spirit will call forth gifts God has placed within.

We began knowing little, but in faith taking each step as we felt led. We created a bowl for the living water, and grace filled it to overflowing. Our prayer is the same for you as you begin your retreat planning.

THE WRITERS

At the debriefing meeting after our fourth Daughters Arise! retreat, someone asked, "Who is going to write a book about this so we can share with other women and girls what we've experienced?" After a short pause, three of us, Donna, Gloria, and Sally, raised our hands.

Although each of us had written for our writers' group, Circle of Stones, and for other publications, none of us had attempted collaborative writing before. We began a writing schedule that evolved into a pattern. Each one would take a portion of our proposed index and write on her selected topic. We drew on discussions, writings, and experiences of the planners and participants in the Daughters Arise! retreat. The writer made three copies of her draft and read it aloud to the others as they read silently from a printed page. We made suggestions to each other. Then, we went home to rewrite. Twice a week, we met to read and revise each other's work. When a piece finally sounded right, we awarded the final copy a pink paper clip while we cheered and applauded.

So this guidebook is indeed a collaborative effort. The "we" of our text is the blended voice of the three of us. We have tried to alert the reader when some part of the text contains specifically the story or thoughts of just one. Any such separation became more difficult as our writing sessions proceeded through weeks and months. As one of us recently said (and we forget which one), "I open my mouth, and your words come out!"

PLANNERS AND PRESENTERS

In the text of the guidebook, we use the first names of those who shaped and presented portions of our retreat. To introduce them in a more complete way, we list them here with some of the pieces they worked to create and present.

AMY WALKER: Girls' passage ceremony, Warrior/Leader archetype, drama

AMY WINDECKER: Dance, movement, crafts

BESS WINDECKER NELSON: Tipi Time facilitator

CLAUDIA WALKER: Harp, songs, Journey Walk Ceremony, the Four-fold Way

Above all, I developed a better relationship with my niece. We learned to share, laugh, and cry together.

—Linda, aunt

DANA CONSUELO SMITH: Tipi Time facilitator, Warrior/Leader archetype

DONNA HUMPHREYS: Healer archetype, midrash

GLORIA KOLL: Importance of names, midrash

JOANNE COLEMAN CAMPBELL: Teacher archetype, midrash, building altar

KAREN DAVISON: Guitar, campfire songs

KITTY ADAMS: Our own stories, Teacher archetype, crafts

LINDA WHITE WADSWORTH: Midrash, campfire story reader, singer

MAUREEN ROWLEY: Meaning of pouches, Warrior/Leader archetype, Journey Walk

PAULA PUGH: Food coordinator, mind-body connection

PEGGY RUDOLPH: Schedule organizer, Tipi Time facilitator, campfire games

SALLY WINDECKER: Host, midrash, wise grandmother crone, building circle and altar

SUZANNE SCHLICKE: Visionary archetype, girls' passage ceremony, crafts

WE GIVE THANKS

For editors. We are indebted to six talented and perceptive women who met with us in editing sessions over several days. Our thanks to Christina Baldwin, Marsha Base, Marcia Erickson Bates, Joanne Coleman Campbell, Karen Christenson, and Maggie Shelton. They brought keen eyes and encouraging spirits to our project. Their professional strengths in writing and publishing, as well as their experience in church, spiritual, and family life, helped immeasurably as they gave generously of their time to make this guidebook clear and useful.

For contributors. Our special thanks go to Suzanne Schlicke, for her magical illustrations, and to Claudia Walker for compiling our music resource section in the Journey Pouch and for contributing many of her own compositions.

We give thanks as well to contributors from the Circle of Stones writing group; to women who planned and presented our retreats; to the Commission on the Status and Role of Women of the United Methodist Church; and to Bill, Bill, and Bob, our husbands, who have grown in faith with us, for their encouragement and help in this project; and to our seven adult children—Amy, Bess, Clif, Eirian, Evan, Karen, and Rob—who continue to teach and inspire us.

For the work of others. The following books were foundational in the development of our retreats:

The Bible—references are from the *New Revised Standard Version* except as noted.

Angeles Arrien, *The Four-fold Way™: Walking the Paths of the Warrior, Teacher, Healer, and Visionary* (San Francisco: HarperSanFrancisco, 1993).

Christina Baldwin, *Calling the Circle: The First and Future Culture* (Newberg, Ore.: Swan, Raven & Co., 1994).

Clarissa Pinkola Estés, *Women Who Run with the Wolves: Myths and Stories of the Wild Woman Archetype* (New York: Ballantine Books, 1992).

Mary Pipher, *Reviving Ophelia: Saving the Selves of Adolescent Girls* (New York: Ballantine Books, 1995).

OTHER CONTRIBUTORS

Kind and generous permission has been granted by the following authors to reprint these original contributions from *The Daughters' Journey:*

Kitty Adams: "The Young Girl Within," page 133; "Reflections on the Story of the Bleeding Woman," page 157; "The Way of the Visionary 2," page 184; "The Way of the Teacher," page 186; "Losing Connection," page 197; and sidebar quotes and photographs interspersed throughout without attribution.

Karen Anderson: "Walk at Ebey's Landing," page 192.

Annette Andrews Lux (compiler): "Gospel Passages about Women," page 173.

Paula Pugh: "Our Mind, Body, Health, Wisdom Connection," page 195.

Maureen Rowley: "Tipi Prayer," page 170; "Cortez Island," page 171; and "Pouches and Power," page 193.

Suzanne Schlicke: "The Way of the Visionary 1," page 183; and original artwork and illustrations.

Dana Consuelo Smith: "The Way of the Warrior/Leader," page 178.

Linda White Wadsworth: "The Way of the Warrior/Leader," page 179; "Midrash of Mary Magdalene," page 146.

Claudia Walker: "Overview of the Weekend" (with Donna Humphreys), page 123; "Why We Use These Resources," page 125; "Introduction Ceremony to the Four-fold Way," page 175; the compilation and annotation of the "Music Resources," page 201.

Amy Windecker: "Making Masks," page 189; photographs of the demonstration of "Sun Salutation," page 53.

Using this Guidebook

Creating a retreat for girls and women is joyful work. But it is work! We offer you in our *Daughters Arise!* guidebook what we have learned during five summers of presenting our retreat. Here are a few clues about using this guidebook.

TWO MAIN SECTIONS

SECTION ONE

Leading you through our planning process and into the retreat itself are these major parts:

- Preparing the Planners
- Essential Elements
- Weaving the Parts Together: Integrative Vision
- What We Learned: Experience as Teacher

Look for the "pouch" symbol which will refer you to the Journey Pouch section of the guidebook.

SECTION TWO: JOURNEY POUCH

- Practicalities and Program Resources

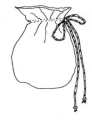

Here you will find a collection of menus, invitations, songs, stories, and ceremonies. We have listed supplies used in our retreats that we think will be helpful to you. Some ideas and examples will be useful just as they are; others will spark activities of your own creation. At the end of this section, you will find a list of inspiring and helpful books and articles.

We encourage you to live through the process of creating a retreat by moving through the guidebook from beginning to end. Preparing yourselves as planners, understanding the essential elements, and seeing how the parts fit together will ready you for the nitty-gritty practicality of the Journey Pouch collection. In the words of poet Harriet Kofalk:

> first
> I taste the morning light
> with which to create
> food for my soul
> then I can cook.[1]

Using the Daughters Arise! Journal

Daughters Arise! A Journal for Girls Approaching Womanhood is available from The Pilgrim Press and is designed to spark writing and drawing and will be a companion for each girl and woman during the retreat, as well as a book of thoughts, feelings, and memories for her to take home.

Quotations on the journal pages may elicit a direct response or may generate topics waiting within the artist or writer. As in Circle times, journaling may raise difficult questions and responses. We refer you to "A Practice of Circle: Our Check-in Time," page 130 and, beginning on page 76, "Be Prepared with Safety Resources."

The quotations in the journal correspond to many facets of the *Daughters Arise!* guidebook. As you plan your retreat, the following guidebook page references may be helpful:

Section One

Preparing the Planners

Circle Is the Heart:
First Catch Your Peacock . . .

. . . is the title of a medieval Welsh cookbook. Bobby Freeman, the author of its 1980 reprint, dedicates the collection, "For my Daughters, Orphans of the Kitchen," for it harkens back to a time of basics long since lost to memory or "orphaned" by supermarkets and processed and fast food. Those medieval foremothers didn't assume or omit any basic step. To prepare the family recipe for roast peacock, they began, "first catch your peacock!"[1]

BASIC RECIPE FOR HOMEMADE COMING-OF-AGE RETREAT

Throughout this guidebook, we use a capital "C" in "Circle" when we refer to an intentional gathering, following the guide-lines and expectations of Circle that we describe here. Circle with a small "c" is just an arrangement of bodies or other objects in a circular pattern.

Our guidebook for preparing a Daughters Arise! coming-of-age retreat is like a recipe book. As with any recipe, we give you our basic version expecting that you will, in time, add ingredients and spices for variety and your own unique flavor. Our emphasis on "basics" may, at times, surprise or amuse you. But many of you have tried treasured family recipes only to discover that some critical ingredient or step in the process has been omitted in the retelling—maybe about something as basic as the container (what was that about a copper bowl for increased volume while beating egg whites?). Like the medieval Welsh cookbook, **we are reaching back to elemental basics**, some forgotten in our contemporary culture. And we do **begin with the importance of the container.**

THE CONTAINER OF THE SACRED

Find a container large enough and strong enough to mix well all the ingredients. The secret of our successful recipe is not an ingredient, but it is the container

- large enough to hold all our dreams and visions for our daughters
- large enough to hold all our own fears, unshed tears, past grief, and regrets
- large enough to hold the vintage wine of our ancestors' journeys with God
- large enough to hold our interaction with the past, the present, and the future
- large enough to hold the new fermentation of the Holy Spirit within us and within our daughters.

Circle is the container large enough.

    Circle is the container of the possible.

        Circle is the heart of the Daughters Arise! retreat

NEW WINESKINS

We found that two scriptural metaphors were helpful in understanding Circle as a container, as well as a way of being together. The parable of "New Wine and Old Wineskins" told by Jesus is recorded in both Matthew and Luke.

> Neither is new wine put into old wineskins; otherwise, the skins burst, and the wine is spilled, and the skins are destroyed; but new wine is put into fresh wineskins, and so both are preserved. —Matthew 9:17

The wine was considered the spirit of the revelation of God at work (at ferment) in the people, and the wineskin the vessel of teaching, ritual, and creeds. These contain what has been understood about the Spirit—a container to preserve the wine and share it with others.[2] Using this interpretation, Circle can be seen as a vessel, a container, for teaching and for ritual.

Taking the metaphor a step further, we might consider Circle as the chalice that brings the wine to our lips and we become the wineskins. We are thus "strong, supple, subtle creatures"[3] to carry and share the wine of the Spirit of God. We, then, containers of the sacred, come together to become the Body of Christ on earth, a larger vessel to contain the sacred.

ONE BODY, MANY GIFTS

The second scriptural metaphor is the Body of Christ. Circle is the way of being together to understand and learn the paradox of different—but equally important—parts making one whole unit or body. As Christians, we are familiar with this concept. Indeed, the entire twelfth chapter of 1 Corinthians is devoted to explaining this concept, though we have not formed our institutions or our ways of working together (our group process) on it. **It was, and still is, a new vision of leadership,** rejecting the model of one strong leader who has subject followers. In the new vision, we learn that each member is a strong leader among other strong leaders in order to incarnate the body of Christ,

> For just as the body is one and has many members, and all the members of the body, though many, are one body, so it is with Christ. For in the one Spirit we were all baptized into one body. . . . —1 Corinthians 12:12–13

> The eye cannot say to the hand, "I have no need of you," nor again the head to the feet, "I have no need of you."—Verse 21

> But God has so arranged the body, giving the greater honor to the inferior member, that there may be no dissention within the body, but the members may have the same care for one another. If one member suffers, all suffer together with it; if one member is honored, all rejoice together with it. Now you are the body of Christ and individually members of it.—Verses 24b–27

Now there are varieties of gifts, but the same Spirit; and there are varieties of services, but the same Lord; and there are varieties of activities, but it is the same God who activates all of them in everyone. To each is given the manifestation of the Spirit for the common good. —Verses 4–7

What this last verse means is that the body of Christ is not complete until **each one is heard, each one is invited** to give his or her gift—not just those who fit the cultural definition of "leader" or "talented" or "gifted." **It takes all the parts of the body to make a whole body!** Together, we are the container for the Holy. Thus, the true container is the deeper Mystery in which we are all held. Circle is the embodied form of the Mystery—the form in which we can best see the body, the community.

LEARNING HOW WE BECOME THE CONTAINER

You may well say, "I know how to work in a circle. I've been in a reading circle or a quilting circle," or "I've served on a committee that used a team approach to planning," or "We use quality circles at work."

But, reflect on the experiences. You may recall discussion, debate, persuasion, perhaps use of *Robert's Rules of Order*, a majority vote, maybe even consensus; then electing a leader, delegating tasks, reporting back to a main official body. Nothing is overtly wrong with that. It gets the job done or, rather, gets the job done in a certain way.

In our planning group, we considered our own experiences and began to compare our observations. Wasn't there a persistent pattern to the skills and ways of expression labeled as those belonging to "leader?" Wasn't there a persistent pattern to those skills and ways of expression belonging to "helpers or followers?" We asked, "What might we be missing?"

It was not enough to *say* that we wanted to have mutuality in planning and a nonhierarchical mode of leadership. Those of us who expressed ourselves verbally and who were extroverted had no trouble jumping right in and contributing ideas. Those of us who expressed ourselves in writing or art or dance, or those who were more introverted, listened with enthusiasm and support. Even though we might be *sitting* in a circle, it didn't take a heartbeat to realize that if we continued in the same understanding and process of leader and helper to which we were accustomed, we would simply re-create the form people had been living with for centuries, although the labels might be different. What if we took scripture seriously and believed we could give valuable contributions without trying to be like someone else?

As Kitty, one of our shyer members, reminded us, **"Just because someone is silent doesn't mean they don't have something to say."** Learning to invite and wait in the silence is not the norm. Gloria related her experience of how she used to lead a class: "After expounding my own idea or opinion, I'd ask for feedback. But after half a minute of silence, I'd think, 'I guess they would rather hear me speak, so I'll go on.' Now I know that quiet people need a time of silence to gather their thoughts and courage, and sometimes a personal invitation, before they speak."

The largest gift of the retreat was that it became an experience of the Body of Christ . . . not as metaphor or analogy, but as literal truth.

—Sally, mother

JESUS' MODEL OF TABLE FELLOWSHIP

So, how do we live out this new vision? Think of the many times in the gospels when Jesus teaches the disciples around a table at mealtime. In the center are the bread and wine that sustain each one. Recall how many parables and stories focus on meals. Remember whom Christ eats with and invites. **The table fellowship Christ models is a Circle of people willing to be equals to each other**—even servants to each other—willing to be a Circle of the unexpected by forgoing the usual cultural definitions of who is worthy and who deserves the "better place."

Calling ourselves into Circle is to intentionally establish context and expectation for our relating. It begins with acknowledging that **the same Spirit is in the center of our Circle** and that is what we rely on to guide us, each one and together. Sally comments, "In the Circle, God (Holy Spirit, the Divine) is present at our center. Our vision of each other passes through the center, through what is holy. No one is any closer to the center than anyone else, and no one sits alone."

See the Journey Pouch, "Creating Circle," page 127.

A CONTEMPORARY INTERPRETATION OF HOW TO USE THE PROCESS OF CIRCLE

We are deeply indebted to the pioneering work of Christina Baldwin for researching and articulating a contemporary context and guide for this process of Circle. The Circle guidelines that we use in our writing group and in our Daughters Arise! planning are directly adapted, with permission and blessing, from Baldwin's book, *Calling the Circle,* and the facilitator's workbook called *A Guide to PeerSpirit Circling,* by Baldwin and Ann Linnea. **We strongly urge you to begin by reading this book** and the accompanying user's guide, because it takes intentional commitment to unlearn the several thousand years of Western civilization's hierarchical form of organization and leadership that has excluded so many, especially women. From Baldwin:

> The circle is an organizational structure that locates leadership around the rim and provides an inclusive means for consulting, delegating tasks, acknowledging the importance of people, and honoring the spiritual. Circle is a useful structure for learning, governing, creating community, providing services, envisioning, and stating long-range goals.[4]

PRINCIPLES OF CIRCLE

As Baldwin acknowledges, the process of Circle is not new:

> In ancestral times, the circle flourished as the primary social structure in richly diverse pockets of human community. We see the remnants of circle-based culture in archaeological discoveries and among remaining indigenous peoples around the globe.[5]

A participant asked psychologist and author M. Scott Peck what he considered to be the most significant source of social change in the twentieth century. He replied, without hesitation, "Alcoholics Anonymous, because it introduced the idea that people could help themselves." From the onset, AA's founders assumed that a circle of peers was the only form of counsel that could help them (alcoholics) abstain.[6]

Baldwin summarizes the process of Circle into **three practical principles:**

1. Rotating Leadership
2. Sharing Responsibility
3. Relying on Spirit[7]

We need to name and agree on the structure of these ways of interacting. This new way will enable us to create a more wholesome context for our daughters.

1. ROTATING LEADERSHIP

In circle, there is a "**shift in focus** from one 'leader' having innate ability, dispensing wisdom or power, to the focus of each having ability and sharing wisdom and power."

Sally Windecker describes that in Circle, leadership is fluid—it rises or wanes in each of us according to need, according to gift. All gifts are used by the Circle in its workings, each in its own season. Like leadership, responsibility is shared by all. (See page 129.)

2. SHARED RESPONSIBILITY

Baldwin says here that "Each person pays attention to what needs doing or saying next and participates in doing their share."

We asked the others in the planning Circle to say how they understood this process of shared responsibility. Kitty replied, "The center is like a combination communion table and a potluck sharing table. You bring what you have to give, and you take what you need." The mystery is that, together, through the Spirit, all needs can be met; my seemingly small gift may be just what another needs. In this giving and receiving, we know that power is in us, not external to us and we know that **we incarnate—bring to reality—the body of Christ.**

3. RELIANCE ON SPIRIT

Remembering that **there is a sacred center** around which we gather and through which we see each other reminds us to give respect to that higher power and to each other, to monitor ourselves, our emotions, our motives and expression, and to bring our highest intention to the content and process of our work together.[8]

If one member suffers, all suffer together with it; if one member is honored, all rejoice together.
—1 Corinthians 12:26

A REMEMBERING OF WHO AND WHOSE WE ARE

For Christians, the process and form of Circle is much more than an effective organizational tool. It is remembering who and whose we are. It is tremendous reclamation work of the new vision, the new wineskin. The early church was a Circle gathered at someone's home. In that genesis time, women's voices were heard; women's leadership and gifts were acknowledged. Learning to be in Circle is a return to home, wholeness, and the honoring of each member of the body of Christ. It will only be through honoring and inviting forth the voices that have long been silent that we will know fully what has been lost. Through this restoring and this "remembering," we will again make whole the Body of Christ. Specifically, it is how we, the church, will strengthen the selves and souls of adolescent girls.

What a healing thing it is to walk into a Circle of people expressing what I needed to hear.
Peggy, grandmother

How We Do It . . .

Circle Guidelines

Speak only when you are led to speak. It is the invitation and intention of the Circle that all shall be heard. But remember also that silence is a gift to the Circle and that some of us need silence before being able to speak. Silence is not empty; it is holy.

When you speak, imagine that you are laying some sacred part of yourself on the altar in the center; you are **giving of yourself in sacred trust.** When someone else speaks, honor the same for her.

Whoever is speaking has everyone's attention. An equal gift to the Circle is the loving, attentive receiving of others' gifts and offerings.

Speak not in reaction to someone else, but for yourself, from your own heart. **Speak your own truth:** Your feelings are valid.

Try to speak succinctly, without rambling, honoring the time so that others may speak.

Intend in your speaking and in your listening **that love will be known,** that your truth will be told in love, and that the realm of God will be made manifest within us.

USING A TALKING PIECE

On the altar, there is often a talking piece. Respectful of our Native American sisters and brothers, we borrow their custom of having a symbol that indicates a member of the Circle who is speaking and has our full attention. As the talking piece (any mutually acceptable object—a rock, a feather, a stick . . .) is passed around the Circle, each person who receives it has the opportunity to speak or not to speak and then passes it on. Using a talking piece is a process that invites each voice into the Circle, reminding us that all parts of the Body of Christ will be heard.

THE KEEPER OF CIRCLE

See Christina Baldwin, *Calling the Circle*, chapter 6, "The First Gathering" (66–76), for a deeper discussion.

Also in the center is a bell. It can be rung by anyone in the Circle or by a designated **Keeper of Circle** when we have lost continuity, when we have forgotten our center, or when something simply needs to be received in a few moments of quiet. The sound of the bell silences us and calls us back to center, to our highest selves.

The Keeper of Circle, sometimes called "Guardian of Circle," is one who, for that meeting will keep a sort of "third eye" over the workings of the Circle. She will watch to see when we, as a group, have strayed from Circle principles. The Keeper may notice someone in distress or who needs to share joy or who has forgotten the ways of Circle. She may simply ring the bell and we all fall silent. She may speak of what she has noticed or, after a few moments of silence, ring the bell again for the Circle to proceed. The Keeper can be anyone in Circle who feels willing and able; the responsibility can be shared among all from time to time. Learning to be together in Circle is a long and deepening process, and, as in life, we try to get better with practice. Whoever has the role of Keeper, for any meeting, has the responsibility to oversee and to hold us to the best we are and to the best we know of Circle.

CIRCLE IS THE HEART:
Reclaiming Who and Whose We Are

I am convinced that the shape of the soul is a circle. Circles have been important, even sacred, in human experience since people first gathered around a fire to warm themselves against strange and cold nights. Circles lie deep within what makes us human, within our traditions. A circle is as ancient as the shape of our solar system and as new as the shiny gold bands on newlyweds' fingers.

The Circle is the foundation of creation, the loving shape of the birthing God, the force of sustenance. All that is whole mirrors the Circle's shape; it is the shape of the universe, the atom, and the soul. Light is the center drawn from the chaos by the power of love—love inherent, love incarnate. Circle is the shape of covenant and promise, of a hug and a halo. It is the shape of all that is holy. Coming into Circle is coming home—to the locus of our birth and to the promise of rebirth. It is the bowl of baptism and benediction. We must remember it well, and give in to its love for the being of the realm of God.

Sally Windecker

See full text in the Journey Pouch, page 129.

We are making space for each other to come forth, by listening to our stories, by expressing our uniqueness and creativity through crafts, in mystery. By taking time and carefully holding, we remember who we are and recognize ourselves in each other's voice. Like the biblical women, we are the Witnesses to Life.

—Kitty, mother

Learning to Be in Circle:
Soul Retreats and
Head Workshops

In our several conference-wide planning sessions, the women confessed that they hardly knew how to plan a rite of passage for their daughters since many of them could not claim a point where they recognized and celebrated that passage for themselves. They had wandered into womanhood believing that they would become mature women by fulfilling the expectations of what our society said women should do. Many realized that they had followed the exterior model at the cost of losing their authentic self. Pastor Joanne observed, "We do not know our own stories well enough to provide the context . . . [for a rite of passage]."

We had learned early in our planning that if we only talked about ideas or activities for the retreat, we seldom got out of our heads; we forever intellectualized about concepts. We were also learning from our Circle of Stones writing group the power of writing about a feeling or experience, then reading it aloud in the loving witness of friends. When we wrote about a feeling or an experience that we had carefully sealed away in memory—whether to censor or to protect—we found that the emotional sensation of the event was still intact and vivid. We were surprised by the authenticity and honesty of feeling and, therefore, insight. The Circle of loving friends supported our exploration and gave us the courage to choose healing and growth.

As we learn to honor one another through Circle principles and to call ourselves to our highest intention, acknowledging the Holy Spirit in our center, we create safety for each of us to journey deep within to find the Holy Spirit at our individual center. How we deal with that meeting, and call upon it to lead us into new life, takes practice and new forms of expression.

From this knowledge, Joanne envisioned a twofold process to go about the planning. It would necessitate creating a setting with content and experience that would draw us into the intuitive places of ourselves, away from rote responses. We would explore ancient myths of passage and initiation. We would look at scripture with new eyes. It would require an openness to sealed memories of our own adolescence and early womanhood in a fresh encounter with the Holy Spirit. This authentic realization could lead us to recognize and articulate the essential elements needed for the rite of passage retreat. This first phase Joanne termed a "soul retreat."

The second phase would be a "head workshop" where we would talk about what we had experienced and felt at the "soul retreat." We would explore how it related to biblical stories, to our own spiritual journeys, to cultural and personal myths and symbolism. We would talk about

Quite suddenly—a FLOOD of memories—which one shall I choose? How much time am I given? I am energized—a little nervous about revealing. But oh, I feel so connected to the women here . . . hearing their stories, feeling permission to BE and being accepted for that. In reflection, much later, this has been restoring. A broken link has been mended, connecting childhood values to what I need in the present to help me stay centered.
—Peggy, grandmother

how to claim the stories for our own, how to create the stories . . . a "how-to" session.

SOME OF OUR BEGINNING SOUL RETREAT ACTIVITIES

Our first soul retreat began with reading aloud "The Ugly Duckling" from the Clarissa Pinkola Estés book, *Women Who Run with the Wolves*.[9] We wrote silently for ten minutes in our journals before sharing our own memories and feelings of looking for our own kind of "ugly duckling." We knew that we wanted to enable our daughters to develop the certitude, patience, and endurance to become the "swans" they were created to become.

Another pivotal soul retreat was the winter evening when Joanne presented a dramatic portrayal of the Canaanite woman who comes to ask Jesus to heal her daughter (Mark 7:24–30; Matt. 15:21–28). In the soft firelight that evening, we saw and heard the Canaanite woman's conversation with Jesus. We tasted the woman's anxiety and felt her love. That woman who loved her daughter so much, desired her healing so much—that woman who was considered an outcast and unworthy by her culture—that woman was willing to risk asking for what her daughter needed for health and life. What barriers might we cross on behalf of our daughters? What might we risk asking? How might we encourage our daughters to ask for themselves?

One Friday soul retreat, we were introduced to the writings of a Circle of women like ourselves, from the collection of *Anthology/Collected and Presented by Zimbabwe Women Writers*.[10] We accompanied Shingirirai, worried and distracted about her sixth-grade class assignment, when she wandered off her usual path. She found herself welcomed by a baobab tree into "The Secret Cave," where Mbuya Nehanda, the grandmother of Shingirirai's grandmother, awaited her. The story helped us ask, "What is the fire we are building to give courage to our daughters? What music and dance are we teaching? What water do we give to refresh their souls? What stories do we tell to nourish them so that they know, 'You are the new Spirit'"?

We have mentioned only a few of our resources for soul retreats. You will find more in the Journey Pouch; and you will discover more from those in your planning Circle. The richer the diversity of your participants, especially diversity of ethnic heritage and styles of learning, the richer will be your pool of resources.

What we gained from this twofold process was the awareness that we were not just planning for a retreat; we were preparing ourselves to inhabit the retreat as a journey for ourselves. We were not just talking about Circle as a process, we were deepening ourselves as Circle to become the container. For those of you who contemplate planning this retreat, this is also your journey.

How We Do It . . .

Soul Retreats and Head Workshops

We scheduled an overnight stay at a planner's home, beginning Friday after work through 2 p.m. Saturday. We agreed to share leadership responsibilities for the activities listed. Here's what we suggest to you:

Friday. Gather early in the evening for a simple supper together. Then, gather in Circle. In the center, spread a decorative cloth on the floor or on a low table.

- Start with a centering devotion, prayer, or song.
- Invite each one to become present as she shares about an object she places on the altar.
- Light a candle.
- Present a soul activity (see suggestions on page 13).
- Silently transcribe responses in your journals.
- Using Circle guidelines, share responses and ideas evoked.
- From the themes that have emerged, share suggestions to dream on that night for Saturday morning discussions.
- Lead a goodnight blessing.

Saturday. Gather for a fix-your-own breakfast.

- Lead body-awakening meditation (see "Sun Salutation," page 53).
- Relight altar candle; share dreams, if any.
- Invite someone to act as scribe.
- Discuss experiences elicited by soul activity with their possible application for retreat.
- Brainstorm activities, related crafts, songs, scripture, and stories.
- Build agenda together; if it needs adjusting, agree on a new closing time.

(Grazing lunch at table as discussion continues.)

- Request volunteers for detail planning, logistics, and materials needed to create the activity, craft, story, and so on, as each would happen at the retreat.
- This small group would meet before the next soul retreat/head workshop to do the planning and prepare to present the activity at the next gathering for a hands-on experiential tryout.
- Schedule next soul retreat-head workshop.
- Give departing blessing, or invite each to speak a prayer to close.

Seeing Scripture with New Eyes

I liked hearing the "old stories" in a new way—and the emphasis on the strengths of these women.

—B.J., grandmother

My friend Karen listened in amazement to the story of the bent-over woman made straight and tall by Jesus' touch. "What a profound and wonderful story," she said. "I've gone to church all my life. Why have I never heard a sermon preached on this story? Why have I never heard this scripture read in church?" A pastor explained that the lectionary of many church bodies prescribes what scripture will be read each Sunday, and this story from the thirteenth chapter of Luke wasn't included in the lectionary until very recently.

Suppose women had been choosing the Bible stories to be read for congregations. Maybe, then, pastors would have talked about what pushed this woman down until she was bent in half. Congregations could have discussed the meaning of Jesus helping her to stand erect in health and wholeness. What was left out when, through the centuries, sincere and intelligent Christian men chose which scripture to study, never consulting sincere and intelligent Christian women? The retreat planners found this question so intriguing that we smiled, blinked, and began looking again at scripture—**this time through the eyes of women.**

Best of all, we now felt free to play with ideas, with words, with stories, and with worship. We began to trust our women's minds, spirits, and bodies to help us welcome the Spirit of God within and among us. We stopped relying on scriptural interpretations of authorities who saw only one right way (theirs) to view Bible stories. We began learning through our own eyes and ears, through movement and touch, through heart and gut reaction—learning from our whole bodies and with our emotions, as well as through our intellects. **Like the bent-over woman in the Gospel of Luke, we stood up.** We stopped asking permission and started interacting with Bible stories and the Spirit, using our own unique, God-given ways of understanding.

How We Do It . . .

Seeing Scripture with New Eyes

PREPARING THE PRESENTERS

To rub the scales from your own eyes, take some time to read from books on women's spirituality listed in the Journey Pouch section in the back of the guidebook. What will these writers tell you?

> We believe that God chose woman
> to be in partnership with God,
> that God chooses woman
> again and again
> to live and love as God:
> to give birth to deeper values,
> to give flesh to the Gospel,
> to touch, to heal, to listen, to care,
> to feed the multitudes
> with the daily bread of life.[11]

In Circle, focus on the Bible story of the bent-over woman (Lk. 13). Ponder this story. What weighed this woman down and bent her in half? What impact might the encounter of this woman with Jesus have on a woman reader? Would a man reading this story receive it in the same way? Why do you think this story was left out of the lectionary for so many years? Why do you think it was recently included? Retell the story as a play and take turns being the bent-over woman. Take turns being Jesus, the disciples, and the crowd. What might it feel like to be each of these?

DURING THE RETREAT

Reread the creation story from Genesis 1 and 2. Were you aware that the Bible includes two creation stories? Which one were you taught as a child? Have you seen pictures of the creation story? What did God look like? Is that how the creation story describes God? Did you know that *ruah* (the Hebrew word for the "Spirit of God moving over the waters") is a feminine noun? When you see the English translation "wind," "breath," or "spirit" of God in the Old Testament, *ruah* is the Hebrew word originally used. As someone reads the story, act it out. Use music and dance it. Make *ruah* one of the actors. Choose other Bible stories that intrigue you. Use women's eyes and creativity to see, read, act, paint, dance, or sing them.

Have several translations available for your Bible-study reading. Be aware that some versions of the Bible are paraphrases, not translations from the original languages of the Bible. One of the latest and most accurate translations is the *New Revised Standard Version,* rather than the earlier *Revised Standard Version.* Both *The HarperCollins Study Bible* and *The New Oxford Annotated Bible,* which use the *New Revised Standard Version* text, provide helpful notes about the choice of words and the historical context of Bible passages.

Seeing Creation with New Eyes

About ten years ago, our Circle of Stones writing group began meeting in Circle on a farm high above Washington's Puget Sound. Surrounded by cedar, fern, and wild rhododendron, **we beheld the natural world and found fresh understanding of our faith.** We remembered the words of Thomas Aquinas who said that sacred writings are bound in two volumes, that of creation and that of the Holy Scripture.[13]

Martin Luther echoed, "God writes the Gospel, not in the Bible alone, but also on trees, and in the flowers, and clouds and stars."[14] Wise words, indeed, from these fathers of the church.

We felt inspired to add, "Yes! And both the Bible and God's creation are understood in new, life-giving ways when viewed through women's eyes."

If understood only in the centuries-old mindset of conflict and domination, then wild and malevolent nature needs to be conquered. How much of creation has been demolished, we asked, because nature was seen as the enemy? We listened to the words of early church mother Julian of Norwich, holding a hazelnut in her hand, that it exists, both now and forever, because God loves it. **In short, Julian believed that everything owes its existence to the love of God.**[15] We devoured these nourishing berries of women's wisdom. Certainly fang and claw lurk in the forest, but women's eyes see clear details of budding and birth, of milk flowing from doe to fawn, of changing moon, tide, and womb.

We felt intimately connected with the creation. Our new insights about the natural world brought fresh visions of our Creator. Should God be spoken of only in masculine terms as our father, king, or lord? We recalled biblical allusions to feminine qualities of God: Deuteronomy 32:18, " . . . God who gave you birth"; and in Luke 13:34, Jesus' self-portrait as a hen who longed to gather her chicks under her wings. **Could God be called "she" or pictured in feminine words: mother, sister, gentle nurse, dearest grandmother?** This audacious sea breeze of thoughts whipped around in our heads.

How We Do It . . .

Seeing Creation with New Eyes

PREPARING THE PRESENTERS

Walk, stand, sit, be in nature. Make the natural world part of your life every day. Take a walk among the trees; stand and look at the sky; sit on a log and watch the waves; touch and taste a seashell; be attentive to birds, to sea life, and to land animals. Does your direct experience give you a different view of nature than you've had from books, teachers, and preachers? Does nature affect your feelings? Does it calm you, excite you, connect with the rhythms of your body?

Meditate with a part of nature. As a way of opening yourself to the Spirit, hold and intently see a leaf, rock, flower, or some other part of nature. You may find yourself more receiving of the Creator as you read and pray.

DURING THE RETREAT

Find a place surrounded by the natural world for your retreat. We hold our annual retreat on a farm. Search for a place of natural beauty near you. If you choose retreat dates during a weather-friendly time of year, you will be able to have most of your activities outside. The women and girls can feel life in the grass, leaves, water, sun, and wind as they sit, move, talk, and eat.

Meet in the darkness around a fire. Nothing stirs the ancient soul like leaping flames. Sing, tell jokes, share secrets, act out folk tales, warmed by the campfire. The fire pulls girls and women together as it makes a place of light in the dark night.

Take a block of time for a silent nature walk after introducing the main concepts (see sample schedule in the Journey Pouch, page 90). Women and girls may walk within sight of each other, but they will use this time without talk to be listening, seeing, touching, and paying close attention to nature. Some may want to carry a notebook to write down or sketch observations. Others may want to bring back a natural object to share with the group. We provided an hour and a half for walking and wandering at the beach.

Accept nature's gifts during the retreat. If an eagle flies by—or a seagull or robin—take time as a group to watch and delight in the blessing. One year, just as the Girls' Ceremony ended, a strong wind blew through the trees and across the bluff. With scarves and hair flying wildly, we celebrated by dancing with the wind.

Move your body; love your body. Use the dancers and athletes among you to gently lead movement activities to stretch bodies and minds. Look at the sky as you move. See the moods of nature, as changing as your own. Breathe in the fresh taste of trees. Your body is part of the natural world. Moving in nature quickens you. The Creator sees you and declares that your body, with the rest of creation, is good!

Perhaps there are no inherently special places, only places made special by the relationships people sustain with them. Wilderness or city, mountain or prairie, desert or swamp, forest or farmland. In this sense all places on earth are equal and identical, only waiting to be known.
—Richard Nelson[12]

The Four-fold Way: The Bones

The spirit of the Lord brought me to a valley filled with very dry bones. God told me to say to the bones, "O dry bones, hear the word of God: I will cause breath to enter you, and you shall live. I will lay sinews on you, and will cause flesh to come upon you and cover you with skin, and you shall know that I am the Lord." —Excerpted from Ezekiel 37:1–10

[They] gave me inner strength. I felt as if I used the Four-fold Ways, I could accomplish anything.

—Kathryn, mid-teen

They made me realize things about myself and gave me something to think about when making decisions.

—Danielle, mid-teen

The book, *The Four-fold Way* by Angeles Arrien, is a rich resource for the work of the Daughters Arise! retreat. Arrien draws on wisdom from many cultures to illuminate four essential elements of wholeness, four archetypes that can teach us to "live in harmony and balance with our environment and with our own inner nature."[17] The four archetypes, **Warrior/Leader, Teacher, Healer,** and **Visionary,** form a framework on which we place our work of reclamation—the bones on which we hang the flesh and sinew of our retreats. We learn the importance of choosing to be fully present to life from the Warrior/Leader. The Teacher leads us to listen, caring deeply yet relinquishing the need to control the outcome. The Healer teaches us to pay attention to what has heart and meaning. The Visionary teaches us to speak our own truth without blaming or judging.

We human beings try to understand using only our rational capacities. We neglect our spiritual and intuitive capacities for understanding. We also fail to recognize that these capacities reside not just in our brains, but in all the cells of our bodies. We need a way that leads us by experience to expand our understanding. **Jesus knew the need to connect the mind and the body.** His hearers often understood with their minds what Jesus said, but they needed also to act on it. Consider how Jesus physically engaged his followers: "Rise, pick up your bed and go home" (Mt. 9:6); "Peter, get out of the boat and come to me" (Mt. 14:28, 29 paraphrased). In our retreats, the Four-fold Way became a valuable tool to integrate what we learn in our heads with what we experience in our bodies.

While you may decide on another resource, rich in myth and metaphor, make certain it has the scope and power to make visible what has been hidden and that it helps you to see the stories of the Bible with new eyes. In addition to the wealth of the ancient traditions from which it is derived, the beauty of the Four-fold Way is its concreteness and clarity. The visual representations of inner qualities engage all our senses so that with our whole bodies we learn and respond. When **we let our imaginations run free** to speak the words of an archetype, to create costume and mask, to move our feet to different music, all of our senses are engaged. Metaphor and archetype flood our minds with images and awareness. It has been our experience that the journeys begun using the Four-fold Way are trustworthy and abundant; it is worth the stretch that it has been for us.

The Four-fold Way also adapts well to **storytelling.** It leads us into deeper understanding of stories as diverse in form, yet common in content and meaning, as *Cinderella, The Wizard of Oz*, or stories from the Bible. (You can read more about Cinderella in "Folktales, Fables, and Parables," page 65.) In Bible stories we hear:

- the voice of **the Warrior/Leader,** who knows to show up and be present to life. Consider Miriam, Moses sister. When Pharaoh's daughter found the baby Moses floating in a basket on the river, Miriam, in the face of likely personal peril, stepped forward offering to find a nurse for Moses' care (Ex. 2:1–10).

- **The Teacher,** who cares deeply but does not need to control the outcome. "Let anyone among you who is without sin be the first to throw a stone at her" (Jn. 8:7).

- **The Healer,** who pays attention to what has heart and meaning. "Leave her alone. She bought it [the perfume] so that she might keep it for the day of my burial. You always have the poor with you, but you do not always have me" (Jn. 12:7–8).

- **The Visionary,** who learns to speak the truth without blame. "Martha, Martha, you are worried and distracted by many things; there is need of only one thing. Mary has chosen the better part" (Lk. 10:41–42).

We have found many tools that support our work of reclamation. *The Four-fold Way* is one of the richest. Heeding its call, we have listened to and told stories, danced and sung the deepest songs of the soul, and sweetened the stories of the Bible with the perfume of image, metaphor, and experience. The dry bones of our spirits have come alive with joy.

So I prophesied. There was a rattling noise and the bones came together, bone to its bone. I looked and flesh had come upon them. Then God said to me, "Prophesy, mortal. Say to the breath: Come from the four winds O breath, and breathe upon these slain that they may live." I prophesied and the breath came into them and they lived, and stood on their feet, a vast multitude.

—Excerpted from Ezekiel 37:1–10

How We Do It . . .

Presentation of the Four-fold Way

PREPARING THE PRESENTERS

The first year we used the archetypes, Claudia suggested four women in the Bible who represented the main characteristics of each of the archetypes of Angeles Arrien's *The Four-fold Way: Walking the Paths of the Warrior, Teacher, Healer, and Visionary.*[16] Then we asked the planning group:

1. Did someone respond strongly to the suggested woman's story or to the archetype?
2. Which woman in our planning group might well explore, live with, and express an archetype?

Each year, we ask if new individuals wish to volunteer to present an archetype or to suggest a different woman in the Bible to characterize the archetype. Many times, this is an opportunity for exploring and developing the characteristics needed for our own spiritual journey. One year, we selected only one woman of the Bible—Mary, the mother of Jesus—to reflect how the characteristics of all the archetypes are demonstrated in one person.

The self-selected or group-nominated person is asked to prepare the presentation in a way that will:

1. **Summarize or highlight concepts** and principles from the archetype as described in Arrien's book.
2. Relate to or **interweave the archetype with the scripture story.**
3. Refer to **"shadow side"** (negative behaviors or misuse of the characteristics) of the archetype in the presentation or activity.
4. **Consider how our bodies help us learn** and facilitate living out the characteristics of the archetype.
5. **Lead a participatory activity** or a meditation stance as described in Arrien's book that would demonstrate # 4 above.
6. **Coordinate with crafts planners** for something to create or assemble that would represent each archetype and could be kept in the pouches the girls and women would be making and taking home.

We found that it took about three meetings of the Four-fold Way presenters to:

- brainstorm together and design a theme or **consistent approach**
- respond to and **give feedback** about developing presentations of each archetype
- provide **"tryout" practice** for proposed activities
  We tested the effectiveness of our activities.
- Are the **instructions** clear and understandable to a wide age range?
- Does the activity **communicate** the intended goal?
- How much **time** does it actually take?
- What **materials** and props are needed?

I feel the Four-fold Way made the messages from the scriptures come alive with new voices—the same messages with brilliant insights and inspired presentations.

—Diana, mother

DURING THE RETREAT

The second year of our retreat, we introduced the archetypes of the Four-fold Way by using a ceremony written by Claudia.

That year, we also represented the "Wise Grandmother Crone." This character-archetype is not one described in the Four-fold Way, but is a character so familiar and frequent in fairy tales and myths as the wise-woman mentor for developing one's intuitive nature, that we chose to add her. It was this Wise Grandmother who introduced the archetypes dressed in simple costumes and holding papier-mâché masks. One of our planners created the masks we use, but they could be much simpler or created anew each year by the girls.

To enliven and connect body, mind, and spirit, the ceremony uses visual aides of color and costume and auditory aides of instruments and responsive reading.

For the ceremony of introduction, you will need:

See "Introduction to the Four-fold Way" on page 175.

1. **Large basket** to carry the four instruments:

> Rattle—one larger rattle for the Warrior/Leader, several smaller ones to be passed around the Circle
>
> Sticks—two percussion sticks to strike against each other, carried by the Teacher archetype
>
> Drum—round Native American drum that can be carried by Healer archetype around the Circle
>
> Bell—a slender branch with small jingle bells affixed with satin ribbon to be carried by Visionary archetype

2. Costumes. Two yards of colored cloth for each archetype and the Wise Grandmother. We have used various colors for the archetypes, but most recently we tried to match the color of the element or season in the Four-fold Way:

> Warrior/Leader—blue
>
> Teacher—red
>
> Healer—green
>
> Visionary—yellow or gold

For the costume of the Wise Grandmother we chose a multicolor cloth suggesting colors of water.

Reminders of the Four-fold Way archetypes in Circle

After the archetypes were introduced for the first time in the retreat, we used a visual and verbal reminder of their presence. We would bring the masks to the Circle each time we gathered and the facilitator for the Circle time would start by saying:

> We gather in Circle to offer what we can, and ask for what we need.
>
> While in Circle, pay attention to how we are practicing the Four-fold Way:

1. As Warriors/Leaders, we have shown up and now choose to be fully present.
2. As Teachers, we will care deeply but release the need to control outcome.
3. As Healers, we will pay attention to what has heart and meaning.
4. As Visionaries, we will speak the truth of what we feel and see without judgment or blame.

Essential Elements

Sacred Symbol and Sacred Space

"TAKE OFF YOUR SHOES . . . "

Perhaps you have had the experience of coming into a place so lovely, so solemn, that a sigh of awe escapes your lips . . . perhaps in a grove of ancient trees, a quiet cathedral, a tiny chapel in an Indian village. In those often-unexpected moments, we become aware of sacred space. **Busy, preoccupied, we stumble into the presence of God.** At church, we seem somewhat more prepared to find the Holy . . . the right place, the right day, the right clothes. But God invites us to find the Holy in all the places of creation and to mark those times and places with the symbols of our recognition and gratitude. Moses, busy with sheep tending, wandered into awareness of God's presence: "Take off your shoes, Moses, this is Holy ground" (Ex. 3:5 paraphrased). Jacob, intent on his journey to find a wife, lay down to sleep in the desert and, after encountering angels in a dream, remarked in surprise, "Surely God is in this place—and I did not know it!" (Gn. 28:16 paraphrased).

In Circle during the retreat, wherever we may be, **we seek the center first**—take off our shoes, as it were—and become ready to acknowledge and receive the Holy. We learn to slow down, breathe, and open our hearts. When we acknowledge the presence of God, we are moved to make some sign of that experience, to find a marker, a symbol to remind us. We bring reminders of God's presence and unspeakable love, collecting us around the Holy center, focusing us—mind, body, and spirit—on the task at hand. The treasures we place on the altar—gifts of ourselves, prayers and pleadings, confessions and blessings—remind us of our experiences, of God's presence and care, of the brokenness we bring for healing, and of the deepening of attachment, one to another, and all to the Holy One.

SYMBOLS MARK OUR EPIPHANIES

People of all faiths create symbols to mark the places of their Divine encounters. Jacob built an altar at the place of his awakening and called it Beth-el—house of God. As Christians, we have inherited powerful symbols and beautiful sacred spaces. **Often we take for granted the symbolic treasures of our faith,** a cup, a cross, a flame, a dove. These are windows that open our souls to God; they are the bells that arouse our spirits to remember the presence of God.

One of the blessings of Circle is that it awakens us to the larger world of sacred space and sign—**a world full of other expressions of the divine.** We are discovering not only our own private icons, symbols of our faith journeys, but other images and reminders. Madeleine L'Engle, a Christian lay theologian and writer, keeps a small laughing Buddha on her writing

I felt continually aware of the loving Spirit present in all our activities.

—B.J., grandmother

desk. She says its gentle, smiling face helps to keep her in balance, reminds her not to take herself too seriously.

Not only can we discover the signs and symbols that speak to others of faith, we can learn to find and create our own symbols of the sacred. In Circle, we can find new symbols, new icons that bespeak our unique life together.

FINDING GOD
ALL AROUND US

Symbols, **tiny doorways that open our souls to the Holy,** come from the substance of our souls and the stuff of our world. The gifts of the sacred appear wrapped in a maple leaf or sung in the sighs of trees. Contemporary society and contemporary Christianity tend to ignore, even deny, the connection between us and our own and the world's physicality.

Our faith tradition, however, is very clear about the sacred worth of the created world. We are taught to look for the footprints of the sacred in the dust of the earth. Moses was instructed to let nothing come between his feet and the holy earth. He was told to strike the rock so that living water would come forth, water that would literally and spiritually quench his people's thirst. Jesus knelt down and with his own saliva and the dust of the earth made mud. Placing it on the eyes of a blind man, Jesus restored his sight. Listen to still clearer evidence of God's precious love of all creation: "And this will be a sign unto you . . . you will find a babe" (Lk. 2:12). In the deepest way, these ancient stories teach us of the relationship between God, the creation, and us. One can say, "A rock when I'm thirsty, a star when I'm lost, mud when I can't see." As symbols of that relationship, the rock, the star, and the mud draw us into sacred space; they call us to know that the Holy is around and within, accessible, immediate.

Ceasing to relegate God to the Holy of Holies, **we find the greening heart of God all around us.** We learn and teach that what is important is not where we call God to, but where we become aware of God. When we name the intent of honoring the Holy One, we release the stiff-sided assurance of self-sufficiency, create sacred space—Circle—and become vulnerable to the inhabiting Holy.

What spoke to me during Saturday's beach walk was a small shell lying alone on a wide expanse of sand next to constantly pounding waves; a small, breakable, precious gift, somehow able to stay in one piece. She said to me: "You, too, are a precious gift, fragile yet strong enough to be whole."

—Kitty, mother

How We Do It . . .

Sacred Symbol and Sacred Space

BUILDING ALTAR

At each Daughters Arise! retreat and each time we gather in Circle, we build our altar. It becomes a symbol of our faith journey together in Circle. The altar is different each time, because each of us changes as we grow into our lives, and each retreat is different from the others: different people gather, varying gifts are honored, our needs and burdens change. The constant in our altars is a candle—symbol of the Divine Light.

The altar is built in the center of our Circle, sometimes on the ground, when we gather outside, or on a table. Sometimes we use a lovely scarf or cloth, sometimes a flower, a shell is added, almost always a rock. There might be a child's picture, an anniversary ring, a mother's Bible, a broken wing, a cross, a cup, a treasured book, a childhood doll. These things are brought to the altar, offered, and laid in the center to be cherished, honored, or held in prayer. If the Circle moves, the altar moves with it, so it is wise to consider portability if the Circle will be moving often. Some Circles that meet regularly in different places have an altar basket that follows the Circle. As the children of Israel journeyed with the Ark of the Covenant, so we journey with our symbols of faith.

During the retreat, each time the Circle reconvenes, we take a few moments to refocus on the center. Perhaps someone now has something to lay on the altar, perhaps she is now able to speak about it, or she may only silently accept our unspoken receiving of it.

As a reminder, refer to "Circle Guidelines," page 9.

It was wonderful to have the opportunity to bring pictures of other women into worship with our group.
—Cindy and Jean, mother and grandmother

Sometimes we use a **lovely scarf** or **cloth,**

sometimes a **flower,** a **shell** is added,

almost **always a rock.**

Passing Wisdom through Story

WHOSE STORY?

Sharing our stories turns out to be the best way to understand each other and to understand our own deepest self. "Whose story?" you may well ask. *Your* story, *my* story, *her* story.

All we need is a way to get started, and the stories tumble out. One of our first sharing activities starts with talk about names. What's so important about names? Our presenter Gloria tells that she carries her grandmother's name, "Karen," as a middle name and that she and her husband gave the precious family name to their daughter. Others endure a silly or negative-sounding name. Nada carried the burden of having a name that in Spanish means "nothing"! Her Scandinavian parents didn't intend that meaning, but "Nada" was not a terrific name to have growing up, as she did, in Southern California!

"So tell about your name," we invite the girls and women. "Were you named after someone? Do you like—or do you dislike—your name? Have you ever changed your name?" Clustering in groups of two or three, we tell about our first, middle, or last names. In this first storytelling, a few attentive listeners are enough audience. In each small group, the woman's or the girl's story begins to be told. It's a start.

"MY NAME IS SALLY AND I'M EIGHT YEARS OLD"

The next day, a presenter invites each one in Circle to go back in time. "Think back to when you were seven or eight or nine or ten. Where did you live? Who were your friends? What did your school look like? Where was the closest store? What did you love to do? How did you feel about yourself? Start by introducing yourself to us with the name and at the age you were then, and tell us something about the girl you 'are' back in that time."

In the silence that follows, usually another presenter will tell her story to model the way of telling: "My name is Sally Anderson. I am eight years old, and we just moved to the city from the farm I loved. I hate it here. But I do like one new friend, Ann. She likes baseball and swimming, same as me." Each story is fascinating. Some are funny. Some are heart wrenching. We cannot fix or revise anyone's personal history. We laugh with those who laugh; we weep with those who weep. (This self-discovery of grief is one reason that each girl comes to the retreat with her mother or other caring woman.) All in the Circle listen attentively and with great respect to each woman and each girl who tells her story. As always, those who choose to remain silent are equally part of the Circle.

I liked listening to people's stories of when they were children and other times.
—Holly, preteen

I love to tell the story, for those who know it best, seem hungering and thirsting to hear it like the rest. I love to tell the story . . . the old, old story, of Jesus and his love.
— old hymn

TALES OF ADOLESCENCE

At a later gathering, girls and women are invited to remember themselves as twelve, or fourteen, or seventeen. Suggest that each chooses what for her was a pivotal year. Perhaps by now, much has changed in her life. Many felt a loss of confidence during these adolescent years. As we tell our stories, women and girls come to a place of equality and understanding. Although each story is different, we all are on the same journey. The grandmother was once the girl; the girl will become the elder. We start with our own stories, and then move on to gather further wisdom from stories of history, of folktales, and the rich stories of the Bible, the essence of our faith.

How We
Do It . . . *Passing Wisdom through Story*

Stories change the hearts of both the one telling and the one listening. Women and girls can be led gently into sharing their own stories. Using this "Names" session as an example, we suggest these steps for the presenter:

1. **Invite everyone** to be seated comfortably in a Circle.

2. **Introduce the topic** in an engaging way, for example, by telling funny or warm stories about why names are important.

3. **Model the sharing** by telling something special about your first, middle, or last name.

4. **Write clear questions** on tag board or chalkboard. (Tell your first, middle, or last name; or a former name or nickname. Do you like your name? What does your name mean? Have you ever changed your name? How did that feel?) Whatever questions you decide upon, be sure everyone can see them and can hear you read them aloud.

5. **Group the women and girls** in twos or threes with people they didn't know when they arrived. (Do this at least for the first sharing session.) Set a time limit, saying, for example, "Each person will tell about her name for four minutes and then listen to others in her group."

6. **Join a group** to give a sense that you are all in this together.

7. **Call everyone back to the larger Circle** when all have had time to share.

8. **Ask for further sharing within the larger Circle.** You might ask, "What is something new that you learned just now?" After the small groups, some will have the courage to speak in a larger group.

9. **Let the silence work.** Remember that many people need time to collect their thoughts and courage before speaking. If we extroverts jump in at every silence, the quiet folks will never speak. Leave time to ask, "Is there anyone else who would like to add something?" followed by a time of silence, before you move on to a new activity.

10. **Receive each story with honor and respect.** You cannot change or fix a personal history, but you can hold it in the safety of Circle. Be prepared for grief. It's not likely in the first getting-acquainted Circles that deeper emotions or revelations come forth. However, they might, so please see "Experience As Teacher," page 74, for ways to prepare and be helpful.

11. **Give a closing thought or activity** that will anticipate what comes next. Say, for example: "After a ten-minute stretching movement, we'll each be creating a fabric doll. What would be the perfect name for that doll? Maybe the name will come to you as you are making the doll."

12. **Use campfire as another opportunity for storytelling.** One of our favorite games is "Tell three things (events) about yourself—two that are true and one that is not true." Others then guess which is which. This is a good transition activity from campfire songs to the drama of midrash and fable.

Both of us enjoyed the partner sharing of "names." It gave us an opportunity right away to bond with another woman.

—Cindy and Jean, mother and grand-mother

See "Telling Our Own Stories, page 131.

See "Campfire," page 190.

Learning with Body, Mind, and Spirit

WE ARE DISCONNECTED

Remember the Cheshire Cat's head grinning down at frightened Alice in *Alice in Wonderland*? Weird and bodiless, the smiling feline face dodges ahead of her through the forest. Discomfiting, to see a head without a body. Yet, our Greek-rooted Western civilization trains us to think of ourselves in this disconnected way. In that view, our minds, centers of intelligence and learning, are distinct and somehow detached from our physical selves. Further, this teaching sees the mind as superior, able to soar above the crude, embarrassing physical body—like the head of the Cheshire Cat. Thus, we are fragmented. We learn to relegate the body to lower duties of animal survival, while only the mind is for learning.

What about the spiritual self? Through the ages, some authorities within the Christian church have taught that spiritual aspects of a human being, informed by the intellect, are God-like and holy. The physical body, according to this thinking, is corrupt, our lower nature, waiting to lead us into sin. Even more unfortunate, women were often seen as closely associated with the physical, earthbound side of life. Mindless, seductive creatures, daughters of Eve, original temptresses, women were viewed as incapable of directing their own financial, political, or spiritual lives.

Wiser teachings hold that no healthy person, woman or man, can be divided from within—nor can the spiritual be held separate and superior to the physical. Genesis 1:31 declares that God viewed all the created world and saw that, indeed, it was very good. The Holy Spirit is the breath of life—and the body needs this breath in every cell. Christ came as Baby Jesus, *Deo Incarnate*, God in flesh, talking and eating with sisters as well as brothers.

The brain itself cannot be divided from the rest of the body. Though we once thought the verbal and spatial spheres of the brain defined the limit of learning, current educational research shows seven or more "intelligences." Educators now acknowledge that some of us learn best through movement, others through art or music, and still others through nature or through personal interaction. There is evidence that the mind resides in all the cells of the body.

How boring to learn only with the head! How invigorating to absorb wisdom with body, mind, and spirit! Songs, dramas, crafts, nature walks, and other physical movement are not merely camp fun. Each girl and woman will find in these activities her best way of learning. Does she dance with strength? She can model movement to timid shufflers. Does she make wild, fantastic dolls? She will inspire and help beginners. Gifts emerge; leadership is passed from one to another.

WE BEGIN

We begin by shaping this gathering of women and girls into Circle: Each one is the same distance from the center. We see each other through the center, viewing all as having equal status and worth. In the center is the altar. Here is sacred space for bringing images and objects significant in our lives: photographs, gifts, flowers—whatever has importance to each one in the Circle. Some speak of what is placed on the altar. Others hold a silence that is respected. We have prepared a space. We have invited ourselves into the presence of the Spirit—the Spirit of God already waiting among us.

WE RECONNECT

Music enters the Circle—harp, voice, guitar—the gifts of women and girls. Hands create masks and dolls and pouches, crafts passed down through the centuries from old women to young. Up jump the bodies (some faster than others) for line dances winding over the green grass! Now, the physical body empowers the expansion of spirit and mind. Amy starts the song "Mend and Weave" (page 221), and we all follow her, singing and twining, ducking under clasped hands, then miraculously emerging in a single line again at the song's end.

An eagle flies by as a story is told. We take this as a sure sign that something important has been said. The sun warms our bodies down on the beach while we sit without talking, communing with splashing waves and salty wind. Each cell is learning now. The spirit and body are one. We walk in silence back to the grassy farm bluff.

One-by-one enter the archetypes of the Four-fold Way—the Warrior/Leader, the Healer, the Visionary, and the Teacher, each in full costume appropriate to her task. They bring messages to women and girls, helping us connect with strengths already present within us. We learn the power of showing up and choosing to be fully present from the Warrior/Leader. The Healer speaks of paying attention to what has heart and meaning. The Visionary tells us to speak our truth without blame or judgment. We learn to listen attentively and to be open to outcome from the Teacher.

As we relate these archetypes to our faith, they provide form and flesh to biblical women—Miriam, Anna, Mary, and the unnamed anointing woman—who seemed paper-doll, one-dimensional in the familiar Sunday school stories. We look within. Warrior/Leader, Healer, Visionary, and Teacher give face, body, and voice to the spectrum of our own slumbering capabilities, so that we can recognize and honor them in ourselves.

We stretch out our bodies and gaze at the sky through fir and maple branches. We have time to see and hear and smell the creation. Body, mind, and spirit now join in learning. We hold this time together as sacred.

Each talk and ritual touched us on many different levels, emotionally, physically, and spiritually. We needed time in between talks and rituals to recuperate and process.

—Jean and Cindy, grandmother and mother

How We Do It . . .

Reconnecting Body, Mind, and Spirit

PREPARING THE PRESENTERS

- **Connect with each other in Circle.** This retreat is not about a hierarchy—a chain of command. From the beginning, use the Circle, the place of equal honor and voice, to model how gifts are discovered and how decisions are made.

- **Find your inner connections by remembering your girlhood** and by telling stories to each other about that remembered girl. Who or what helped you? Who or what hurt you? These stories will help prepare you to equip the girls at your retreat for their journey into womanhood.

- **Reconnect with nature.** Place a flower or green sprig in the center of your Circle. Pay attention to the birds and animals outside the window as you are meeting. You may want to choose one of God's creatures to be your symbol or totem. Be attentive to the trees in your neighborhood. Thank God for every tiny pink flower.

- **Live in your body.** As you gather to plan, create time for movement activities. Experience moving to music or rhythm. Sing songs together while you stomp your feet or clap your hands. Those not able to move freely can snap their fingers or bang with a spoon. We are wonderfully made, all of us.

- **Pray and meditate together.** You may want to join hands, sitting or standing in a Circle, while a short prayer or thanksgiving is spoken by each one who feels called to pray aloud. For others, silence itself can be a prayer. Simply breathing together can inspire.

DURING THE RETREAT

- **Include nature in your setting.** Seagulls and rhododendrons are native to where we live, and other plants and critters live around you. We walk on the beach. If you live in the city, find a garden or park for an outdoor time with nature. Bring rocks, pets, plants, or flowers into your gathering.

- **Help each one to be attentive and fully present** as she listens to the story of a girl; looks at the rock in her hand; lies on her back and feels the sunshine on her face; touches the bread of communion. All is grace; all is gift.

- **Talk less, move more.** Some information needs to be presented as participants sit, but eyes can quickly glaze over during a lecture. Masks, music, dance, and handiwork all engage the senses and help us learn.

- **Intersperse dance and movement activities.** Encourage girls and women to try (within their safety zone) stretches, dance steps, and wiggles that they haven't done before. Smiles and laughter will follow.

- **Remember that hands can move while the mind is learning.** After you teach doll-making and the girls and women have picked out their fabric, needles, and thread, their hands can be busily creating as they join in stories and songs.

- **Hold the entire weekend as sacred.** God delights in being among us and within us.

I was surprised how much I enjoyed just being "fiddled over" in the mask making . . . lying there for a while, not being able to speak or do, just receive was very restorative. It surprised me, made me realize as mother, we have always been the ones who were doing the fiddling. Who brushes our hair, washes our face, dresses us, strokes us?

—Karen, mother

Crafts: The Work of Our Hands

Sally muses: "If I open my mind's eye and wander ancient pathways, I imagine women and girls gathered, circled around the work of their hands, the bounty of soul made visible and useful, made manifest.

. . . I see a quilt now snuggled safely away, the labor of my great, great ancestor.

. . . I see her sisters and friends as they gathered to make candles, or spin wool.

. . . Drifting to earlier times on this continent, I see dark-skinned sisters shaping pots and bowls of rich, red earth.

. . . Releasing my memory to ancient imprints, I see women gathering, drying, blending herbs and potions for health and sustenance.

. . . Receding into the caverns of early human life, I imagine a woman scraping a hide, cleaning, then working it, softening it with her own rich milk."

Wisdom, health, necessity, and blessing of life have emerged from the gathering of women around the work and wisdom of their hands—their creativity made tangible, connecting body and soul. At our retreats, we have moved from a hunch that our hands needed to be busy to an almost fanatic commitment to the truth that, unless we make our souls' journeys manifest in the work of our hands, we remain disconnected, dismembered.

What fun to become aware of the importance of fun! We tumble all over ourselves in a plethora of possibility—so much to choose from. What will we make, sing, dance, act? How will we find time for all we would love to do? Timidly at first, we learn to sew a pouch, or paint a mask, or create a doll from bits of shell, wood, and yarn. When performance anxiety is calmed, the most wonderful creations emerge, bringing forth parts of ourselves long silent.

We have chosen mask, pouch, and doll-making for our retreats because they are laden with the power of archetype and symbol. Long-hidden personae are gently coaxed into the light of freedom and safety. We often experience reluctance and insecurity, hobbled by childhood histories of rejection and the "mistakes" of long-ago attempts. But as we listen to our stories—hearts traveling down imaginations' long roads—we see emerging from the works of our hands, lost and lovely pieces of soul—selves we learn to celebrate—creation's imperatives. Maureen says, "As I crocheted or hand-stitched or embroidered the [pouches], there was a deep work being done within me. I was creating a space within myself, a reservoir of my own power." (See "Maureen on Pouches" in the Journey Pouch, page 193.

In craft-making, as in dance, song, play-acting, and movement, we recover the physical body's gift, and give thanks that the body and its creative, generative power reminds us we are made in the image of the Creator. Each year, each retreat, the epiphany has intensified. Our minds' work of connecting, reclaiming, and releasing is limp and feeble if it is not spoken also by the loving work of our bodies. The threads are picked up again—the ancient work of women's lives to be woven again in our time by our own and our daughters' hands.

I adored making space for the feminine, making points of connectedness.

—Kitty, mother

I thought making the dolls and the pouches was the most fun.

—Holly, early teen

[Most fun was] making the masks and campfire (after everyone's gone to bed) when the fire is still going and we sing silly songs.

—Colleen, early teen

How We Do It . . .

Crafts

See "Pouch-making" and "Masks," page 189.

And their prayer shall be in the work of their craft.

—Ecclesiasticus 38:39 (Douay Version)

We have found crafts to be an essential part of the retreat—a tool for integrating body and spirit, and for expressing the ways of Circle. In the joy and liberation of coming into ourselves, spirit and body, we understand the importance of working with our hands.

At the very beginning of our retreat, we begin a craft project, making a pouch or a doll. Our hands are busy as we listen to music and story. Later, as the retreat develops, we begin mask-making and decorating the cover of our retreat journals. We learn to entice our creativity out into the open.

As you plan your retreat, brainstorm about those in your group who might teach a craft—many of you can. What do you, or would you, like to make? Great skill is not required, just some experience and interest. Start with the skills and enthusiasm your planners have; just make sure each craft has meaning for the content of the retreat. We chose crafts that traditionally have been passed from older to younger women (doll and pouch-making) and those that helped in self-discovery (masks). **We always have baskets full of fabric scraps,** thread, yarn, beads, and a table laden with paper, paste, pens, paints, and brushes. This smorgasbord approach to supplies seems to free up the creative child in each of us.

We have found that **old-fashioned, wooden clothespins** (not the pinch kind) work well as the form of a little doll. In our most recent retreat, a facilitator gave each one of us a baggie of fabric scraps, feathers, wool, beads, and a clothespin to start us off on doll-making. As we get braver, we use sticks from the beach walk, shells, feathers we find; the dolls become wild and lovely. A pipe cleaner folded in half for a body and a shorter one for arms can also form the framework for a doll.

We make masks using plaster-coated gauze (much like doctors make casts from), available at most craft stores. This requires only minimal experience; then we teach each other. Masks dry quickly and can be painted and decorated. Many of us had some initial resistance to making a life mask, but gradually we all wanted to make one. There may be someone in your group, as is in ours, who will make a mask for each of the archetypes of the Four-fold Way. They are wonderful ceremonial additions.

We also began last year's retreat giving each participant an inexpensive spiral journal (about 4" x 7") and we provided retreat time to decorate the covers of these journals.

We have found that the work of our hands weaves us each to the other and into a deep satisfaction. Perhaps somewhere in us is the memory of generations of women sewing, weaving, gathering, making their world serviceable and beautiful. Maybe we are called back to that gift. Perhaps we weave the patterns of our lives into the work of our hands. Or, it could be that, with our eyes busy helping our hands to create, our hearts are more open to knowledge and understanding. Perhaps it is all of these that make handwork an integral part of the experience of the Daughters Arise! retreat.

Song: Singing Our Songs

Behold! A sacred voice is calling us. Behold . . . from the earth to the sky, a sacred voice is calling us. Behold!
—Marlena Fontenay, adapted by Claudia Walker[25]

A lady at my Mom's assisted living house died yesterday, but I did get to say my goodbyes. I taught her daughter the song I learned at your retreat and we both chanted it to her mom . . . I felt like I gave her a moment of joy before she left this world.
—Suzie, mother

Gloria recalls her first memory of music. "'Rock me, Mama,' I would say at the age of two as I crawled into my parents' bed. Exhausted from a ten-hour day at the mill and four hours after that building our house, Daddy turned over to sleep as best he could as my mother rocked me and quietly sang me to sleep. More than half a century later, I still hear that little tune in my mind some nights as I go to sleep. I think it's a Swedish melody. Maybe my grandmother Selma sang it to my mother. Maybe my great-grandmother Johanna sang it to her babies."

A song is primary and elemental. A song hums through our bones. As we look at our retreat schedules, we see that our opening activity each year was a song. One year, we formed a circle of all the women and girls on the lawn and sang, "Behold, behold, a sacred voice is calling us, behold, behold." Another year we formed two circles, one inside the other, and rotated the circles so we could greet each other, one-by-one, singing, "I greet you sister (name) from the earth to the sky. We are connected by love."

Spoken words are analyzed. The listener selects what she wants to receive. Sing the words and they zing right into her heart. In our greeting circle, we meet each other eye-to-eye and hand-to-hand, more open and less self-conscious as the music and movement disarm us.

Claudia, our lead musician, chooses our songs during the months before our retreat. The words in the songs she selects for the Daughters Arise! retreat speak of God's delight in all of creation, including us: "And all creation's straining on tiptoe just to see the children of God come into their own."[20] The songs tell of the tender, mother-love of God: "Mother, hold me, Mother rock me in your arms."[21] They speak of our hurts: ". . . to You we bring, all broken hearts, all broken wings."[22] They sing of growing confidence in the Spirit within each of us: "You are a rock and an anchor for yourself and those you love."[23] Weeks after the retreat, someone will say, "I have that melody with me all the time. Those words sing to me just when I need them."

Claudia looks for and writes **songs with singable melodies.** She introduces the songs to the other presenters at planning meetings. Claudia asks for our feedback about the songs themselves and about the best way to teach them. In happy, duplicate purpose, the singing of these songs enlivens and inspires our planning meetings while giving Claudia information she needs about what works with untrained singers—and what doesn't. She finds that "just join in whenever you can" doesn't work nearly as well as "lining" a song: Claudia sings a line; we echo it back. She repeats this until we feel confident.

Songs breathe life into ceremony and worship. Musical instruments, including harp, drums, conch, and rattles get us moving with the music. We hear the wind, seagulls, eagles, and chipmunks as accompaniment to our voices: "Let all life sing, with earth, with beauty, let all life sing."[24]

How We Do It . . .

Singing Our Songs

PREPARING THE PRESENTER:

- **Find a musician who likes to sing, to teach, and to have fun with people.** The dance-movement leader will work closely with this person. A musically talented, outgoing girl may fill either of these roles if given the proper support.

- **Choose or write songs that average singers can learn and enjoy.** Intersperse new songs with familiar ones such as campfire, popular, or well-known church songs. A familiar tune may be used with new words.

- **Look for songs that express themes of the Daughters Arise! retreat:** Lullabies help to heal emotional injuries. Women and girls are beloved daughters of God. We belong in God's creation; we are related to eagles and salmon, to wheat and hyacinths. The Spirit burns within each of us, and we trust her guidance.

- **Change a word here and there in songs** if that will make them welcoming to girls and women. Picturing God as our loving mother nudges "God the Judge" out of our souls for this blessed time.

- **Gather musical instruments and musicians to play them.** A guitar, small harp, drums, rhythm sticks, a flute, a violin, a harmonica—all these are easily transportable to a place under the sky.

- **Try out songs on your fellow presenters.** You will quickly see what works. Better to find out at planning sessions than at the retreat that a song falls flat!

DURING THE RETREAT:

- **Use songs often throughout the retreat.** Meaningful times for songs include the first greeting time; calling back into Circle; creating altar; campfire; some of the movement exercises; before meals; meeting the Warrior/Leader, Teacher, Healer, and Visionary; Journey Walk; Sunday morning worship; and the Girls' Ceremony. Participants may volunteer their own favorite songs.

- **Teach the songs by "lining"**—the leader sings a line and the others echo it. Or by "call and response"—the leader sings the more complicated part and the others answer with a learned chorus or a simpler part. This gives everyone confidence to sing. Telling people to "join in whenever you can" means most folks will never join in.

- **Compile a temporary songbook.** Try to include music as well as words on the more difficult songs. (Be sure your church has permission for copying the songs or get permission). No need to include easily learned choruses.

- **Put music, words, movement, nature, color, and rhythm together** to enliven body, mind, and spirit.

Mother and God, to you we sing, Wide is your womb, warm is your wing.

—Miriam Therese Winter, composer and liturgist[18]

I am a child of God, nothing can shake my confidence. I am a child of God, no one can take my inheritance. Never alone I'll stand, strengthened by God's own hand. I am a child, I am a child, a child of God.

—Tom Walker, composer[19]

Dance: "...with Tambourine and Dance"

This is so foreign—so forgotten. Dance and instruments were daily joy for me in childhood, but set aside when demands were made to explore ... responsibility.

The body connection is seeming so much more important.

—Peggy, mother and grandmother

'Round and 'round we go, we hold each other's hands and weave our lives in a circle. The day has come, the dance has begun.

—traditional German folksong

When asked why dance is important in our retreat, even in our lives, Amy, a young facilitator and dancer, replied, "Because when you open your body, you open your spirit ... open body, open mind, open soul."

Learning to dance—risking the discomfort of stiff bodies and embarrassment of stumbling feet—has brought us retreat planners and participants into a whole new (for most of us) world of joy. Perhaps we learned ballroom dancing from "Miss Twigget" when we were ten years old or even folk dance or girlhood ballet. Perhaps we remember a few times as adults that we were partnered to the sounds of Benny Goodman or the Beatles. But for most of us, the freedom of movement and dance was left somewhere in childhood, lost in adolescence when we were taught to be guarded about how we move our bodies.

In the Daughters Arise! retreat, we find again **the joy of the spirit expressed in dance.** We do not learn formal dances, or complicated steps—just the freedom to run, or leap, or toe tap, or stretch to the music of our hearts and of the world around us. We have learned the beauty of dance as praise: One blessed retreat Sunday, after the young girls had made their beautiful ceremony of becoming, the wind rose off the water, blew through the tall firs, and teased us to follow her. Hair askew, skirts flying, we circled and laughed, filled with the grace of the Spirit, convincing us rooted ones that our bodies indeed are the wings of the Spirit, meant to be free, alive, vibrant.

The prophet Jeremiah writes of the rebirth of Israel—the coming time when God will restore the people to wholeness. We experience our restoration to the family of God in the work of the Daughters Arise! retreat. Jeremiah writes of the joyous time: **"Then shall the young women rejoice in the dance ..."** (Jer. 31:13).

How We Do It . . .

Dance and Movement

See page 53 for "Sun Salutation" meditation.

See the songs in the Journey Pouch, page 201.

PREPARING THE PRESENTERS

Musicians and dance-movement leaders work together. You don't need professionals, but you do need people of talent who will have fun finding or creating movement activities. Not all movement activities involve singing, but a drum, rattle, or other percussive instrument adds to the drama of the activity.

In planning, find dance, stretch, and other movement activities that 1.) are fun; 2.) are within the ability (or can be adapted to the ability) of all participants; and 3.) enhance the educational and spiritual purpose of the Daughters Arise! retreat.

Try the activities out at one or more of your planning sessions. Lead your frank and verbal woman and girl coworkers through a movement activity and you will quickly find out what instructions are unclear, which stretches are impossible, and when an activity has gone on too long.

DURING THE RETREAT

Be clear in your instructions and have fun. If you're having fun, so will the others. Here are a few movement activities selected from several of our retreats:

We begin by greeting each other. After asking us to form two circles, one within the other, Claudia instructs us to say our own name to each woman or girl we face. Then we all sing, "I greet you sister _____," each filling in the name of the person facing us. After each singing, the circles rotate one person, and we sing the greeting to the next person. You can find or invent similar activities. The key elements are speaking each name, saying or singing a welcome face-to-face, and using movement and music to scatter constraint.

Amy forms us into a line on the lawn for "Mend and Weave." The words and tune are easy to learn: "Mend and weave, mend and weave, gather the golden fragments of our sacred lives, O sisters . . . mend and weave." Amy leads us into a circle and then into a spiral as we sing our song, again and again. We weave more and more tightly into the spiral, and then unwind until we find ourselves in a circle again, grinning at the surprise of it.

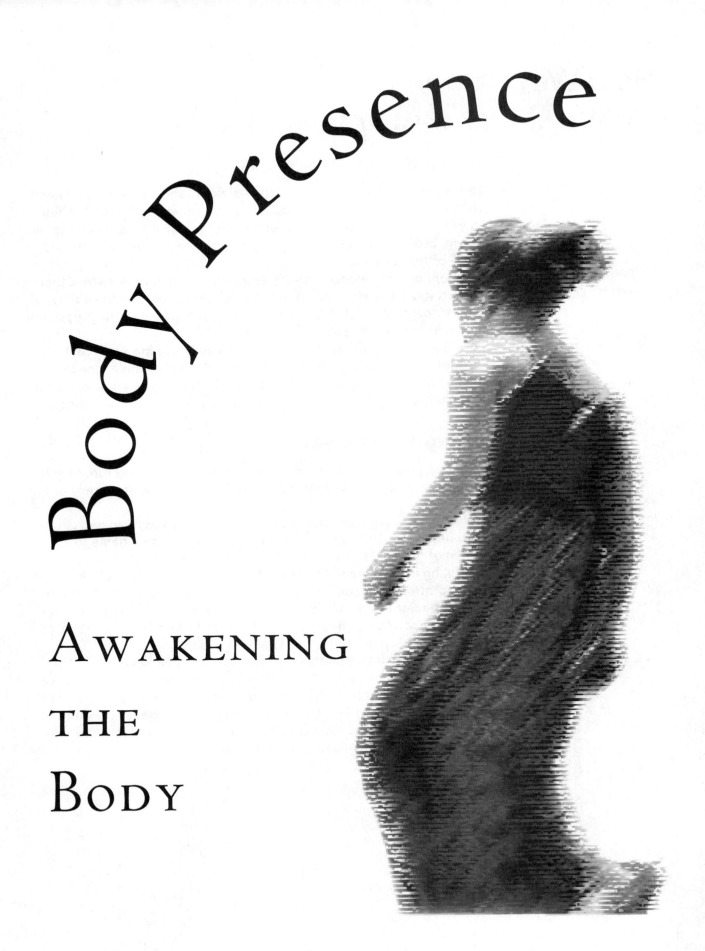

Body Presence

AWAKENING THE BODY

When we first arrive at the Windecker farm, each of us knows only a few of the other women and girls lugging sleeping bags and clothes into bedrooms and tents. In the way of well-meaning strangers, we smile at each other, introduce ourselves, and try to make some connection: "Oh, you're from Tacoma. I went to school there." Friendly but superficial.

But before that first hour is over, Claudia invites us onto the grass. She teaches us a simple song: **"I greet you with my heart and hand."** Following the words of the song, we touch our hearts and touch the hands of the woman or girl facing us. Our eyes meet her eyes in mutual welcome to this place. When, in the midst of one verse, we mix up the words and movements, we laugh. Laughter, music, hands, feet, voice, eyes, earth, and sky join to assist us in forming ties of respect and love at the beginning of our retreat.

See page 41 for "How We Do It . . . Dance and Movement."

The following evening, when the archetype Warrior/Leader (see "The Four-fold Way: The Bones," page 20) enters our Circle, she dances close to each one and shakes a gourd rattle, calling out a positive attribute of the Warrior/Leader: "Show up! Respect limits! Right use of power!" Then, she circles again and shouts a warning to each of us of the shadow side, the misuse of Warrior/Leader traits: "Rebellion! Fear of accountability! Giving away authority!" Gloria recalls meeting the Warrior/Leader: "The sound of the rattle and the strength of her dance propel her words into my body and brain. Next, I learn to call out in a low, loud tone from the gut while stomping on the earth and raising my arm in the Warrior stance. **At first, I feel silly. But I am surprised and pleased at the power coming from my body."**

By flexing arms and legs, voicing "unfeminine" sounds, shaking ourselves awake, we electrify learning receptors. Recent research shows that body movement itself is talent and intelligence, and that **movement enhances learning.** But we women and girls are not thinking about research. We are merely feeling alive, pleased with ourselves and with our sisters.

Each morning when the conch shell is blown to signal the body wake-up time on the lawn, we stumble out into the day, heads fuzzy, bones creaking. Then we see Amy, smiling face alight with the early sunshine. Girls and women stand, waiting for Amy to help us coax our bodies awake.

Bare feet on cool, morning grass, we wake our bodies and souls, greeting the new day with every fiber of being, giving thanks to our Creator. Later in the day, moving to the beat of a drum or the sounds of harp, guitar, and our own voices, stretching and leaning, touching hands and earth, humming, hearing, following the awakening of our bodies—all this teaches the soul to speak. Movement of our bodies deepens our souls' praise.

We are adopting new forms, trying on personae to see if they fit. Such simple effort amazes us with its power and just plain fun. No longer stilled by outside authority, **our bodies are in motion.**

Campfire

It will probably come as no surprise once as planners you have begun to experience Circle and you have felt the power of storytelling, that you are drawn in your retreats to create campfire. You will no doubt remember Camp Fire Girls or Girl Scout experiences—s'mores and all. We are drawn back to those girlhood experiences. You may remember from Christina Baldwin's book, *Calling the Circle*, that the tradition of **circling around a warm fire as the day's light dims is an ancient memory in our bones.** So, if it is possible, try to find a retreat setting where you can build a campfire. We even did it indoors one rainy night, circling in front of a wood stove! If campfire isn't possible in your retreat setting, try circling in the evenings around a huge collection of candles.

In spite of some of the inconveniences of campfires as we get older—drifting smoke, hard logs to sit on—the power of circling around a fire in the dark, telling stories, playing games, singing songs, is one that all generations at our retreats treasure. Our annual retelling and enacting of the "Vasalisa" story at the very first night's campfire never fails to amaze and enthrall us; we shed the cares and postures of our daily contemporary lives and become the myth. It speaks deeply and clearly.

You can choose the campfire setting to introduce basic retreat material or just to play games and sing songs. We usually save s'mores until the last campfire as celebration. We try to end the planned campfire activities early enough, with all present, so that any who would like to may leave for bed, and those who would like to linger around the fire may do that, too. Often, some participants' tents are pitched nearby, taking advantage of the soft firelight. So, as you plan your retreat, consider campfires as a meaningful part of each retreat day.

How We Do It . . .

See "Vasalisa the Wise," page 191, and "Presenting Midrash," page 135.

Campfire

1. We usually gather and begin campfires by singing. It is wise to sing songs everyone knows or is mostly familiar with, as the dim light and informal setting don't lend themselves to reading music and words.

2. There are many games that work in a campfire setting. One of our favorites, which is also a good opportunity for storytelling, is "Things about Myself." Each person tells three things about herself. Two of them must be true—events, accomplishments, hobbies, habits, or talents; and one thing isn't true but might be, or will be, or is a dream to come true, or is a plain, outrageous concoction. The person to her right must guess which thing is not true or not yet true. This is a good getting-to-know-ourselves game. It also speaks aloud some of those things we each might be hoping or dreaming to do.

3. Tell stories: We have found Clarissa Pinkola Estés book, *Women Who Run with the Wolves* to be a rich resource for myths and stories. While her version of "Vasalisa the Wise" is our favorite, we have also found "Sealskins, Soulskins," and "Crescent Moon Bear" to fit well with retreat themes. It is fun to have a few women and girls act out the stories as they are being told or read aloud. (See "Folktales, Fables, and Parables," page 64.)

4. Early evening campfire is also a great place to share plays written from scripture stories. We have usually written a play for the first evening, asking for volunteers at dinner, and using an hour or two to prepare. The plays should be simple and easy to read. We've included a couple of ours in the Journey Pouch. They will get you started on your own. This is one form of retelling Bible stories called midrash. In our experience the girls, with only a little help from a friendly adult, then love to create their own plays.

Bridge to Tipi

As women and girls begin discovering the strength of storytelling voices, of stomping, dancing feet, of clapping hands and doll-making fingers, it becomes clear that the God-created capabilities in each one of us are good—very good!

But girls wonder about another, sometimes confusing, mix within and around them: emotions that overwhelm or feel strangely numb. Body changes that come too fast or not fast enough. Friends who are faithful—and friends who are not. Social classifications that mark one girl popular and another left out. **Strong attractions and glimpses of intimacy, delightful and frightening.**

What about that one creative aspect of life that in our culture is more exploited than explained? What about feminine re-creative, generative power? What about intense feelings ignited by another? What about "I love you so much I can't stand it!" What about—sex?

Our first retreat year, we did not provide a time for the girls to have their own separate Circle, a time to be together, speaking of their own lives and asking their own questions. Our omission was an honest and intentional one. Not feeling that we had the girls' confidence or permission, we were conservative and erred on the side of caution. Our first retreat was only two days long. Our hesitancy was perhaps justified: a longer retreat is necessary to build the setting of safety and the freedom to speak honestly.

Once again, we were about to learn from the girls. In response to our request for feedback after the first retreat, the girls gently, but pointedly asked, "How come we didn't talk about dating, or sex, or friendships, or how our bodies are changing? We want to talk about these things."

We realized we weren't addressing the whole person if we excluded relationships and sexuality. The girls needed a time apart to talk about their interests and concerns, helped in the discussion by adult women facilitators. Speaking from her own experience, Maureen, one of our facilitators, has written: "So many young women make decisions that diminish the quality and potential of their lives because they do not understand the special power that is within them—and how to hold it."

Why is it important to have this discussion in the setting of the Daughters Arise! retreat? Part of our cultural and religious bias is to separate body and spirit. In our discomfort with matters sexual and in our uneasiness and displeasure with our own bodies, we as parents, mentors, pastors, and teachers often do not provide girls with needed guidance and understanding about these aspects of life. We, in the Daughters Arise! retreat, want the girls to know that they are part of a larger Circle of loving women of faith, more experienced than they are in life and upon whose strength and stories the girls can call as they learn to make their own decisions.

In our retreats, we are coming into fuller knowledge that we are created for joy—both spiritual and physical. Each one needs to be aware that the decisions she makes about sex are an expression of her whole personality and affect her entire life.

As women, we have a special power of life within us. This is our gift. We must learn to identify it. We make choices every day that channel our personal energy.

—Maureen, mother

See page 193 for full text.

How We Do It . . .

Bridge to Tipi

DURING THE PLANNING

Because you will want to respond to questions and comments of the girls honestly and sensitively, here are some items to consider:

- Invite girls who are at least eleven years old or beginning menses.
- Inform the women and girls in the printed materials you send out before the retreat about Tipi Time and that girls may, among other topics, ask questions about sexuality during the discussion.
- Tell them in this advance material that an alternative Tipi Time is available for girls who choose to discuss school and friendship concerns but prefer not to discuss sexuality, because they are younger or for other reasons.
- During planning, use the discernment of the Circle to choose two secure, caring, nonjudgmental women who can gently guide the Tipi Time discussion. These facilitators need to feel comfortable talking about sexual matters in the context of the girls' own life decision-making.
- As your reservations come in, look at the ages of the girls. If you have an older grouping—eighteen to twenty-four for example—you may want to provide these young women with a space for their own discussion.
- Invite several presenters to search their own memories for times of insight and growth in their young womanhood. They will create a way of telling these experiences to the girls and women at the retreat, as did Maureen and Paula (see below).

DURING THE RETREAT

Before the girls depart with their adult facilitators for the tipi, prepare for the separation with wisdom pieces that come from the life experiences of the presenters. Here are examples of sharing from our retreat:

- The first story is told by Maureen, about a time in her life when she discovered the importance of understanding and using well her power, of setting boundaries and holding her power, as she was able to hold small treasures in the pouches she made. As we hear her story, we create and decorate our own cloth pouches.
- A little later, Paula speaks about coming to an awareness that changed the direction of her life: She tells us that she learned to recognize the connections of mind, spirit, and body and how the health of each influences the health of the whole person.
- After the girls leave for Tipi Time, the Circle of women remains to speak of "Holding and Letting Go." Mothers and other women share resources and support in the gradual release of the daughters and young friends to their increasingly independent lives. We recognize the push and pull of the girls needing both closeness and independence. We speak of the skills we need in enabling our daughters to become strong, faithful young women. We are moving from mothering to supporting.

[There was] a significant change in our relationship . . . the conversations were truly between an older woman and a young woman. [The Daughters Arise! retreat] was as much for me—enabling me to make the shift, to let go, to bless—as for my daughter.

—Joanne, mother

See full text of these three wisdom pieces in "Bridge to Tipi," page 193.

Tipi Time

In a tall, white tipi set under the stately firs, young women who choose to participate gather to talk of the wonderful and fearful changes in their own bodies, of how they are received by others, of faith, of friendship and its cost, of popularity and its elusiveness, and of the pressures and joys of sexuality.

Accepting the guidelines of Circle, the girls build their own altar, their own sharing space. With the assistance of two older, wiser women, the girls are offered the freedom of a safe place to be heard, to share hopes, dreams, fears, and the realities of life for adolescent young women in our culture. We also offer an alternative Circle for girls (usually the younger ones) who have chosen not to participate in the more mature discussion in the tipi.

The girls have initiated discussion about the difficulties different generations have in understanding the issues girls face today—pressure of drugs, sexual experience, and the fear of pregnancy, disease, or violence. The girls talk about having and losing friends, how to be a friend, personal boundaries, learning to make decisions, learning to honor one's own and others' feelings and decisions. In a safe place, with privacy honored, these **girls-becoming-women search out ways to be themselves, beautiful, and whole.**

The discussions and sharing often form the basis for the girls to plan their own ceremony of passage for Sunday morning. Once they begin to understand the reuniting of their spiritual and physical selves, they try out the freedom to enjoy their femininity. Shedding the restrictions and expectations our culture places on physical beauty, the girls find the joy of adorning themselves with pretty things—scarves, make-up, clothing—just for themselves. They find words, music, and dance to express the joy and hope of their young womanhood and to ask for the blessings and support of the older women of the retreat. They begin to become, as Angeles Arrien has said, **"the strong, supple selves"** they were meant to be. These beautiful ceremonies witness to us older ones, too, the joy of coming into our own power as daughters of God, fully present to life's struggles as well as blessings, in a strong community of faith.

How We Do It . . .

Tipi Time

The Tipi Time is rather like a blending of a little girls' secret club, a long conversation with a loved and trusted aunt, and a sacred ceremony, for it includes the crucial elements of confidentiality, of trust, of wisdom, and of the Holy.

BEFORE THE TIPI

1. We have found it important that **the girls be at least eleven years old** or have already begun to menstruate.

2. The young women need to understand that the tipi discussion will be **a nonthreatening forum** for them to openly discuss concerns about their sexuality, family, friendships, and choices.

   Be aware that there may be someone present who is gay or who has gay family members. No one should be made to feel excluded.

3. In our retreat mailings, we **give information about the form and content of Tipi Time.** Early in the retreat, we introduce the Tipi Time facilitators, encouraging girls and their mothers to ask questions of the leaders. We offer another tipi discussion for those girls who don't feel ready to talk about sexuality.

4. We have used the traditional shelter of the Plains Native Americans for its simplicity, beauty, and power. If you do not have a tipi available, **choose a similarly special setting apart from the others.**

5. **Allow about 1 1/2 hours** for the first discussion early in the weekend. We have scheduled it after the introduction of pouch-making, so the girls may take their pouch work into the tipi with them. We share "Bridge to Tipi" stories (see previous pages) with the whole group just before the girls go to the tipi.

6. **Schedule time during the retreat for at least two more tipi gatherings** for the girls to continue planning their ceremony. (See "The Girls' Ceremony," page 56.)

IN THE TIPI

1. **There is soft music** playing (flute and drums) when the girls and the older women (we believe two is appropriate) enter the tipi.

2. **The altar is created** in the center. The candle is lit when all are seated.

3. The girls are reminded that this is a sacred Circle and what is discussed is confidential. They are asked if they agree to the **guidelines of Circle and confidentiality.** (See also "Be Prepared with Safety Resources," page 76.)

4. The **facilitators and girls introduce themselves.** The girls may add what year in school or where they're from—as they choose.

5. The concept of an **"ask-it basket"** is explained: Given paper and pencil, the girls may write a question or topic and, without writing their names, fold the paper and put it in the basket. Each girl then takes a question from the basket and reads it aloud for the group to consider. Sometimes discussions begin spontaneously and the basket is not used.

6. We suggest that the facilitators remain as objective and nonintrusive as possible, intervening only if someone is dishonored or her opinions or ideas are threatened. In the main, **allow the young women to conduct their own discussion.** Beginning to trust their own inner voice, they learn to honor their own deepest discernment in the choices they make. The facilitators encourage the girls to think about the importance and consequence of the decisions they make. Considering the best wisdom of family and faith tradition, they are encouraged to honor themselves as well as others.

7. There is also a basket of **shells, pretty stones, and feathers** from which each girl may choose a memento. Perhaps she will want to lay it on the altar to be claimed later or put into the pouch she is making.

8. **The girls will probably begin thinking about the ceremony of passage** they might like to create. We offer them a basket filled with scarves and other pretty ornaments, to which they can add their own things to adorn themselves for their ceremony.

Ceremony and Celebration: Circle Is Sacred Space

We have spoken of the importance of Circle in how we relate to each other, not only during the retreat, but also in the work and planning for each retreat.

Circle is also the shape of our relationship to God and to each other in worship and ceremony. For many, if not most of us, our experience of God in worship has been the usual, formal church setting: congregation sitting in rows facing the pastor and the altar or communion table. While the focus was on God, it was God "out there" or "over there," not God among or within us. Now, some congregations are choosing to shape their worship space in a circle or semicircle around the altar or communion table. **Circle calls us back to the immanent God, God in the midst of us, God at our center.** When we create or name sacred space in the retreat, we choose to gather around it, around the flame of the Spirit, around the symbols that mark our sacred journeys of faith.

While our Sunday morning retreat worship service is a retelling and remembering of the more familiar Sunday worship of our faith, and while we anticipate its blessing on our retreat experience, we have learned to celebrate ourselves as daughters of God in other ways, times, and places. We are learning to **"Sing God's song in a new land" in a very real way. It is the land of our own experience, ringing with the words and music of our own songs.**

We intend to affirm to ourselves and to the girls the freedom to create meaningful ceremony. It is a deep gift of the Daughters Arise! retreat. We are empowered to have confidence in our own expressions of faith and divine encounter.

Saturday night, it hit me big time how important it is to share! The Circle is not complete without each of our gifts. Mine are as blessed as others; this I must remember. . . . It is a blessed thing when one values herself enough to realize she is a gift to herself and others.

—Kitty, mother

circle is sacred space

Matins, Meditation, and Body Presence

We encourage any retreat participant to contribute a short thought, poem, or prayer in the morning at our five-minute matin service and to share a blessing before lunch or dinner. Each morning before breakfast, there is a half-hour opportunity to gather under the big trees in silent meditation.

A less usual form of meditation we are learning is to call the body into presence. Amy and Dana, two of our facilitators, have training in dance and body movement. One leads us each morning after breakfast in a series of gentle body movements. For example, as in the photos, Amy leads us in part of the "Sun Salutation," reaching down to the earth, then up to the sky, causing us to connect our bodies to our physical world. Our morning awakening can include waking the voice by humming and reaching out to each other to connect ourselves. Angeles Arrien points out in *The Fourfold Way* that each of the four archetypes has its own special posture for meditation: the Warrior/Leader is a standing meditation, the Teacher, a meditation while sitting, the Healer, lying down, and the Visionary's is a walking meditation. These undemanding but powerful experiences call us into our bodies—into the created homes God has given us—strengthening our connection to the natural world and waking our bodies, too, to praise.

into the **created homes** God has given us—**strengthening** our **connection** to the natural world and **waking** our **bodies**

How We Do It . . .

Meditation

An example: We awaken our bodies with a "Sun Salutation."

Place your heels together, toes spread, palms together in the prayer pose. It's easy to mirror Amy's actions as she gently leads us into this meditative practice. Fingers dive toward toes, leading the body downward from the waist. Arms circle overhead, pulling the body up. Eyes look through raised hands into the blue sky. We are fully awake.

1. Stand feet together, palms pressed together near heart

2. Raise arms straight overhead, palms inward, inhaling, looking skyward

3. Back flat, exhale, and bend over, extend arms toward feet

4. Inhaling, lift arms straight out to sides . . .

5. . . . and overhead again

6. Bring arms down, palms together in beginning position.

The Journey Walk

A ceremony we have come to treasure is the Journey Walk. Saturday at dusk, a large spiral of cedar and fir is lovingly laid on the lawn under the tall trees. At intervals along its winding way are unlit white candles set in bright apples. Deep in the fragrant center is the lighted altar candle, surrounded by symbols of faith. We form a large circle around the spiral, and after a few words of instruction, the girls are invited to walk the spiral one at a time, slowly toward the center. As we sing during her solemn walk, each one will pick up a candle, carry it to the center, and light it. She may pause for a moment or two to pray, to consider her own journey, to give thanks, to commit her way—it is a private time, upheld by the presence and voices of the other women and girls. As she returns from the center, she sets the candle down somewhere in the cedar boughs to light the way for another to begin the walk.

The Journey Walk is evocative of other sacramental moments . . . confirmation, marriage . . . a person makes an individual commitment, upheld by gathered witness.

—Sally, mother

When the young have finished, other women, too, can choose to walk the spiral and light a candle—perhaps for rededication, perhaps for forgiveness or thanksgiving or healing. **All who choose to take the Journey Walk seek a moment with the Holy, then return, lighting the way for others.** It is a singular walk to the light in the center in the beauty of the natural world, and there is power in the naming and witnessing of each one's journey. The peace and beauty of candlelit faces, the fragrance of the evening and the boughs, voices softly singing—all are the loving Body of Christ gathered there in deep and joyful blessing.

How We Do It . . .

The Journey Walk

The Journey Walk seems loveliest at dusk, before the evening's campfire. Maureen and Claudia and others leave supper early to lay out the ever-green spiral while the rest of us are occupied elsewhere. It becomes a gift when we are led to it for the ceremony.

[Lyda] come forth, let your light pour out of the rainbow of love at your core . . .
—"Daughter Come Forth" (page 211)

- The spiral we create is usually about twenty to thirty feet in diameter and made with freshly cut boughs of cedar and fir. (You may wish to choose other greenery.)

- Often our center is a tree-round, but it could be a stump (also honoring the tree that was) or a rock, a small table, a drum, or just a pretty cloth on the ground. Again, the candle is symbol of the Divine Light; those who set up the ceremony select a few particularly meaningful objects from the retreat altar to place in the center.

- You will need one apple and one candle for each participant, anticipating that all might be moved to take the Journey Walk. The apples are cored and a candle is inserted in each one. They are then placed along the spiral on the green boughs. We add flowers, feathers, perhaps ribbon. Choose whatever you wish for making the spiral beautiful.

And all creation's straining on tiptoe just to see the children of God come into their own.
—"The Tiptoe Song" (page 229)

- We all sing while each one walks. "Daughter Come Forth" (see page 211) is particularly meaningful, sung for each woman and girl who chooses to make the Journey Walk. We have learned that it is wise to become familiar with one or more appropriate songs for this ceremony, so that printed sheets are not needed in the dimming light. Another approach is for one person to sing the verses and all to join in an easily learned refrain. We all learn the verses as we repeat them. Taizé songs, from an ecumenical community in France, are lovely in this setting, and quickly learned. Singing continues as long as someone is walking.

- We leave the boughs and candles on the ground until the end of our retreat, enjoying their beauty as we pass by.

The Girls' Ceremony

What has stayed most in my thoughts is the advice [blessings] given to me in the ceremony.

—Kathryn, mid-teen

A highlight of the retreat is the rite of passage ceremony that the girls create. They delight in the freedom to create their own joyful and solemn celebration—their own passage of praise. The beauty of these ceremonies captures the hearts of all the rest of us. With loving adult conspiracy, the young women retreat into the big, white tipi to discover for themselves what will meaningfully mark their passage—music, words, dance, costume, symbol—and what they would like to receive from the older women.

The creation of this and other ceremonies during the retreat collects us around the liminal times of our lives, causes us to witness to our journeys as women, and women-becoming. When we attend to what has heart and meaning, the moment is crystallized, and the Divine enters and is received.

The most wonderful highlight of the retreat was the [girls'] ceremony at the end. It developed from the girls' creative imaginations and ended with the spontaneous gift of the Holy Spirit. . . . The Spirit was truly among us.

—Linda, aunt

How We Do It . . .

The Girls' Ceremony Planning

Further details are in the Journey Pouch, page 162.

One of the lovely blessings of the retreat, and of the Girls' Ceremony in particular, is the returning to the retreat of girls who have participated before. They act as guides and attendants in the ceremony-planning for the girls who this year have chosen to participate.

Be sure to allow time in your retreat agenda for the girls to prepare for their special ceremony. In our retreats, they return to the large, white tipi— the one in which they have met in Circle throughout the retreat. The girls choose at least one adult to help with their planning. Sunday morning, they ready themselves for celebration—special clothes, make-up, if they choose, often flowers in their hair, anointing one another. Often, the adult women are asked to make an arch at the door of the tipi. The girls emerge to song, then move singly around the Circle, each one receiving a blessing from each woman. They select music and dance; a favorite is "Mend and Weave" (page 221). We often use instruments, a harp, guitar, tambourine, drum . . . the important thing to remember is that the girls plan the ceremony and request how they would like us to participate.

Sunday Morning Worship

For most of us on retreat Sunday morning, it seems natural to return to our more familiar form of worship service. Although we still meet in Circle and under the sky in places that have become sacred to us in our time together, on Sunday, we gather around the treasured essentials of Christian worship: prayer, scripture, and Holy Communion.

Heather M. Elkins, in *Worshiping Women*, speaks of the importance of participatory worship and ceremony. Elkins says that in childhood, when we first encounter the Divine, "something inside (our)selves knows (it) to be absolutely real—**the child has a vision . . .**"[26] Creating joyful celebration, rich with ancient experience and image, reclaims the first and truest experiences of God and teaches us to remember and cherish those divine dreams. Worship then becomes a blessed opportunity to reclaim, awaken, and honor that spiritual experience as it gives us confidence and leads us into womanhood.

Because we reach out into our larger community with invitations to the Daughters Arise! retreat, some of the girls and women attending are not connected with a church. For them, worship is a new experience and their acquaintance with God perhaps not specifically Christian.

Though it springs from our familiar church form, our Daughters Arise! retreat Sunday morning **worship is fresh in understanding and gentle in invitation.** We welcome all in joy and thanksgiving. We use the liturgical order, leading those gathered from the longing and painful parts of their lives into God's loving and healing embrace. We use easily understood (rather than traditional Latin) names for these parts of the service: "Gathering in Joy," "Confessing Our Pain," "Asking for Healing," "Responding with Gratitude," and "Committing to a Loving Life" are examples of terms we use.

We let go of other nonessentials in order to make this worship as accessible and user-friendly as possible. At the same time, we avoid "dumbing down" or generalizing. Rather, we search for fresh, powerful poetry, prayers, and songs. We weave these into our own music and litanies, creating a worship service reflecting the pain and joy in the lives of women and girls. As prayers, songs, bread, and wine pass among us, Christ's transforming love holds each one, mends the broken places, and promises new life. As each forehead is blessed with anointing oil, a reminder that we are loved and called to love, God gives us strength for the days ahead.

We do not rely on ordained pastors to lead us, but they have been part of our worship celebration. Laywomen and girls creating and leading worship attest to the ministry of the Divine in and through every one of us. In this worship, for this time, we feel the power and servanthood of attending to each other's needs, rather than always receiving these gifts of God from the hands of priest or pastor. **To each of us belongs the privilege of inviting others to the holy table.** We bring ourselves into the presence of our loving God, who is already waiting for us. This is not a service for those who have their beliefs all down pat. This is a gathering of seekers, ministering to each other.

It has been such a blessing for us (grandmother, mother, daughter) to experience women sharing and worshiping God from a feminine perspective.

—Cindy, mother and daughter

My overall delight was in our claiming ourselves to be beloved daughters. All my life I have heard about beloved sons, and now we are intentionally claiming our birthright.

—Kitty, mother

How We Do It . . . *Sunday Morning Worship*

See " Worship,"
page 154.

*Even though I'm not
Christian, I enjoyed
this, because it relates
to all religious
peoples' reverence
toward God.*
— Sarah, older teen

*That two young
women felt drawn to
plan the closing wor-
ship points to the pro-
found impact shared
leadership and
intergenerational par-
ticipation have in this
process.*
— Claudia, mother
and daughter

PREPARING THE PRESENTERS

- **One or two planners may take responsibility for gathering and writing liturgy.** You will find poems and prayers from many sources: creative friends, books, and church worship materials that use inclusive language. Shape these together with your own worship sense, creating a space for the Spirit's grace.
- **A musician will work with the worship planners** to make musical instruments, singing, and dance an integral part of worship. You are co-creators with all the worship musicians and poets who have come before—Hildegard of Bingen, Julian of Norwich, and King David, to name a few.
- **Leading worship does not mean coercing people** into mouthing the words you want them to say. After our first retreat, when one girl was brave enough to tell us that her beliefs didn't fit with our service and that she preferred to take a walk to meditate in her own way, we have offered that option.

DURING THE RETREAT:

- **The retreat altar,** often a colorful cloth on the lawn or deck, can be tidied up and lifted to a table or bench, creating the communion table. Here you may wish to place meaningful objects from the retreat or other art and symbols that inspire worship.
- **The shape of the Daughters Arise! retreat worship is Circle.** Early in the retreat, invite participation at a worship-planning meeting. During worship, those who have individual parts sit in the Circle and their voices emerge from the Circle. A dancer or singer may move to the center for a short time, but she returns to the Circle. Leadership is shared, and the Spirit moves among us.
- **A short sermon may be part of your worship.** Even today, some have never heard a woman preach. Women have much spiritual wisdom to share, and this is a welcoming place to do that.
- **As free as the wind, as fresh as the Holy Spirit,** your worship will be able to use feminine language for God and womanly context for scripture. Choose what speaks to your hearts and time, and do not feel you need to rely only on traditional words and patterns. Your own inspired words, combined with ancient forms, slide the gathered community into hallowed space.
- **If you choose to share communion** in your worship service, you will need bread. (A round, crusty loaf is nice.) You may wish to offer both wine and juice, tying a ribbon around one as an identifying mark.
- **Here is an example of how we have celebrated communion.** Gloria acts as celebrant, sharing the words of invocation and blessing of the elements. She begins with the story: " Jesus—descendant of Israel's liberator Miriam, born of mother Mary, recognized by the prophet Anna, and anointed by an unnamed woman— this Jesus broke the bread." Gloria serves the bread and wine or juice to one in the Circle, who then serves the next, until each woman and girl shares in the meal.
- **As a psalm is read, anointing oil may be passed** as each one blesses the next.
- **We are led to places God has promised** but which tradition has blocked. To paraphrase Miriam Therese Winter, we are pioneers of the Spirit.

Weaving the Parts Together: Integrative Vision

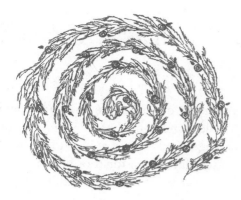

Midrash: Crawling inside Bible Stories

In our quest for the new, we discovered the very old. Since time before memory, talking and writing about scripture has filled the lives of Jewish scholars. It is, for those in the faith of Sarah and Abraham, the highest calling and the greatest joy in life. "Midrash" is a Hebrew word for one way of exploring scripture. In this centuries-old method, rabbis and their students read a biblical narrative closely and then ask questions of it, filling in gaps in the story. Midrash looks for truths about our relationship with God, with each other, and with the rest of creation.

As we began to explore midrash, we found examples of poems and stories in which the ancient narratives of scripture are shaped in new ways. Sometimes a minor character tells the story. Sometimes the story is moved to another time and place. Questions and insights jump out of each new telling.

Maybe midrash, this historic tool from the Jewish tradition, could help a Circle of Christian women crack open the tough nut of church teachings about Bible stories. We gave it a try. Several writers chose fascinating but puzzling stories from the Bible. One chose David and Bathsheba; another picked Mary Magdalene's encounter with Jesus; still another retold the story of the bleeding woman who touched Jesus' garment and was healed.

At the retreat, the writers read or acted out their stories as women and girls sat in the sunshine on the deck. **We learned what it is to crawl inside a Bible story,** gather up ancient fragments, and discover how the hardened clay can be softened and shaped into a vessel useful for our time.

One afternoon, we handed out illustrated pages of scripture stories quoted directly from the Bible. The women and girls were invited to read and contemplate a story and then to write a midrash: a poem, play, or story seeking the truth of the scripture in a fresh, personal form.

In retrospect, we realize we should have offered more assistance in writing and presenting midrash. The girls and women hesitated—and then chose to make facemasks or pouches instead of writing midrash. Though disappointed, we presenters were about to relearn an important lesson: In Circle, leadership is passed from one to another, and new leaders rise up as they are needed.

That evening, Amy, our high school-age leader who had participated in two previous retreats, and Cindy, a woman participant who is skilled in drama, offered to draw out the girls' talents in writing a midrash play for that evening's campfire. **In an hour's time, the girls wrote and rehearsed "Eve and Adam."** They understood the essence of the biblical story. By reversing roles and placing the story in a contemporary setting, the girls used dialogue and action to shape a hilarious play. They demonstrated amazing insight into the push and pull between men and women today. This play became a highlight of the retreat, both in what the girls were able to create and in what we learned once again about leadership emerging from the strong-woven basket of Circle.

What a wonderful way to breathe a new perspective into well-known Bible stories.
—Cindy and Jean, mother and grandmother

Donna's story of Mary was a highlight for me. Enactment of the bleeding woman healed by Jesus was wonderful.
—Unsigned retreat evaluation

How We Do It . . .

Midrash

See "Presenting Midrash," page 135.

If Bible study is about wrestling with the word of God, midrash is about jumping into a Bible story and dancing around in it. To do it yourself and to teach others, it helps to know some steps.

1. **Start with scripture.** Find an accurate, recent translation, such as the *New Revised Standard Version.* Many Bible "translations" are really paraphrases.

2. **Pick a story that challenges or bothers you.** Retell the story from the point of view of an intriguing character, using her voice. You might choose to write this midrash as a story set in a different time and place. You may want to fill in missing details or go on from where a story stops in the Bible.

3. **Present your story at the retreat.** Use props, music—whatever will make your midrash come alive. Your midrash may be happy, sad, or angry. You are shedding new light, giving a different view, of an old familiar story. You are also giving an example of what midrash is and how to do it. You are giving others the courage to do their own midrash.

4. **Have a midrash script ready.** Early in the retreat, tell the girls and women that you need actors for your story. **Keep it simple.** We chose the story of the bleeding woman touching Jesus, as rewritten by one of our presenters, using the woman's voice and point of view. After some rehearsal, the girls acted out the story at campfire while a woman read it.

5. **Offer help** to the girls and women in creating and presenting their own midrash play: "Cindy will help you choose and create a play. Some of the Bible stories you might like to use are 'Adam and Eve,' which you might call 'Eve and Adam,' or 'Baby Moses in the River' as told by Miriam and Pharaoh's daughter." (This will be a couple of days into the retreat, and the girls will know that Cindy is helpful and that acting at campfire is fun.) Girls in our retreats have chosen "Eve and Adam," with Eve as the breadwinner and with the serpent selling steroids to body-vain Adam; "David and Goliath," about a bully on the playground; and "Jesus Casting Demons out of the Man and into the Pigs," with crowd and pig roles for all of us!

6. **Plan adequate time** for the girls and helpers to choose and create the play without feeling rushed. They will probably need 1 1/2 hours to prepare.

7. **Schedule a good time for the presentation** when all can be present and enjoy it. The flickering campfire adds to the drama. The story reader can use a flashlight to see her printed page. Staging the play at the beginning of campfire time, when there is still some daylight, also works well. Actual presentation time for our girls was about ten minutes.

Folktales, Fables, and Parables: "The Tortoise and the Hare"

Remember Aesop's fable of "The Tortoise and the Hare?" Do you remember how that story turned out? Who won the race? Donna tells how this story (fable) made it possible for her daughter, the tortoise, to coexist with her brother, the hare:

Whoever can give the people better stories than the ones they live in is like the priest in whose hand common bread and wine become capable of feeding the very soul.

—Welsh saying via Hugh Kenner[32]

The light of the camp-fire illuminated each face in the Circle, and we were young and old, new and ancient. We had gathered in the way of the centuries to hear the stories.

—Gloria, mother

> Can you imagine what it would be like if you were the tortoise?—to watch a hare running past you, constantly achieving and winning awards, seemingly without effort?—always there before you, waiting for you, while you toiled away to reach the same achievement or recognition?
>
> Every once in awhile a turtle figurine or picture would appear for our daughter when she was discouraged. No big pep talks, just a turtle as a reminder that the race wasn't over yet. When she graduated from college, at the family celebration party, we each had words of congratulations for her. The most significant words came from her brother, the hare, who told her that she was his hero for her willingness to risk new things and her ability to really give herself to a project without giving up, even if it looked like it would take too long or might be boring at first. Her determination and perseverance were sought-after traits for the hare. "I was never able to do that," he said, "and I know I missed out on a lot."

Metaphors represent a compact or condensed language, somewhat like icons on the computer screen, which represent lots of information. When we use a metaphor, our minds are flooded with associated images, words, and stories that make it possible to perceive multiple levels of meaning at the same time. Folktales, fables, and parables are metaphorical stories that help us bring a concreteness to abstract concepts and ideas.

METAPHOR: HELP OR HINDRANCE?

Because metaphors are useful shorthand communicating much information in few words, certain metaphors become woven into common use in a family or in a culture. The double-edged quality of this practice is that frequent use of a certain metaphor may limit how a culture is able to think because of the limits of the metaphor. For example, if a frequent metaphor is from military strategy, the words "winning" and "losing" influence relationships and ways of solving problems at the expense of thinking about cooperative metaphors evoking teamwork or consensus.

The additional quality of fables and parables is that they are intended to frustrate our logical thinking, to get into our perception beyond our rational expectation. Of course one would expect the much swifter hare to win the race. It startles us into questioning, "How could a very slow tortoise win that race?" "Tell me what happened." "Who am I in the story?" "What does this mean for me?" "Who do I want to be in the story?"

Earlier in this guidebook when we discussed "Midrash" and "Looking at Scripture with New Eyes," we were reminded that the Bible was written by men, using metaphors that had meaning for males. And, later, the same was true because men were interpreters of the Bible. Yet, Jesus' use of parables was a way to shatter the limits of his culture's metaphors that limited people's understanding of the nature of God.

The word "parable" comes from two Greek words, *para* (alongside) and *bole* (thrown). "Parable" literally means "thrown alongside" as an emphatic way to show that parables are not meant to be a logical teaching form. Rather, their images are designed to collide paradoxically against each other and, thus, to collide with our preconceptions in order to bring new insight. In Jesus' case, the new insight from a parable is "so compelling that it causes a prompt reorganization of our life."[33]

In both the Old and New Testaments, the phrase, "not counting women and children," was used frequently when relating numbers of people in stories, because women and children were not considered important enough even to be counted, let alone have their stories told. The use of that phrase signals that metaphors meaningful to women and children are likely to be missing in the accounts and interpretations passed on to us. It does not mean that the stories were not there, but that they were neglected and lost.

In our scriptural heritage, we can recover some of these stories by retelling what is there, such as telling Jesus' parables with women as the central characters, and by rediscovering and presenting the recorded stories of Jesus' conversations with women (frequently left out of the lectionary). We can use the tool of midrash and women's metaphors to "flesh out" the bones of some of these stories, until now told only through male metaphor.

It does mean that **we must dig for fragments of stories** just as an archaeologist digs for broken pieces of pottery, sorting and selecting to fit together the whole pot. These fragments of pottery are called "potsherds." Recovering women's stories and metaphors is like that.

FOLKTALE AS A TOOL TO RECOVER WOMEN'S METAPHORS

Many of the ancient teaching stories, folktales, fables, and parables of other cultures are valuable because they are full of these "potsherds" of women's stories and metaphors for life. That is why a story like "Vasalisa the Wise" (which we use in the retreat) is so important. It is a recovered initiation or quest story of a young girl's journey, discovering her inner guidance. You might recognize elements of the story in our culture's domesticated version called "Cinderella." After you have heard the story of Vasalisa, you can realize how much was lost when it became the story of Cinderella and told within the metaphorical constraints of our culture, washed clean of the metaphors of women's power and wisdom.

We use the Cinderella story as an example because it is such a prevalent folktale, told over and over again in each generation in our western culture. Again in 1998, the story was retold in the movie, *Ever After* (20th

The first morning of the retreat I awoke with this thought: I wish that growing up I had been asked "What do YOU think of you?" rather than, "what will others think of you?" as a guide for my actions.
—Kitty, mother

Century Fox; director, Andy Tennant, 1998). The archetypes of the "step-mother" and "stepsisters" are symbolic and, as author Claudia Pinkola Estés explains, can be understood as internal "elements of the psyche," as well as an external family or culture that cannot understand or appreciate a girl or woman.

> The stepmother and stepsisters can be understood as creatures set into a woman's psyche by the culture in which a woman belongs. [an internal stepfamily] . . . who taunt, "You can't do it, you're not good enough . . . you're only allowed to do this much and no more."[34]

I valued the honoring of women's ways: Stand up, Speak out, "I am!"
—Kitty, mother

It can represent the parent and siblings, whether biological or adopted, who do not nurture a child they feel is different or who will not conform. In our contemporary times, there are nurturing stepparents and adoptive parents who have actually rescued children from biological parents who were abusive or neglecting. The reference is in no way disparaging of those courageous, giving women who raise or mentor children not born of their bodies but is symbolic of negating rather than nurturing influences.

The Cinderella story portrays a dependent girl with an ineffectual father, unable to protect her from abusive elements and people in her life. Her deliverance is not achieved through her own knowledge, courage, or self-determination, nor through compassion, insight, or justice on the part of others. Rather, with the help of a fairy godmother, Cinderella is assisted in acquiring the desirable traits for a female as defined by a male culture. The godmother outfits her with the right clothes, which display her physical beauty, and **she waits to be noticed** and come under the protection of a strong male who "saves" her from her abusive family. One might well ask, saved her to or for what? And one might well ask, **what does it say about a society where a woman derives her existence only from someone else's power?**

But, in the Vasalisa story, the young girl receives a gift from her dying mother, a little doll, the symbol of her own inner knowing. The girl learns how to rely on that gift when she is sent from her home by the stepmother. This story is a girl's "quest" story. Most quest stories, which remain in our western tradition, are for young men. Most have been Christianized by retelling them as the search for the Holy Grail. In quest stories, the journey through wilderness, inhabited by mysterious people and powers, is a metaphor of the inner search for a personal encounter with the Divine. Finally, finding that the **"inner knowing" is the Spirit of God** within enables the quester to return to the real world to speak and act, guided by this newfound spiritual wisdom.

In the Vasalisa quest story, after her time with the Baba Yaga, Vasalisa's inner knowing has grown so powerful that it becomes visible, represented as light emanating from the skull the Baba Yaga gives her. This lights her way home and casts a burning light on those who would try to harm her. Therefore, the damaging influence of her stepmother and stepsisters is made manifest to her, and it sets her free from their control and domination; it had "burned up their power over her."[35] She no longer defines herself as they had defined her, nor does she live her life subject to their approval. This is no longer dependence—existence derived from the power of others—this is the full knowledge that one is a beloved daughter who has resources and power of her own.

Until we heard the original story, we had no idea what had been lost: The Baba Yaga, in compelling contrast to the sweet fairy godmother, and Vasalisa, carrying the glowing skull in contrast to the pastel Cinderella holding the pumpkin, startle us with vivid detail, design, and power.

RICHNESS AND RESTORATION THROUGH FOLKTALE, FABLE, AND PARABLE

In our planning and in the content for activities and stories in our retreat, we use the parables of Jesus—life examples told in paradoxical images and metaphors to give immediacy and new insights to his teachings.

We focus especially on stories of women in the scriptures. The same themes of worthiness, self-knowledge, and right use of power that we hear in "Vasalisa the Wise" are plentiful in the stories of heroic women like Miriam; Queen Esther; Ruth and Naomi; Mary, the mother of Jesus; Elizabeth; and especially in stories of Jesus' interactions with women; they just need to be retold.

When we are assisted by the stories and metaphors of women from ancient folktales and fables, the "potsherds" of these stories take shape and volume, showing us characters of depth and complexity, emerging from the shadows of the uncounted women to reenter the stories of the Bible.

For example, author Angeles Arrien gathers these potsherds from indigenous cultures. By using the descriptive characteristics of the four archetypes in *The Four-fold Way*, we have a new way of seeing familiar Bible stories.

We recognize Miriam as a Warrior/Leader who chose to be present, coming forward to speak to the Pharaoh's daughter.

We recognize Queen Esther as a Visionary, telling the truth without blame or judgment.

We recognize Mary as a Teacher, being open to outcome when she replies to Gabriel, "Let it be with me according to your word" (Lk. 1:38).

We recognize the woman who anointed Jesus with oil as a Healer, paying attention to what had heart and meaning.

Guided by the Holy Spirit, we use our creative imagination to reclaim the scripture stories in a way that brings inclusion, wholeness, and healing.

It might be an apt metaphor to say that the tortoise (women and children of the Christian faith) is catching up with the hare, not to pass and leave the hare sleeping, but to complete the "race" together with him and rejoice in a full chorus of all of God's children.

I feel the Four-fold Way made the messages from the scriptures come alive with new voices. The same messages with brilliant insights and inspired presentations.

—Unsigned retreat evaluation

How We Do It . . .

Folktales, Fables, and Parables

At our first retreat, we presented two folktales at campfire time. One of these was "Vasalisa the Wise," a girl's initiation quest story (ancestor of "Cinderella") from the book, *Women Who Run With the Wolves*.[27] This story was so popular with the girls that it has now become a tradition, a permanent part of the curriculum.

We recruited actresses from our facilitators and a daughter who was experienced in drama. In subsequent years, we have had girls volunteering for the roles. The only requirement was to read through the story several times before presentation night. Costuming was kept very simple:

Vasalisa—red dress or skirt, apron with pocket, head scarf, and small doll dressed in same colors to fit in apron pocket

Dying mother—sheet

Baba Yaga—black cloak and hat or wig

This was dramatically narrated (with assistance of a flashlight) while actors mimed action. Time required was about fifteen minutes.

The results were electrifying. The resulting conversations and questions over the remaining days of the retreat revealed to us that our intuition about using folktales had been correct. The daughters, young and old, found themselves moved by the drama. The metaphorical language spoke to them and helped them talk about life issues that concerned them. They also spontaneously started to relate and compare these stories with scripture stories. At the request of several mothers and daughters in more recent retreats, we have initiated discussion right after the folktale with prepared questions.

Other folktales we used from *Women Who Run With the Wolves*: "Sealskins, Soulskins": Returning to one's soul; one dries up and withers when one leaves the "waters" of one's soul (ancestor of the story and movie, *The Secret of Roan Innish*).[28]

"Crescent Moon Bear": Love overcoming fear and rage; taking action for love, not knowing the outcome; learning that you have the resources within you to deal with the troubles you will face in life, but a mentor may have to help reveal that to you.[29]

"The Ugly Duckling": learning how to claim who you are, and finding those who will affirm and honor your best self.[30]

We found that there was as much learning by mothers and guardians about parenting, as by daughters for their journey, in these rich resources of metaphor and tradition.

The first year, we over-prepared the opening introduction. We tried to present the theological, sociological, and psychological rationale for the weekend to assure mothers it had been well thought-out. We lost the girls. The next couple of years, we had a very abbreviated introduction. It was too vague. Then, based on the success of the "Vasalisa" experience,

[Myth] gets under our skin, hits us at a level deeper than our thoughts or even our passions, troubles oldest certainties till all questions are reopened . . .

—C. S. Lewis[31]

we wrote an introduction based on a contemporary fable, *The Wizard of Oz*. This is presented by two facilitators alternating the paragraphs between them. We print the first paragraph here below; the full text is in the Journey Pouch.

FABLE AS INTRODUCTION TO THE WEEKEND

"We want to spend a few minutes telling you a bit of what to expect this weekend. Many of you know the story of Dorothy and the Wizard of Oz. Well, this story is a good way to think about what this weekend is about. In fact, it's a helpful way to begin to understand what happens to us when we grow from one phase of our lives into a new one. Right now, like it or not, each of us is growing, changing, becoming something new. Remember when Dorothy woke up and looked outside after her house plopped down in Munchkin Land? Anybody remember what she said? 'Toto, I don't think we're in Kansas anymore!'"

See full text on page 123.

The Four-fold Way:
A Metaphor for Integrating

You have read about the important role *The Four-fold Way* plays in our retreats. The four archetypes and their characteristics bring us visible, unexpected ways of seeing inside ourselves, of understanding the gifts we are created to give. In them, we see the ways in which we might serve the Spirit as whole human beings.

The myths and Bible stories around the campfire . . . allowed sharing with one of my daughters at a very deep level . . . very great gifts that came not through anything didactic or ritualistic but . . . from the storytelling process.

—Joanne, mother

Why not just stick to Bible stories? We do tell many stories from the Bible, but *The Four-fold Way*, unfamiliar to most of us, shifts us out of the habitual patterns of seeing ourselves and the world. The Bible stories most of us have heard all of our lives then become filled with new breath, take on new light. *The Four-fold Way* helps us to see more clearly.

You may decide on another resource to assist in the work of integrating the experiences of the retreat. Other metaphors and myths might also serve so long as they strike to the heart of what needs to be awakened. It is essential that whatever you choose helps to make visible the inner selves we have abandoned or forgotten; that it opens you to the transforming power of the Spirit; and that it helps you to see the stories of the Bible with new eyes. **It is not that we are exchanging one metaphor for another, but rather that we are enlarging our understanding of what we hold dear.** In addition, as in the parable of the new wine skins, we are pressing new grapes and need new containers for the sweet wine of our rebirth.

In our retreats, the voices of the Warrior/Leader, Teacher, Healer, and Visionary speak to ancient soul and call it forth, as Lazarus (Jn. 11:1–44) was called from the cave and bindings of death. Much as the woman at the well saw herself whole and forgiven in the eyes of Jesus, the stories of courage, wisdom, and faith inspire unimagined possibilities for our own lives. **The archetypes put before us a model of ourselves we didn't even know to imagine.** The power of archetype is that it leads us into the deep springs of our souls.

When Moses struck the rock as God had asked, he had no way of knowing the hidden water that would spring forth (Ex. 17:6). In our retreats, the sounds of bells, rattles, and drums and the scent of sage pique senses that have lain dormant in our sanitized and insulated lives. They call out to us, "You need to be digging here . . . there is crystal water deep inside." Could we have imagined calling a teenage Jewish girl named Mary a Warrior/Leader just because she was willing to "show up" to God's call? Could we have imagined what a difference another Jewish girl, Anne Frank, centuries later, would make because as Visionary she simply spoke her own truth?

Our contemporary culture is like a desert or a prison for young girls. Thirsting for the sweet water of confidence and assurance in a prison of others' expectations, the girls find archetype and myth leading them toward the voice of the Holy. They are called to strength and wholeness, to deep spiritual waters, to the truth of their own souls, and to their own inherent worth. **This is the power of story at the mythic level;** it lifts us out of our habitual, cognitive processes and wrests us free from the complacency of familiarity to see truth that lies beneath. Not myth as fiction, but myth as truth deeper than mere fact, as God's own truth, and its power to redeem and set free.

. . . voices of the

WARRIOR/LEADER,

Teacher,

Healer, and

Visionary

speak to ancient soul

What We Learned

Experience as Teacher

Experience as Teacher

No matter how carefully you plan, plan on the unexpected. Murphy's law also operates in a Daughters Arise! retreat. From our experience, we emphasize the following:

See "First Steps," page 84.

1. After checking church and other community calendars, **set the date** for your retreat as early as you can—six months lead time is not too much! "Get there first!"

2. **The abilities that you will need already exist** in your Circle of planners. Historically, we women have not been affirmed in our insights and abilities. Often, we have had nowhere to try them out, or even to imagine them. Rotating leadership gives all a chance to try unpracticed abilities. The Daughters Arise! retreat is just the place to dream and imagine. It is not only the young ones' gifts we are enabling.

3. Be specific about:

   - **ages of the girls** you feel appropriate to your retreat—and stick to your decision.

   - **each girl having an adult participant** arriving with her, willing to be her mentor.

   - **who participates in which activities.** Example: Tipi Time might not be appropriate for the younger or less mature girls; and girls who wish to participate in the Girls' Ceremony need to participate in ceremony planning.

4. **Be clear about setting boundaries.** Be sure to articulate that each participant continually chooses to be part of what is going on or chooses not to. One year, a young girl felt confident enough to decide not to join in our Sunday communion service. In our time together, we learn to recognize our own limits, to state them comfortably, and to have them honored. What a treat! Also, encourage yourself and others to stretch those boundaries; **welcome your growing edges.** Help each other to try new things, confronting the difference between comfort and safety.

5. **Structure the schedule** for the retreat. Timing is critical to both the experience and the flow of the retreat. (See "About Schedules," page 86, in the Journey Pouch.)

6. Leave a few minutes each retreat day for questions or needs that arise. We found that **a check-in time** just after matins works well, providing everyone an opportunity to share needs or requests before they become problems.

7. Be sure to have a **facilitators' Circle** at the end of each retreat day. If little problems have arisen, Circle wisdom can help solve them, preventing their becoming more difficult and destructive. Not all problems take the full Circle to solve; an individual may be asked to mediate the misunderstanding.

8. No matter what happens, stay in Circle to deal with it. **Remember that the Holy Spirit is at the center.** Troubles happen when we forget that.

9. **The unexpected will happen!** It will be joy; expect that it will also be grief. Circle creates safety for the emergence of long-buried feelings. As a difficult story is told, a friend might say quietly, "Would you like me to stand behind you?" or offer other support. Someone may disclose that she is gay; or that her marriage is crumbling; or that she has suffered date rape. When grief arises, the Circle is not responsible to find solutions, only to listen, receive, and hold loving witness. Determine to stay in Circle, fully present, focusing on the Light of the Spirit. (See Baldwin, *Calling the Circle,* ch. 8.) Consider beforehand what you might do if a woman or girl tells of a present danger to herself. What would be a responsible and caring follow-up? (See page .;p76.)

10. Sometime after your Daughters Arise! retreat, it is important to **review the overall effectiveness and quality of your retreat** and of each activity. Get this post-retreat evaluation date on the calendar as you are making the rest of your schedule. We recommend scheduling this debrief and evaluation at least a few days or up to two weeks after the retreat. Immediately after the retreat, there is a mixture of celebration, elation, and exhaustion that makes analysis difficult.

11. We have learned that it would be a **great benefit to the girls** who have experienced our retreat if there were a way **to continue the community** they have formed at the Daughters Arise! retreat. This could happen through e-mail, or regular mail if they live in different locales, or by returning to the retreat the following year to be "big sisters" for the new attendees, or by beginning their own Circle to continue the journey together. We have experienced the gift of girls returning to our retreats. We know from their feedback that without continuing community, the experiences of the retreat can fade. If the girl has success in applying experiences from the retreat to her own life, she longs for a place to share that and to mentor younger girls. We have considered a women's lodge for the women and girls near or in our community. Such a group, meeting even quarterly, would provide continuity and an ongoing experience of Circle.

12. **Your own Circle of planners may want to continue** after the retreat as a writing, reading, Bible study, or other sharing group.

BE PREPARED WITH SAFETY RESOURCES

In Section One, "How We Do It . . . Passing Wisdom through Story," page 31; "How We Do It . . . Tipi Time," page 49; and again in "Experience as Teacher," page 74; we repeat that: "**The unexpected will happen!** It will be joy; expect that it will also be grief. Circle creates safety for the emergence of long buried feelings."

While we are committed to confidentiality, and while we know that for the most part we are not responsible to find solutions to problems that are revealed, **there are two situations that require referral and outside assistance if they arise.** We recommend that you prepare for this possibility. These two situations are if a girl shares about abuse or potential harm that is happening to her or if she expresses fears of harming herself.

In the Pacific Northwest, we are fortunate to have the resources of the Center for the Prevention of Sexual and Domestic Violence. This organization was founded by the Rev. Marie Fortune, who has a close affiliation with all denominations in their training programs and groundbreaking video study courses. There are policies and training regarding clergy misconduct in the Pacific Northwest Annual Conference of the United Methodist Church, as well as in other denominations. There has been a mandate for each individual church in the Pacific Northwest Conference to write its own sexual misconduct policies and guidelines and supervision for adults working with children and youth. Check to see what resources your denomination has available.

Another good resource is found in *The Stephens Ministries Manual* in the training presentations on "Confidentiality" and "Ministering to Suicidal Persons and Family and Friends."[36] School districts also have policies for teachers and counselors facing similar revelation.

Begin with your local church and community to find out what resources are available. Establish an emergency contact person who is willing to advise or be present should you need assistance.

In the years of our retreats, we have not had any problem of a serious nature arise. Learning from the experience of one of our writers, however, we have chosen not to be complacent. Her middle-school-age daughter attended Bible camp with a new friend and returned home to relate that her friend had revealed, to the pastor leading the camp, the sexual abuse by her stepfather. (The pastor took appropriate action.) Following our advice is like carrying the proverbial umbrella—if you have one, it probably won't rain.

If you do not have local training programs, or if you need help in locating resources, please contact the Center for the Prevention of Sexual and Domestic Violence at 206.634.1903; fax: 206.634.0115; e-mail: <cpsdv@cpsdv.org>; and Web site: <www.cpsdv.org>.

Journey Pouch

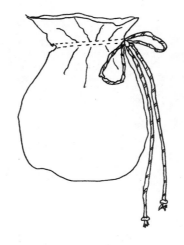

Journey Pouch Contents

Gathering women and girls in a Daughters Arise! retreat is fun and inspiring. But as you create your own retreat, planners' heads will be rattling in the months before the retreat with details, details, and details of the program and the practicalities of living together. We've tried to save you some of the struggle by providing, in this section, examples of practical items: schedules, menus, and budgets. We also include program ideas and samples of songs, stories, and activities.

Journey Pouch
PRACTICALITIES

CHOOSING YOUR DATE AND SITE

Set the date for your retreat 9–12 months ahead! Get there first! Of course, this is after checking church and community calendars, but we cannot emphasize enough the importance of setting intention and asking people to reserve the date. This early reservation is especially true if you will be using a church or youth organization camp such as Girl Scouts or YWCA.

THE POWER OF PERSONAL INVITATION

Start thinking about women friends and their daughters who you know would really enjoy this retreat. Think about women who have already dreamed about a rite of passage for girls. They may have a granddaughter, niece, godchild, or other special girl in their life, if not a daughter. Think about girls—friends of your daughters, relatives, girls in your church or school.

For your first year, consider handwritten individual invitations or face-to-face, personal invitations. Many moms are already nervous about the variety of offerings for their daughters, from "New Age" to pop culture, and will need a sure articulation from you of the foundation of this retreat.

Our first year, women in our planning group had daughters of the right age range to invite. Added to that core group were the daughters and granddaughters of women in our friendship and church groups who had expressed a strong desire to participate and contribute to a first retreat. This made it possible to invite the girls as colleagues for testing a "pilot" retreat. We shared with them that we had an idea, but it needed testing before offering it to girls we didn't know.

DECIDING ON YOUR AUDIENCE

While you will need to include all the "Essential Elements" in the Guidebook (pages 26–59), you can fine-tune the retreat schedule according to the ages of girls attending your retreat (more about that under "About Schedules").

- You may want to invite girls from a single-age group for your first retreat, such as a class from Sunday school or a middle-school youth group. This could be a great way to start your first retreat. A skit or activity could be presented to the group to generate interest and to get the necessary peer support ("I'll go if you'll go.")
- An added benefit in having a group begin a spiritual journey together is that it offers unique possibilities for developing new themes each summer (or whatever time the retreat is scheduled) and the potential of deeper conversation and support for one another through these shared experiences.

First Steps

- We have learned that you will not need this single-age group in subsequent retreats, but for your first year, it might feel reassuring to the planners to have a ready-made, cohesive group. Our happy experience has been that the nature of the retreat invites relationships beyond age boundaries and beyond school or friendship groups.

One caveat regarding the age issue, however, is that the girls are initially more comfortable at the retreat when there are at least two girls in the same age grouping if you have a wide-range of ages. Our retreats usually span ages eleven to eighteen. As long as each girl could find at least one other girl about her own age at the retreat, a natural camaraderie of shared interests provided the security and comfort as a foundation for then reaching out to other ages in the activities.

And, from experience, the couple of times that we were persuaded by eager mothers to include girls younger than eleven, we learned that their maturation level was not on a par with the older girls for it to be an optimum experience for either. On the evaluation forms, older girls advised us not to include girls younger than eleven; their observation was that discussions and group decision-making were hampered by the younger girls. It caused ambivalent feelings—the older girls felt protective about wanting to include the younger ones and, at the same time, felt guilty about their frustration that their own needs weren't being met because of the caretaking needed for the younger girls.

This dilemma produced creative discussion about how the retreat might be extended and developed to be more of a "Women's Lodge," including very young ones. Special attention would need to be given for their roles and inclu-

sion for certain activities, reserving their participation in the Girls' Ceremony until they reach age eleven. There could be other ceremonies for older women who had never experienced a rite of passage for themselves or were ready to celebrate entering menopause or the age of "Elder." All of this suggests fertile ground for you readers to plow. But for the Daughters Arise! retreat, we simply advise inviting girls eleven years and older.

THE WRITTEN INVITATION

As you review our sample invitations, you will observe the increased specificity of some items. For example, note "What to Bring." We weren't sure at our first retreat that the girls would want to dress up for their ceremony. The girls told us that it added greatly to the feeling of celebrating themselves and to the expression of their full femininity. So, we pass that along to you to be specific about bringing dresses, skirts, blouses, scarves, and other ornamentation for this special ceremonial time.

SELECTING A SITE

We refer you to "How We Do It . . . Seeing Creation with New Eyes," page 19. Even an urban setting will yield spaces of nature to become acquainted with and provide the setting for most of the activities, even if the location will be treated as a "day camp" with overnight indoors.

About Schedules

We want to point out some aspects about designing the retreat schedule that can be influenced by the age group(s) of your girls.

BALANCE PHYSICAL ACTIVITIES

Balance the day among sitting activities, light physical activities, and more energetic physical activities. We are greatly indebted to Maggie Shelton and Stephanie Weller for an analysis of this balance for each day of our fourth retreat. Their focus was to balance the needs of eleven- and twelve-year- olds (the age of their daughters at the retreat.) They reasoned that girls of this age share a common school day schedule for nine months of the year and that could be a good starting guide for activity balance during the retreat. They estimated that the girls' average fifteen-hour day looked like this:

SITTING TIME	LIGHT ACTIVITY	HEAVY ACTIVITY	PERCENTAGE RATIO
(class time, homework, TV time) 6.75 hours	(meal time, between classes, after school, chores, playing) 5.25 hours	(physical-education classes, after-school sports, private participation in gymnastics, dance, swim teams, etc.). 3.0 hours	45/35/20

Comparable activities in the retreat were:

SITTING TIME: Crafts, altar time, stories, songs, Four-fold Way presentations, tipi time, campfire, worship

LIGHT ACTIVITY: Meditations that required movement, meal preparation and meals, some games/ crafts, campfire dramas, midrash planning and acting out, ceremony planning, Journey Walk, some Four-fold Way activities, some parts of Girls' Ceremony

HEAVY ACTIVITY: Body presence exercises, some games, songs with dance movement, dance, beach or forest walk, some Four-fold exercises, dance and game parts of Girls' Ceremony

If the age range of your girls is older, the ratio could be more like 50/30/20. Nevertheless, since a significant emphasis in the retreat is reclaiming the body as gift and expression of the spirit, we need to continue to incorporate physical interaction in the learning process as much as possible. Our own goal each retreat is to **strive to include more movement. Anticipate that it will be a good struggle to do so!**

If you have a wide-range of ages participating, one suggestion is to provide a discussion Circle for girls over eighteen or a Circle for girls who have attended the retreat in a previous year and are ready to apply what they have learned in a deeper manner. Our experience has been that many of these alumnae want to come back and take on a more active role in mentoring and facilitating activities for new girls. At these "older girl" times, the younger girls could have more free time to enjoy nature, do more crafts, take a nap—simply enjoy more unstructured time for their developmental needs.

BALANCE CONTENT FOR THE LENGTH OF THE RETREAT

In one planner's evaluation, she suggested, tongue-in-cheek, that we have four plans from which to select: Basic, Economy, Middle-of-the-Road, and Deluxe. But this smorgasbord or cafeteria-style selection belies how integrally woven the content and activities are over the several days of the retreat. Your challenge will be to include all the "Essential Elements," within the time frame you set for your retreat. Rather than eliminate an essential element, you may need to have fewer related activities with each element.

Compare our schedules from the following first-to-fourth-year retreats. Our first year, as we have related, was more of a pilot retreat. We started with only one overnight meeting, from Friday at 1:00 p.m. through Saturday at 6:30 p.m. We (planners) presented most of the midrash scripture experiences or had scripts prepared for the girls to read. In the following years, we found that for each new activity, we needed to add more retreat time.

At the second retreat, we added one more overnight and a half-day because:

- the girls were ready to develop their own midrash and plays

  Need: more planning and presentation time for the girls' midrash and plays

- we introduced Tipi Time at the suggestion of the girls from the first retreat

  Need: time for introduction as well as the Tipi Time itself

- we introduced the Four-fold Way

  Need: time for introduction, four presentations, and related participatory activities

- we added scheduled morning "Awakening the Body" exercises

  Need: time as a whole group each morning

For the third retreat, we added one more evening and overnight (Thursday dinner–Sunday noon meal) because of additional goals:

- we added small group (2–3) interaction for shy participants before introducing to large Circle participation

  Need: time for opening activity and time in campfire schedule for get acquainted game

- we added more movement and more participatory activities

  Need: time for modeling, time for girls' participation within each presentation

- we included more integrating of parallels between scripture stories and Four-fold Way attributes

  Need: more examples of midrash and girls' discussion of how characters in scripture displayed attributes of Warrior-Leader, Teacher, Healer, and Visionary

- we added staff meeting after campfire each evening to deal with inevitable questions or difficulties

  Need: campfire closure for all with request for fire monitor for those staying up later

For our fourth retreat, we did not add more time, but we worked with adjusting the schedule, and we did add two more scheduled events:

- a new "introduction to the weekend" using the familiar *The Wizard of Oz* story

  Need: a shift in timing of opening evening schedule

- a time before dark prior to our last campfire for participants to show and tell about their artwork and crafts over the retreat—masks, dolls, pouches, personal-journey altar boxes, journal covers, poems, dance

BALANCE INPUT WITH PROCESS TIME

How you balance these two needs will vary with your individual participants and your age groupings. Some individuals simply need more process time regardless of age. It is their individual learning style. This is one reason it is so important to include two opportunities to make adjustments in your schedule:

1. to begin at least one Circle each day with a check-in time framed as "asking for what you need"

2. to discuss necessary schedule adjustments every evening at your staff meeting time

As we planned our fifth retreat, we focused on lightening up our Friday schedule. On her evaluation, one adult participant from the previous retreat said, "There were so many new concepts introduced for me, I felt like I was sitting in a puddle I couldn't absorb." In previous years, however, at what we had planned as "process time" or free time, the middle-teen girls were asking us what they could "do" or "work on."

Other factors will affect how much content and explanation will be needed. How much your adult participants know about church history will affect how open and able they are to understand the correlation between scripture, folktales, and other cultures' wisdom stories. Very young girls need more explicit explanation of the Four-fold Way archetypes and guided questions about how they can recognize these characteristics in everyday life. Conversely, older teens like to be left with the metaphorical ambiguities to search out their own meanings.

As Stephanie said, "When input and process are out of balance, fatigue and confusion are emotions that can arise and behavior might express as irritability, resentment, or inability to absorb further concepts."

Checklist for Deciding Whether to Include an Element, Experience, or Activity in Your Retreat

Have you planned elements which

❑ Welcome girls and women as equally valuable, all beloved daughters of God?

❑ Provide enough variety of stories of courageous, creative, strong, intuitive women and girls to expand vision beyond cultural nearsightedness?

❑ Provide experiences that help see scripture and creation with new eyes—reintroducing the perspective that, rather than inviting God into our presence, we bring ourselves into God's presence, which is all around us?

❑ Provide opportunities for expressing gratitude and praise?

❑ Provide for ceremony, in supportive witness of the gathered community, that celebrates the understanding that the self is a gift of a loving God?

For each proposed element/activity ask

1. How does it increase awareness that we are each needed, and that the way we relate to each other invites us to make complete the Body of Christ?

2. How does it increase awareness that our bodies are a gift from God—which we learn through body, mind, and spirit?

3. How does it increase awareness in the girls that they are surrounded by a supportive community of women of faith—those who came before us and those present with us today?

4. How does it increase awareness that the Spirit resides within us to guide us—that we can increasingly trust our inner knowing as we feed it with wisdom from stories, song, dance, prayer, and worship?

5. How does it increase awareness that the inner knowing and all our abilities are gifts to use, not only for our own benefit, but for others as well?

6. How does it increase awareness that the earth, our home, is a gift from God—that we are a part of all creation—which we are called to learn from, to protect, and to cherish?

For physically active experiences, add these questions to those above

7. Does the activity promote encouragement and support rather than competition?

8. Does the activity reward knowing when to keep one's own safety boundaries by being able to say "no" when necessary, as well as rewarding taking reasonable risks and stretching personal limitations?

9. Can all ability levels be welcomed into the activity?

SAMPLE OVERVIEW SCHEDULE

Sample Schedules

Thursday

5:00 p.m.	Women and girls arrive and register
6:30 p.m.	Greeting; dinner
7:30 p.m.	Beginning activities
8:30 p.m.	Campfire; get acquainted games
10:00 p.m.	Planners' meeting

Friday

7:00 a.m.	Meditation; breakfast
8:10 a.m.	Awakening the Body exercise
8:30 a.m.	Introduction to crafts: masks, rattles, dolls
9:00 a.m.	Circle; altar
	Sharing stories, "when we were seven to ten years old"
11:00 a.m.	Games
11:30 a.m.	Songs; introduction to the Four-fold Way
12:30 p.m.	Lunch
1:15 p.m.	Pouches
1:45 p.m.	Sharing stories, "when we were eleven to seventeen"
3:00 p.m.	Girls—Tipi Time; Women—Holding and Releasing Our Daughters
4:30 p.m.	Midrash; craft time
6:00 p.m.	Dinner
7:30 p.m.	Four-fold Way: Warrior-Leader
8:30 p.m.	Campfire; "Vasalisa the Wise" play
10:00 p.m.	Planners' meeting

Saturday

7:00 a.m.	Meditation; breakfast; exercise
8:30 a.m.	Songs; Four-fold Way: Healer
9:15 a.m.	Movement song; Four-fold Way: Visionary
10:00 a.m.	Beach walk
12:00 p.m.	Lunch
12:30 p.m.	Sharing of gifts from the sea
1:15 p.m.	Crafts: altar boxes, pouches, rattles, masks
2:45 p.m.	Songs; Four-fold Way: Teacher
3:30 p.m.	Ceremony planning; crafts
6:00 p.m.	Dinner
8:00 p.m.	Journey Walk
8:45 p.m.	Campfire; sharing what we have made; s'mores
10:00 p.m.	Planners' meeting

Sunday

7:00 a.m.	Meditation; breakfast; exercise
8:15 a.m.	Girls prepare for ceremony; Women prepare blessings
9:15 a.m.	Worship service
10:30 a.m.	Girls' ceremony; blessing by women
12:30 p.m.	Closing lunch

SAMPLE COMPLETE SCHEDULE

Thursday

5:00 p.m. Registration—Dana

      Matins sign up—Gloria

6:30 p.m. Greeting song—Claudia and Kitty

      Dinner—Sally, Paula, Donna (See "Feeding The Multitude," Journey Pouch, page 109.)

      Dinner theater; "Rules of the House"—Sally and Amy Wa

      Overview of weekend (*The Wizard of Oz*)—Donna and Claudia

7:30 p.m. "You Have Called Me By Name" song—Gloria; form small groups (2 or 3)

      Rejoin Circle; each one introduce another in small group

8:00 p.m. Pass out journals—Kitty

      Creating altar or sacred space—Sally

      Understanding Circle—Sally

      Music introduction—"Take Off Your Shoes" music to place object on altar

      All join in song

      Midrash introduction; invite girls to work on play—Sally

8:30 p.m. Campfire

      Gathering songs—Linda and Claudia

      Mention opportunity to talk to Tipi Time facilitators—Peggy

8:50 p.m. Game, exercise (getting acquainted)—Peggy

      Story—"Mary and Elizabeth" play—Linda, Suzanne, Sally, and girls

      Closing song—Linda and Claudia

10:00 p.m. Staff meeting

Friday

7:00 a.m. Meditation—Dana and Peggy

7:30 a.m. Breakfast—Donna

      Blow conch shell—Amy Wi

8:00 a.m. Matins (5 minutes)

8:10 a.m. "Awakening the Body" exercise—Amy Wi or Dana

      "Round and Round" song—Claudia

      Explain concerns; check-in time—Kitty

8:30 a.m. Introduction to crafts—symbolism of working with hands—Suzanne

      Masks, rattles, dolls—Michele passes out doll kits

9:00 a.m. Circle-altar time—Sally

      Concerns; check-in—Kitty

      Personal stories of when we were seven to ten years old—Kitty with Linda assisting

      Peggy's story closes

      Stretch at halftime—Dana and girls

11:00 a.m. Movement: games ten-year-olds play

      (Balloons, hopscotch, follow the leader, blow bubbles)—Dana and girls

11:30 a.m. Song—Claudia

      Introduction of Four-fold Way (Wise Grandmother and Archetypes)

      "They'll Know We Are God's Children" song—Claudia

12:15 p.m.	Silent wandering time—Peggy introduces
12:30 p.m.	Lunch—Kitty
1:15 p.m.	Introduction to pouches—Suzanne, Maureen; altar boxes—Sally
1:45 p.m.	Sharing personal story (when we were eleven to seventeen)—Gloria with Donna assisting
	Continue crafts
2:45 p.m.	Introduction to Tipi—Paula
3:00 p.m.	Tipi Time—Dana and Suzanne
	Circle of mothers and others: holding and releasing—Peggy and Paula
	"Letting Go" song—Linda
	Resources—Donna
4:30 p.m.	Midrash; girls work on play—Gloria, Linda, Amy
	Free time: dolls, pouches, altar boxes
6:00 p.m.	Dinner—Claudia
7:30 p.m.	Circle sharing time—Sally (She then uses rattle to call in Warrior/Leader)
8:00 p.m.	Introduction to Way of the Warrior/Leader—Dana
	Song
8:30 p.m.	Campfire—gathering song
	Game—Peggy
	Story: "Vasalisa the Wise"—Linda reads, Claudia, Amy Wa, Suzanne act
	Wise Grandmother asks questions for discussion of story—Sally
9:30 p.m.	Closing song—Claudia
10:00 p.m.	Planners' meeting

Saturday

7:00 a.m.	Meditation—Dana
7:30 a.m.	Breakfast—Linda
8:00 a.m.	Blow conch shell for matins—Amy Wi
	Check-in; concerns—Kitty
8:10 a.m.	"Awakening the Body" exercise—Amy Wi or Dana
8:30 a.m.	Call Circle with song; Claudia calls in Healer with drums
	Introduction to way of the Healer—Donna
	Story and meditation
	Song
9:15 a.m.	"Mend and Weave" action song—Amy Wi
	Short break
9:30 a.m.	Circle gathers; Linda rings bells to call in Visionary
	Introduction to the way of the Visionary and story—Suzanne
10:00 a.m.	Beach walk—silent walk and meditation—introduction, Gloria
11:30 a.m.	Break
12:00 p.m.	Lunch—Peggy
12:30 p.m.	Regather Circle—share gifts from the sea—Gloria
1:15 p.m.	Reintroduce crafts—Suzanne
	Altar boxes, pouches, rattles, masks

2:30 p.m.	Transition time—singing, movement—all musicians
	Convening Circle—Gloria hits sticks together to call Teacher.
2:45 p.m.	Introduction to the way of the Teacher—Kitty
	Song—Claudia
3:30 p.m.	Girls' ceremony planning time in tipi—Dana, Suzanne, and girls
	Free time for others; women plan blessings for girls
	Continue crafts
4:30 p.m.	Small groups: Girls create story, midrash—Amy Wa and drama group
	Prepare for sharing art at campfire—Peggy and Suzanne
5:30 p.m.	If girls' midrash needs daylight, present here.
6:00 p.m.	Dinner—Dana
7:00 p.m.	Celebration of our creativity—share artwork, masks, dolls
	Sally explains personal altar sharing.
8:00 p.m.	Journey Walk with candles and song—Claudia
8:45 p.m.	Campfire opening—Peggy, Suzanne, Claudia
	Humming, rhythm instruments, circling masks
	Girls' midrash play, shared drama, songs, dance, art.
	Campfire closes with s'mores.
10:00 p.m.	Planners' meeting

Sunday

7:00 a.m.	Meditation—Dana
7:30 a.m.	Breakfast—Suzanne
8:15 a.m.	Girls prepare for ceremony—Dana, Suzanne
	Women in Circle create blessings for girls.
9:00 a.m.	Planners prepare for worship
9:15 a.m.	Worship—Gloria, Sally, Claudia
10:30 a.m.	Girls' Ceremony
	Wise Grandmother—"What do you wish from us?"—Sally
	Women's blessing for each girl
	Celebration and games
12:30 p.m.	Closing lunch—Gloria and Paula

COMMITTEES

Drama: Gloria, Linda, Amy Wa; **Crafts:** Suzanne, Kitty, Michele, Amy Wi; **Movement, Body Presence:** Amy Wi, Dana; **The Four-fold Way :** Donna, Kitty, Suzanne, Dana; **Tipi Time:** Dana, Suzanne, Peggy, Paula; **Registration:** Sally (brochure), Gloria (letter), Donna (mailing), Dana (sign-up); **Guidebook:** Sally, Gloria, Donna; **Food:** Gloria, Linda (shop), Peggy (chart and nametags), Paula (coordinator during retreat); **Worship:** Gloria, Sally, Claudia

Promotional Materials

Girls and women! Look ahead to August on your calendar and save these days: Thursday evening, August 6 (dinnertime), through Sunday noon, August 9 (lunchtime). For the third year on Whidbey Island, a retreat for women and girls will explore and honor the passage from the years of childhood into the journey of womanhood. The retreat is hosted by Circle of Stones, a South Whidbey women's writing group, and sponsored by the Commission on the Status and Role of Women (COSROW), Pacific Northwest Annual Conference of the United Methodist Church.

Sally Windecker opens her home and land overlooking Puget Sound for these summer days of storytelling, singing, crafts, and campfire dramatics. Women in the Bible, folktales, and our own personal stories all remind us of our God-given creative strength as girls and women.

Later newsletters will provide more information about this event, but save the dates! Gloria Koll is a retreat planner and participant each year, as well as a contact person for Trinity Lutheran. Space is limited, so call Gloria at (phone number) if you would like to sign up at this time.

RETREAT PUBLICITY

Daughters Arise! Retreat
From August 6 through August 9, girls and women will gather for the fourth year on the Windecker farm overlooking Puget Sound. We bring sleeping bags, Bibles, journals, and jeans. We bring tacos, vegetarian lasagna, and artichoke dip. We sing, dance, and dip our toes in tide pools. Sound like camp? Sort of—but the challenge of the journey into womanhood in our society demands much more than that!

Something dramatic happens to girls in early adolescence. Just as planes and ships disappear mysteriously into the Bermuda Triangle, so do the selves of girls . . . crash and burn in a social and developmental Bermuda Triangle. In early adolescence, studies show that girls IQ scores drop and their math and science scores plummet. They lose resiliency and optimism and become less curious and inclined to take risks. They lose their assertive, energetic and "tomboyish" personalities and become more deferential, self-critical and depressed. They report great unhappiness with their own bodies.
—Mary Pipher, *Reviving Ophelia: Saving the Selves of Adolescent Girls.*

Of course, adolescence has never been easy. The Christian church has always tried to equip our young people to resist the siren call of the world's destructive temptations. But as Mary Pipher, clinical psychologist for adolescents, observes: "Girls today are much more oppressed. They are coming of age in a more dangerous, sexualized and media-saturated culture . . . a girl-poisoning culture . . . What can we do to help them? We can strengthen girls so that they will be ready."

At the same time that Pipher was writing her best-selling book, members of the United Methodist Conference Commission on the Status and Role of Women (COSROW) were making observations parallel to those of Pipher and echoing a similar declaration, "Our daughters deserve a [church] in which all their gifts can be developed and appreciated." After several conference-wide planning discussions, COSROW invited a Circle of women writers on Whidbey Island to collaborate in creating a rite of passage for girls, anchored in Christ's teachings, which would honor, strengthen, and encourage their journey into womanhood.

As we women of faith began this task, we acknowledged with sadness that the Christian church has given women and girls mixed messages. The liberating news of the life and teachings of Jesus has been shrouded by millennia of cultural contaminations of hierarchy, temple patriarchy, and of philosophy which split asunder the wholeness of spirit and body and its further distortion of identifying women's bodies with the "weakness of the flesh." Yet we read scripture's stories of how Jesus called women to discipleship, friendship, and witness and encouraged them in ways in juxtaposition to his time and culture. We yearn to hear Jesus and the church speak clearly to our daughters and to us in our time and culture.

We knew we needed to reintroduce our daughters and ourselves to the authentic gospel of Jesus' accepting love. We also wanted to reclaim women's way of working and storytelling in circle as women always had done—around a quilt, the village well, the birth of a child, sharing the work, stories, and wisdom.

Reflecting on our own lives, we became convinced that choices a woman makes out of respect for her inner knowing can be both wise and liberating. Rather than being an object for someone else's demand, a young woman can become the subject of her own story, confident that the Spirit will call forth gifts God has placed within her.

As older women of life experience and faith, we have wisdom to pass along. At the retreat, girls and women tell and act out stories filled with resourceful girls and women who are heroes in the Bible, in folktales, in history, and in our own lives.

We sing songs telling each girl, "you are a child of God, nothing can shake your confidence; you are a child of God, nothing can take your inheritance!" As we walk the beach, gather in tipi, make pouches, as we eat and worship together, our stories and songs pass wisdom from women to girls—and from girls to women.

You are invited to participate in this four-day retreat exploring and celebrating the life-journey of girls and women. The retreat is scheduled this year from 5:00 p.m., Thursday evening, August 6, through the noon celebration meal, Sunday, August 9. Please call for a letter of further details and for reservations:

Gloria Koll, Trinity Lutheran Church, at (phone number)

Donna Humphreys, Langley United Methodist Church, at (phone number)

Planning a Budget

DAUGHTERS ARISE! BUDGETS

The Daughters Arise! retreat can be planned on a "shoestring" budget as evidenced by our first year's retreat, especially if the site is someone's home property and if the food is basically potluck.

OUR FIRST RETREAT BUDGET

Everything was donated
Total: $0.00

OUR SECOND RETREAT BUDGET

Photocopy costs (invitation letters, schedule, scripts)	$20.00
Postage for invitation letters	8.32
Plaster rolls for face masks (2 masks per roll)	50.00
(All other craft supplies were donated)	
Food to supplement potluck items for lunch and dinner	91.90
(See "Feeding the Multitude," page 109)	
Total:	$170.22

To cover costs for 30 participants (this included facilitators), each would need to pay $5.67. We charged a participant fee of $5.00, plus food to share.

OUR THIRD RETREAT BUDGET

We increased our budget to publicize the development of the retreat at the Annual Conference of the United Methodist Church; we purchased more craft materials, and we asked for support from our sponsoring United Methodist Commission, COSROW, to cover purchased food costs so that the facilitators would not have to donate both time and food.

Photocopy costs were covered by our local Langley United Methodist Church.

Craft Supplies	$77.95
Food	226.72
Total:	$304.67

At 28 participants, we would need $10.88 per participant to cover costs. We charged a total participant fee of $10.00, plus food.

OUR FOURTH RETREAT BUDGET

We realized that whether costs were covered by donation or sponsorship, it would not reflect a realistic total if we did not track and record them, so for purposes of assisting other groups to compile a realistic budget, we attempted to list our real costs.

Crafts

30 boxes for personal "altars"	$27.81
Candles for altar and other ceremonies	8.36
Candles for Journey Walk Ceremony	11.83
Apples to hold candles	6.00
Fabric for Four-fold Way and Grandmother Archetypes	37.07
Plaster rolls for masks	62.96
40 small, spiral-bound journals	43.01
40 tiny mirror rounds for Healer Archetype presentation	5.96
Wooden clothespins to make doll kits (30 count package)	3.59
Nametag materials for 40	11.07
Craft Total:	$199.83

Food

	$411.47

Miscellaneous

Batteries for tape player to use for outdoor meditations	$ 8.50
Photocopies for songbook and confirmation letters	28.00
Site preparation	50.00

(This will be a much larger budget item if your retreat is at a campground or retreat center. We hired a housecleaner for the private home where our retreat was held.)

Long distance phone calls	50.00
Mileage and ferry tolls to purchase food at grocery store	20.00
Postage to mail confirmation letters	12.80
Miscellaneous Total:	$109.30

Promotional Brochure

1 ream of #60 paper	$30.00
1 ream of letter weight matching paper	20.00
500 matching envelopes	25.00
Copy center cost for 165 brochures	17.00
Postage to send brochures to district COSROW representatives	16.54
Brochure Total:	$108.81

Promotional color flyer

Photos	$ 5.93
Color copy (20 copies)	47.67
Postage to closest churches in our district	11.00
Flyer Total :	$64.60

Retreat Total:	$584.01

At forty participants, we would need to charge $14.60 each to cover costs. We did not want facilitators to have to pay, however. This would mean 28 participants would need to pay $20.85 to cover costs.

To ease the transition from the previous years' low costs and retain some of the great flavors of the potluck tradition, we had two different fees: one for local participants, which was $10.00, plus one salad or vegetable dish and one dessert. We had another fee for participants traveling from a distance: We charged $25.00 for adults and $15.00 for girls, and they did not have to worry about bringing food.

Of the forty registrants, thirty-four attended. We had twenty-seven paying participants for a total of $335.00. Our Pacific Northwest COSROW underwrote the balance of the cost.

SPONSORSHIPS, CAMPERSHIPS, SCHOLARSHIPS

To make sure that you will have funds to design and mail promotional materials, find a sponsor or an organization willing to underwrite the costs of promotion. Our Commission on the Role and Status of Women was willing to make this retreat possible and to cover other costs if there were not enough full-paying participants. The Conference United Methodist Women was willing to provide scholarship money to make sure that all who would like to come would be able to attend.

Along with the Daughters Arise! retreat brochure, which they mailed out, each district representative in our Pacific Northwest Conference also sent a letter to potential attendees in their district offering to find scholarships, camperships, or travel subsidies for those wishing to attend the retreat.

We believe this was a remarkable "good buy" for three days and three nights, and we know you can do as well or better. Have no fear! You can do it!

Scheduling and Planning

To assist in your planning process, the following are selected notes and agendas from a few of our planning sessions. It is important to remember in your planning sessions to practice Circle together and to explore your material together. Try creating midrash, practicing songs and dances, sharing story. This will strengthen your own relationship in Circle and enhance your ability to lead others.

Agenda for the February 13 planning meeting:

1. Shape, size, and location of worship service; the Girls' Ceremony—place? Before or after worship?

2. How or if to use the Grandmother tree?

3. Structure: What are the bones?

4. Dream sharing activity

5. Committees and leadership;

   Food committee:
   Meal teams:
   The Four-fold Way:
      Warrior-Leader:
      Healer:
      Visionary:
      Teacher:
      Wise Grandmother/Crone:
   Crafts: Kitty
   Worship: Sally
   Newsletter: Dana
   Brochure: Sally
   Music: Linda, Claudia
   Drama: Linda, Amy Wa

6. COSROW funding: need budget by February meeting

7. Time in weekend for participants to "check-in," feelings, reactions, problems . . . when?

8. Prepare explanation to Tipi Time for mothers

SAMPLE LETTERS FROM
THE PLANNING STAGE OF SEVERAL RETREATS

April . . .
Dear Midwives of Daughters Arise!, enclosed are items for your immediate attention.

Please note the wonderful letter that Joanne Coleman Campbell mailed to all the COSROW representatives. They all affirm and appreciate the long birthing process of this creation.

Please look over the working draft of the schedule. Look where your name is—did you remember you said yes? Have you conferred with others (if listed) for that activity or committee?

Look where your name is not listed—please let Donna know if your name was inadvertently omitted somewhere on schedule or committee.

VERY IMPORTANT! The "Reporting" meeting is Friday, June 5, 9:00 a.m.–2:00 p.m. at Sally's. This means you will have met as many times as necessary for your activity or committee so that you are prepared to report, or prepared to request specific help. Please, please clear your calendar, provide other care for husbands and children (including phone contact), so that you can participate the full time without distraction. The meeting is 9:00 am–2:00 p.m. (yes, bring food). Committees will report; introduction to The Four-fold Way will rehearse/perform; Claudia will teach music (1/2 hour time slot).

EMERGENCY! FOOD COMMITTEE IS STILL NOT STAFFED NOR HAS MET!

If you can help, please call Donna.

Enclosed are two brochures and registration letters—keep one each for your notebook; please give the other to a girl and mother you hope will come. Note that there are two different letters—one for Whidbey Island residents, one for off-islanders. Let Donna know if you need more copies of either.

Thanks to Dana for update of schedule.

Four-fold Way four meet Thursday, April 30, 7:00 p.m. at Dana's, and Friday, May 8, 9:00 a.m. at Donna's.

Tipi Committee met April 7th—is there another meeting?

Joanne mailed letter to COSROW representatives and set up accounting system with Conference.

Sally did a wonderful job on the brochures! THANKS!

Donna mailed brochures and registration letters to COSROW representatives.

Manual/guidebook committee has met twice—concurred on table of contents.

For the upcoming June Meeting . . .

Planning Notes: Things/ideas to consider/include that we haven't finished with yet, that you have suggested, possibilities, impossibilities . . . please add your own.

—Gloria is working on a letter describing/inviting—to be mailed soon

—We came up with a slightly different title (other than "Becoming Woman") but I can't remember it

—More time for the further telling of our own stories, like when we were sixteen or twenty . . .

—Spaces for quiet time

—Other kinds of body time

—Dance, play, song, "random acts of mirth" (leaving spaces for)

—What other songs?

—Focusing/refining the work of the weekend

—Can we make/find images of each "Way" to put in our pouches?

—Can we make rattles?

—What are the small group times; are there enough?

—Some things we have said, questions we have asked, that we need to keep in mind:

> "What are your dreams for yourself?"
>
> "We are working to elevate the young women's and our own lives."
>
> "What makes you feel alive?"
>
> "Strength implies remaining the subject of one's own life and resisting the cultural pressure to become the object of male experience" (*Reviving Ophelia*)
>
> ". . . valuing all parts of the self whether or not they are valued by the culture" (Ibid).
>
> "We are creating a safe place for belief, doubt, and exploration."
>
> Our deepest fear is not that we are inadequate. Our deepest fear is that we are powerful beyond measure. It is our light, not our darkness that frightens us. We ask ourselves, who am I to be brilliant, gorgeous, talented and fabulous? Actually, who are you not to be? You are a child of God. Your playing small doesn't serve the world. We were born to make manifest the Glory of God within us. It's not just in some of us; it's in everyone. And as we let our own Light shine, we . . . give other people permission to do the same.
>
> —Marianne Williamson

EXAMPLE OF AN AGENDA FOR AN OVERNIGHT PRACTICE MEETING FOR PLANNERS

"Joining the Circle of Women"
A Coming-of-Age Retreat for Our Daughters

Dear stone sisters and all midwives of the retreat:

This is a bold reminder that our most important planning retreat is only a week away!

NEXT FRIDAY   MAY 17   5:00 P.M.   SALLY'S HOUSE

Agenda: To add sinew and flesh to the bones of the retreat so life may be breathed into the experience at the retreat of AUGUST 9, 10, 11.

FRIDAY:	**ARRIVE 5:00 P.M. SHARP WITH POTLUCK DISH TO SHARE.**
5:30–6:30 p.m.	Eat and cleanup
	Stretch, stake out sleeping space, push-ups
7:00 p.m.	Focus intention; call our Circle
	Cedar bough "Journey Walk" ritual—Maureen
	"For the Greening" hymn—Claudia
	Building our altar—Joanne (bring an article which symbolizes the wisdom you wish to pass on to our daughters)
	Recalling and remembering intention—
	Practicing a new way of work in Circle—Donna
	Song "Gathered Here in the Mystery of This Hour"
	Naming the "bones"—core essentials and framework
	Claudia begins process—all to contribute
	(WE WILL NEED YOUR DRAFT SCHEDULES HERE)
8:30 p.m.	Celebration break—Bodywork/dance—Dana
8:35 p.m.	Reconvene with song—Karen
	Refocus intention and energy—Gloria
	Naming the "sinews and flesh" needed—Circle—Suzanne start
	Prayer for discernment—Peggy
	Song—"Let Us Go Now to the Banquet"
	Poem—"There Will Come a Day"
	Speaking from the Circle—
	Gifts I observe for this work—mine, others
	Prayer for wisdom and quickening of hearts—Sally
	Naming the call of our hearts
	Asking for collaboration
	"To be with me in my struggle, I need . . . "
9:30 p.m.	Sacred commitment to the calling of our hearts
	Closing of large Circle
	Song—"What You Hold"—Claudia, Sally, Amy

| 9:45 p.m. | Campfire: Story sharing, poems, songs, dances, random acts of mirth, merriment, and silliness |

Saturday:

7:00–8:00 a.m.	Awaken
8:00 a.m.	Breakfast
8:30 a.m.	Drumming, chanting, body prayers—Suzanne
8:45 a.m.	Calling the Circle—Refocus intention and energy—Gloria
	Dreams and visions in the night
9:00 a.m.	**Attaching "sinews and muscle"**—work in small groups on fleshing out elements, including costs
10:30 a.m.	**Celebration break outside**—Karen
10:45 a.m.	**Tryout new experiences**—outside, weather permitting
11:30 a.m.	Adjust schedule—Sally
12:00 p.m.	Prayer and song—Linda
	Lunch—cleanup
1:00 p.m.	The Great Communication: Dana and Susanne
	Invitation list
	New letter of invitation
	New flyer/poster
	Budget request
	Outline of schedule
	Working notebook
	Equipment/crafts list
	Menu and shopping list
	Ideas for sharing chores—drawing from a hat, etc.
1:45 p.m.	Set next meeting date, volunteers to convene small work groups—Joanne
2:00 p.m.	Closing ritual—Kitty and Maureen

THIS IS A WORKING DRAFT—PLEASE CALL AND CONFIRM WILLING-NESS TO FACILITATE ITEM LISTED OR CHANGE WITH SOMEONE OR VOLUNTEER TO ADD AND/OR INSERT SOMETHING.

RSVP TO DONNA.

SUMMARY OF THINGS TO PREPARE AND BRING:
Yourself, for the entire time if at all possible.
Something for the altar that symbolizes wisdom you would like to pass on to our daughters.

YOUR DRAFT OF THE REVISED SCHEDULE FOR AUGUST 9, 10, AND 11, with elements, activities listed. THIS IS FOR EACH OF US TO DO AHEAD OF TIME.

POTLUCK DISH FOR DINNER AND SALAD FOR SATURDAY LUNCH.

August . . .

Tasks, Dear Circle of Stones: Our special weekend is here! This is a reminder of little details that will help Sally relax and participate. We are each asked to serve as a hostess in her home.

1. Parking—Karen and others

2. Introductions—several and all

3. Secretary (note taker)—All (Stones) take journal notes of the workshop, (Dana to collate later?)

4. Food prep (before 1:00 p.m. Friday)—everyone come around 10:00 Friday morning (bring sack lunch). We will tend to last minute details including any necessary food prep.

5. Food buying (Costco)—Karen

6. Bringing:

   tomatoes, pickles, napkins, plastic cups—Claudia

   ketchup and mustard, paper plates—Donna

   vegetable lasagna (16 servings)—Karen's recipe (?),—Karen, Gloria

   coffee, communion goblets, wine, and grape juice—Sally

   plastic forks—Karen

   copies of *Women Who Run With the Wolves*— anyone who has one

   Conch shell—Donna

   Pocket Doll, Bell—Kitty

   Each Stone bring:

       her own mug

       any "sit-upons" (like the blue, plastic cushions)

       books that have been important to us on our journey (we'll set up a book table for browsing)

   Sketchpad, workshop journal, nametags—Sally

   Floor pillows—Gloria

   Craft supplies—all can bring any fabric, beads, needles, yarn, floss, etc. for pouches, and small stones for stone painting

7. Food prep and cleanup (each meal)—sign-up sheet

8. Help greet our guests, show them around, especially necessary information:

   stow gear on deck around hot tub (or by your bed or sleeping place)

   show where available beds are: priority to those with special physical needs, elder guests, otherwise it's "first come-first serve"

   hang bath towels on hot tub railing if necessary (there will be ample hand towels in each bathroom)

   choose a mug and keep throughout weekend

   available food, when and where

   boundaries of property and access

   nametags

We'll go over this Friday morning—see you then!

Donna and Sally

The Paper Trail

Paperwork is not the number one favorite occupation of any creative person. Nevertheless, orderly forms and records work for us as a reference librarian to jog the memory, as a secretary to contact participants, as an auditor to check on finances, and as a firm taskmaster to see that chores are completed. If we can't hire a staff of professionals, we must rely on well-organized paperwork.

Here are sample mailings, registration and release forms, nametags, meal team and other signup sheets, and evaluation and participant-list forms for you to consider as you develop your own paper trail.

To: Interested Women

From: Circle of Stones; a women's writing Circle, an *ad hoc* committee of COSROW of the Pacific Annual Conference of the United Methodist Church

Regarding: August Women's Retreat

Greetings:

We would like to invite you to a retreat for women interested in creating a rite of passage from childhood to womanhood. In a pastoral setting on Whidbey Island, overlooking Puget Sound, we will hold council in Circle, share story, sing, and play, evoking the Holy Spirit/Ruah's inspiration in developing this rite of passage.

If you would like to join us and have not already registered, please call_____.

If you wish to prepare ahead of time, we ask that you read from the following texts and consider the questions we've included:

Holy Bible: Mark 5:25–43
> What is it that Jesus is calling forth in these women?
> Which of these women do you identify with at this time in your life?

Women Who Run with the Wolves by Clarissa Pinkola Estés
> Chapter 3:   What are the gifts of the mother?
>   What are the necessary tasks to become a woman?
> Chapter 9:   Consider what robs you of your soul ("pelt"). As author Estés might ask,
> "What is required to put us in our rightful wildish natures?" (page 268)
> "How can we share and teach the ways we become overdrawn and the ways we become replenished?

Circle of Stones: Woman's Journey to Herself by Judith Duerk
> How might your life have been different?
> How can our daughters and other young women's lives be different?

We hope you'll join us.

Registration for the Daughters Arise! Retreat

Registration for the **Daughters Arise! retreat** is very easy. The cost is nominal. The question is—who wants to come? **This may be the last year** this retreat is offered on Whidbey Island. **The hope** is that women and girls from around the Conference will attend and then begin their own Circles to create retreats for their own communities. **The women from the Circle of Stones, as well as COSROW members, are offering technical support for new groups.** There is also a manual being written for those who attend the retreat to assist in the re-creation of **the Daughters Arise! retreat**—a re-creation that is as unique and specific to a community or culture as each of us is unique.

If you believe that girls need this kind of supportive community as they move into womanhood, we urge you to make time on your calendar and attend this retreat. However, space is very limited—we want you to register **now**! If you have any questions, you may track down a COSROW member (see list below). You may also turn your registration in **now** to Joanne Coleman Campbell. Registration deadline is July 10. There is a waiting list of people from Whidbey Island who wish to attend—we are holding spaces open until the 10th for those out of the area. **Please Register Immediately!**

COSROW Members Attending Annual Conference Are:

Joanne _____ , Tacoma District

Karen _____ , Seattle District

Keat _____ , Spokane District

Reta _____ , UMW, Tacoma District

Donna _____ , Puget Sound District (Saturday only)

Phyllis _____ , Spokane District (Saturday only)

Karen _____ , Vancouver District

George _____ , Spokane District

Cottie _____ , Walla Walla District

The Daughters Arise! Retreat: A Celebration of Passage

Details and Registration

Who: Minimum Age for girls—11 years old or have begun menses. We have had a range of participants from 11–18 years old.

Grandmothers, other women relatives, or mentors can be the "Mom"/sponsor.

Three-generation groups have been especially fun: grandmother, mother, and daughter (or two).

When: 5:00 p.m., Thursday, August 12, through noon meal, Sunday, August 15.

Where: Windecker Farm on Whidbey Island, Washington. Please turn to back of this page for directions and important ferry information.

What to Bring:

1. Sleeping bag and pillow—there are some beds and floor spaces available inside.

2. Your own tent if you would like to sleep outside—there will also be two tipis.

3. Towel, wash cloth, and personal toiletries—(Yes, there are regular bathrooms and showers.)

4. Clothing: Include outdoor clothing—temperatures in the Northwest can vary from rain to sunny and warm to very cool evenings by the campfire. Include sturdy shoes for walking (beach and woods). Please note: Girls and moms may also bring a festive dress or skirt, colorful scarves, etc. Previous years revealed that some girls like to dress in flowing skirts or dresses for the ceremony they design for themselves. Girls have told us to urge you to bring them.

5. Items to share: Pictures of women important to your life, items/symbols of your faith and spiritual journey—these have been everything from angels, to teddy bears, to beads, to Bibles. Bring songs, poems, and prayers to share during matins and/or worship. Also bring journal or notebook and books and articles for our resource table. If you have attended before, please bring things you made—doll, mask, pouch.

Questions? Please call Kitty at_____

Please note: There will be an opportunity for girls to talk and ask questions about sexuality in a confidential setting with prepared facilitators. An introduction and a Q & A time will be provided first before girls go apart with facilitators. (An alternative activity will be provided for those girls who do not wish to participate in the discussion.)

- -

(Clip and mail)

Registration: Fee—$25.00 each

Adult_____Age_____Daughter_____Age_____

Address_____

Phone_____Total $ Enclosed_____

Please make checks payable to_____and send to Kitty at _____

_____

Current ferry fare—cash is best, checks are accepted:

Car and driver—each way: $5.75

Passenger (in vehicle or walk on): $2.50, collected in Mukilteo only.

Youth fare—(5–18 years): $1.80

Senior fare—(65 and older): half the regular passenger fare

Directions to the Windecker Farm . . .

_____

_____

_____

- -

Please let us know:

If registration fee assistance is needed_____

Vegetarian meals are requested _____

Need to have a bed inside_____

Other special needs _____

"FEEDING THE MULTITUDE"

Food supplies:

We've tried **three different ways** of gathering food for the retreat. They all work, and each way has certain advantages. Whichever method you choose, you will need a menu planner and a food buyer. Consider providing vegetarian alternatives and allowing for other dietary needs.

1. **Ask everyone to choose two of the following food items to bring: main dish, salad, and dessert.** You will need lots of refrigerator and other food space. Unless you like surprises, you may want to check ahead of time that not everyone is bringing the same thing. The fun part of this method is that wonderfully tasty creations walk through the door as people arrive. Your menu planner will make a list as items arrive and will decide which food will be used at which meal. Food buyers will supply breakfast items and drinks.

2. **Have only local people bring food items.** As compensation, they will pay a bit less for the weekend. Those coming from a distance will pay slightly more, but will not have to juggle food as they travel to the retreat. This way, you will still have some homemade treats, but planners will have to supply more store items for the weekend.

3. **Don't ask anyone to bring food.** A few may still bring treats, but planners will supply all food needed for the weekend. You will, of course, have to factor this expense into the cost of your retreat. You will have better control over what will be served at each meal, but you may have to rely on many pre-made items from grocery stores or other markets.

Meal preparation and serving:

1. **Most items should require very little preparation—ready-to-eat or heat and serve.** Our parting meal on Sunday became a celebration with oven-ready chicken one year and salmon another. This special dinner honored Sunday worship and the Girls' Ceremony.

2. **Retreat participants are happy to help, but someone needs to preplan and organize.** You may want to post a color-coded poster of food preparation teams, one team for each meal. Each woman and girl will have a ribbon of her team color attached to her nametag. Balance the number of women and girls on each team and mix in folks who don't know each other. For each team, designate one woman who is acquainted with the kitchen and food plan to be team leader and to answer questions.

3. **This team approach is a good get acquainted time and a generational mixer, and it spreads around the duty and the fun of hosting a meal.** If retreat planners try to serve every meal, you will have little time to be co-participants in the retreat. (You will also find yourselves grumbling under your breath as you welcome others to the table.)

IT'S TIME TO EAT!

Ideas for Breakfast:

Bagels and cream cheese with jam
Cereal and fruit
Sweet muffins and English muffins
Milk, juice, coffee, tea, hot chocolate

Ideas for Lunch:

Salads
Tortillas or pita bread
Cheese, meat, chopped veggies for filling
Bread and sandwich makings
Fruit, guacamole, salsa
Sun tea, lemonade, sparkling water

Ideas for Dinner:

Oven-ready lasagna
Stuff-your-own burritos (rice, beans, and cheese)
Hamburgers/veggie burgers
Precooked chicken
Salads
French bread
Cookies, cake

Special Treat: S'mores—marshmallows, chocolate bars, graham crackers (for campfire on the last night)

LODGING

Whether you plan your retreat at a church, a private home, a retreat center, or a camp, you need to learn what accommodations and supplies are available in that setting so that you can let your participants know well in advance what they can expect:

- Will they need to bring their own bedding, towels?
- Should they bring tents and sleeping bags?
- Will they have beds to sleep on or will they want to bring air mattresses or cots?
- Will there be separate bedrooms or dorm-like accommodations?
- Will there be provision made for people with special needs?

In your communication with retreat participants, be sure to ask if there are special needs. Decide if you will be able to accommodate these circumstances. Plan on poor weather, especially if your accommodations include camping out. If the sun shines—so much the better.

Near the end of your retreat, engage the participants one last time: someone (not the host) needs to call everyone's attention to leaving the retreat site as you found it—CLEAN! Remember the scene in the Disney *Snow White and the Seven Dwarfs*, where the birds and little animals helped Snow White clean the dwarfs' cabin? Also, implore everyone to find and take home with them ALL of their belongings. Retreat "lost and founds" are a pain in the "keester" to deal with!

Arrival, Registration, and Sign-up Sheets

As participants arrive, a host greets each one, confirms her registration, and receives any unpaid fees. You may also provide sheets for retreat participants to sign up to offer a blessing before a meal or a morning's short devotion. Make sure these sheets are available throughout the retreat for anyone to add her name as she feels called. Also at the registration table have release forms to sign, if necessary.

RETREAT PARTICIPANT LIST

Before the end of your retreat, ask the women and girls if they would like to have a list of the names and addresses of the retreat participants. If it is agreeable with all to have their names included, that can be done following the retreat as a nice way to thank each one for her participation.

NAMETAGS AND MEAL TEAMS

Each retreat participant should receive a nametag at the beginning of the retreat. We have tried to make them interesting and attractive so people are more likely to wear them.

One way we have linked nametags to meal duty teams is to give each team a color. Teams are then color-coordinated by a ribbon on each nametag. A chart is posted in a conspicuous place showing the names of individual team members, designation of which meal each helps with, cued with a strip of the matching color ribbon. Each team has a leader (name underlined on the chart). Team members are asked to refer to the chart for their assigned meal and to report to the leader at the appropriate time.

Retreat Evaluations

We highly recommend that you ask your retreat participants for feedback after the retreat. We like to hand each participant an evaluation form at the retreat's end and ask that they take some time before they leave to fill it out to leave with us. However, some take them home to mail in later. The paragraph below was mailed to each participant in September following an August retreat. While a more immediate opportunity is advisable, even if you ask later, getting responses about the experience of the retreat from each one who attended elicits valuable information for your future planning. Much of the substance of our retreats has come from reactions and suggestions from participants. Plus, the positive feedback always feels good!

Following are four different ways we have asked for feedback.

EVALUATION FORM I

Dear Sara,
With leaves turning and storm winds blowing, the "Visions of Womanhood" retreat on Whidbey Island you attended in August may seem a distant memory, but we are already planning next year's retreat, and we need your input. Please complete this evaluation quickly with your first responses, put it in the enclosed stamped envelope, and pop it in the mail. Our first planning meeting is November 8th. We all treasured the experience of getting to know you. Thank you for your help.

VISIONS OF WOMANHOOD RETREAT:
What touched you—tell us why. (Please use additional paper for longer responses.)

> Sharing stories and introductions in Circle
>
> Storytelling at campfire time
>
> The Four-fold Way concepts: The way of the—
>
> Warrior/Leader (showing up and choosing to be present; honor and respect)
>
> Teacher (wisdom, trust, open to outcome)
>
> Healer (paying attention to what has heart and meaning)
>
> Visionary (telling the truth without blame or judgment; life dream)

Stories from the Bible

Crafts (masks, pouches, dolls)

Movement—exercises and dance

Silent beach walk

Designing and participating in a ceremony celebrating you

Being with a wide-range of ages

Getting acquainted with girls you didn't know previously

Did you understand and relate to the "Circle" framework and guidelines we used for leading the weekend process? Did you feel comfortable sharing in Circle?

If you were to tell a friend about your experience, what would you tell her?

Has this experience made a difference for you? How so? What has stayed in your thoughts?

If you were to invite a friend for a retreat, how would you like to see things improved, changed, remain the same?

Other comments:

Thanks for your help. Hope we can have a reunion. We miss seeing you. For the Visions of Womanhood Planning Circle_____

EVALUATION FORM 2

September . . .
We all treasured the experience of getting to know you at the "Visions of Womanhood" retreat on Whidbey Island in August. There has been enough time for some of the experience to fade as you returned to your "regular" life and prepared for school and/or work. In some ways, the retreat may seem a distant memory. But we hope there remain some lasting memories, learnings, and inspiration. It is a very important gift for us to receive your responses about your experience at the retreat: What was meaningful? What could add to the experience or work better? We wish to begin planning for next year's retreat greatly based on your input. Please complete this evaluation as soon as possible, put it in the enclosed stamped envelope, and pop it in the mail. Our next planning meeting is October 10. Don't get hung up on a particular question; answer it as best you can or go on to the next if you wish. Thank you for your help.

VISIONS OF WOMANHOOD RETREAT:

What was most meaningful about the retreat for you?—tell us why.
(Please use additional paper for longer responses.)

What was significant for you in each of the presentations of the Fourfold Way concepts and their parallel stories of women in scripture?

The way of the:

Warrior/Leader—the story of Mary, the mother of Jesus

Teacher—the story of Anna

Healer—the story of the unnamed woman who anoints Jesus

Visionary—the story of Miriam

Using the enclosed retreat outline as a reference, what did you like or what would you change about the following?

Introduction to retreat

Sharing introductions and personal stories in Circle

Campfire songs and games

Introduction to the Four-fold Way and meditation on "Why are you here, my daughters?"

Acting out of the stories of "Ruth and Naomi" and "Vasalisa the Wise" at campfire time

Other midrash stories from the Bible: Mary Magdalene, David and Bathsheba

"Eve and Adam"—girls' original midrash of Genesis story

Crafts (masks, pouches, dolls) and their symbolism for you

Meals

Morning meditations and matins (devotions)

Movement, exercises, and dance

Songs and music

Tipi Time (girls answer)

Letting Go Time (moms/sponsors answer)

Beach walk

Journey Walk

Worship service

Designing and participating in a ceremony celebrating you!

In any of the above items, how could we invite your participation more?

Did you understand the purpose and guidelines for sharing in "Circle"?

How was it for you—being with a wide-range of ages? Getting acquainted with girls you didn't know previously?

Has this experience made a difference in how you think about yourself and your future? Tell us about it.

What has stayed in your thoughts?

If you were to tell a friend about your experience, what would you tell her?

If you were to invite a friend for a retreat, how would you like to see things improved, changed, remain the same?

Other comments:

Thanks for your help! We look forward to seeing you again.

Additional questions for moms and/or sponsors:

Did you feel the retreat assisted your relationship with your daughter? Please tell us how.

Did the stories and process convey values you believe will assist your daughter to believe in herself, in the work of the Divine in her life, and the importance of choices she makes in building her future life? How?

How could we do better in this?

How could we invite greater participation of those new to the retreat?

Several of you commented that it was not clear to bring celebration clothes for the ceremony. This is what we said in the letter, "At the conclusion of the weekend, some may choose to design a ceremony celebrating their passage into the journey of womanhood. You are welcome to bring whatever you wish, including clothing and adornment, to help with this ceremony."

How can we word this to be clearer and more specific?

Did the retreat generate good conversations between you and your daughter after your return home? What items or remembrances started these?

Any other comments or suggestions:

Again, thanks for your help!

EVALUATION FORM 3

Please help us consider/evaluate the workshop.

What was(s) the most meaningful part?

What was missing?

Help us evaluate the different parts of the weekend.

(Good, not too good, indifferent)

> Circle
>
> Crafts
>
> Storytelling ("When I was ten . . .")
>
> Campfire stories
>
> Beach and silence
>
> Singing
>
> Eating
>
> Closing
>
> Other stuff

What would you change or eliminate?

Daughters Arise!
August 6–9

You are important to us, so your feedback is really important to us, too. Every year we learn so much from your responses about how to make the retreat experience more meaningful and more fun.

Please take a few minutes to answer these questions. If you can do that before you leave, that would be GREAT! Otherwise, please mail your responses to Sally. THANK YOU!

The following is a summary of responses from girls and women to the questions of Evaluation Form 4. Questions on the form are in bold.

1. Were The Four-fold Way presentations helpful or meaningful to you? In what way?

"It represents all four of our different personalities that are important to understand about ourselves."

"They made me feel connected to other people and made me feel good about myself and others."

"They made me realize things about myself and gave me something to think about when making decisions."

"They taught me that you need inner beauty more than outer beauty."

"Tools to take away and use."

"I would have liked time to interact with what was offered in a way to remember more."

"Yes, they were informative as an introduction. I found myself wanting more concrete information as to how to apply the Four-fold Way to my life. It was obvious that others were further along in their integration of these concepts into their daily thinking, living, and attitudes."

"These are four characteristics that are important in my life. The Leader/Warrior is one I need to feel confident in my professional life."

"They gave me a lot of 'food for thought.' I would have been helped by having a handout summarizing the main characteristics—or a copy of the song describing them—to take along with me."

"They will be. I need to spend more time understanding them. I believe they'll help me put names to parts of myself that I struggle to understand."

"Very much. A reinforcement of the workshop two years ago and of my reading the book. The women were well prepared which always helps to clarify."

"They will be. Perhaps for my children—perhaps for my future purpose."

"Lovely synthesis of idea and story; wonderful color and imagination in costume."

2. **What were the most meaningful activities for you in the retreat?**

"Singing, the ceremony, and the Journey Walk ceremony."

"I liked listening to people's stories of when they were children and other times."

"Just working with other people, sharing thoughts and experiences."

"The ceremony."

"Personal sharings, singing, beach walk"

"Interacting, crafts with a meaning, singing around fire, spiral lighting of candles, silent time at the beach."

"The girls' ceremony was great, but I didn't know most of them very well. I found myself wishing there had been perhaps some kind of small group opportunities—don't ask me what!"

"The company and the hospitality and place. Not enough time for one-on-one, so there were many I didn't get to share time with."

"It was all important! Coming together in a Circle of love and friendship with other women made all the activities meaningful."

"The Journey Walk ceremony was beautiful and meaningful, the worship service, and the girls' ceremony. I also appreciated the Four-fold Way presentations."

"Sharing of stories, quiet time to talk and walk with other women."

"Sunday worship—young women's celebration"

"Getting to know the women, watching and listening to the stories; feeling unconditional caring."

"Worship service—Circle—body movement."

3. **What was the most fun?**

"The girls' ceremony."

"I thought making the dolls and the pouches was the most fun."

"The stories."

"Making the mask and campfire (after everyone's gone to bed) when the fire is still going and we sing silly songs."

"Singing around the fire, games, crafts."

"Celebrating the young ladies."

"The beach walk, without a doubt!"

"The girls' ceremony, the crafts, the plays."

"I love working with my hands. It was especially nice to keep working on our creations when someone began another activity, or when someone talked."

"Sharing time around the campfire and singing."

"Games, dancing, singing around the campfire!"

"Songs, dances, and games."

"Talking, bonding, sharing, listening, playing."

"Crafts and body movement and kids' plays and midrashes."

4. What changes would you make in the retreat?

"Just make sure all feel included with everyone not just adults."

"I can't think of any."

"More free and think time. There were a lot of things I wished I had more time to think about."

"More time on the beach."

"Nothing in the format, but that more girls could experience it."

"Increase the images of Names of the Holy."

"Address list of participants."

"Friday left little time for reflection. I felt like a wet sponge in a puddle! What are some ways others have made changes in their lives to be true to the Four-fold Way? Just as examples, not as models."

"Much, much, much more downtime to process, to talk with folk, to walk and move, to let spontaneous things happen."

"Nothing!"

"Keep ages of girls old enough to be meaningful."

"Call me when I've had time to digest it all."

"Honestly cannot think of any."

"Not change, just development of Amy Windecker's and Paula's piece . . . the body connection is seeming so much more important."

5. Any other comments?

"It was GREAT! I really want to come next year, and bring my mom—I think this would be a good experience for her."

"I had FUN."

"Thank You!"

"Time for the oldest to meet together and share too."

"It was wonderful. The planning group and Circle of Stones group did a wonderful job being all-inclusive. I never felt left out in any way. It is obvious that a great deal of work and planning went into the weekend. Thank you from the bottom of my heart. What you have accomplished comes directly from God; a sense of the holy and sacredness exists in this place. Thank you! Thank You! Thank You! I look forward to the completed manual so I can bring this to my other daughters in California!"

"Hospitality is always superb and gracious—thank you, Sally. The planners, the gifts each of you gave to the retreat leave me in awe. I am so grateful my sister, niece, and Steph and Kathryn could all experience this."

"It was wonderful! Thank you for all your hard work and effort in putting this together. It is a wonderful, meaningful time, especially for mothers and daughters! Thank you so much!"

"Glad I came. Thank you."

"This was a good retreat. I loved the returning girls and their big-sistering of the younger ones."

"Just Thank You. Bless you all. It is plain to see all your hearts are totally into this and that you've all put thousands of hours into this. Love, Susan K."

Journey Pouch
PROGRAM RESOURCES

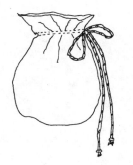

Welcome

"RULES" OF THE HOUSE

Wherever you choose to hold your retreat, you will need to include in your opening remarks and welcome specific information about your site—simple things like where people eat, sleep, where the bathrooms are, and what are customary practices and peculiarities of your retreat setting. The following is what we tell our guests.

"Rules" really is too heavy a word, except for one important exception: The Cliff!! Stay off the fence, don't go over it! Stay on this side of it! The view is beautiful, but falling is a 200-foot one-way trip!

If you haven't already determined your sleeping spot and need some help, please let someone know. There are towels in each bathroom and the beds are clean and intended for your use. If you do sleep in a bed, please strip it and put the sheets in the laundry on Sunday. Towels, too. There is a sign-up sheet in each bathroom for shower-taking times. It should be self-explanatory. You should find extra toilet paper in each bathroom. Please flush only as necessary—a slightly indelicate but useful ditty says it all: "If it's yellow, let it mellow. If it's brown, flush it down." The toilet in the family room is a water-saver. There will be break times in the schedule, but they may not suit your particular constitution. You needn't wait for permission. We're learning to respect our own individual promptings for many things. The outhouse down the lawn is for your use, too; it is clean and does not smell.

You have been assigned kitchen duty, perhaps more than once. When you're on duty, please show up in the kitchen at least fifteen minutes before mealtime or when Circle has recessed. There will be someone on each team who knows her way around the kitchen. You'll be setting out food, plates, utensils, and cleaning up afterward. Let me start the dishwasher. Please feel free to look for what you need in the kitchen. If you didn't bring your own mug, choose one in the kitchen and make it yours for the whole weekend. Keep track of it, wash it if you want to, and don't use anybody else's.

One of the biggest headaches for me is what people leave behind. I haven't yet been able to find owners for some of last year's lost-and-found. Please check around before you leave on Sunday to make sure you've got all your stuff.

Craft supplies are on the table in the breezeway and are intended for your use. Enjoy them and please put them back when you're finished so someone else can find them.

You are welcome to wander anywhere on the farm—fields or woods. Shoes, socks, and long pants are a good idea. Please remember to close any gates you open or you will be responsible for rounding up stray cows! Better not to go barefoot anywhere on a farm.

We seem to be a refuge for lost animal souls: They just wander in. The friendly cat is Hannah, the three shy ones are her kittens and don't have much use for human sorts; they are just great farm cats. Hannah would like you to believe that she never gets anything to eat or any love. Don't fall for it. She is not to be indoors—she's a farm cat, and she is not wary about getting out of the way of cars.

Here are three different openings we've used, speaking them conversationally, rather than reading.

1. OVERVIEW OF THE WEEKEND

We want to spend a few minutes telling you a bit of what to expect this weekend. Many of you know the story of Dorothy and *The Wizard of Oz*. Well, this story is a good way to think about what this weekend is about. In fact, it's a helpful way to begin to understand what happens to us when we grow from one phase of our lives into a new one. Right now, like it or not, each of us is growing, changing, becoming something new. Remember when Dorothy woke up and looked outside after her house plopped down in Munchkin Land? Anybody remember what she said? *(Toto, I don't think we're in Kansas any more!)*

The story of Dorothy is what we call an "initiation story," it's an adventure quest of a girl discovering who she is and how to get "back home" to this place (point to the heart). This place is what life is all about. Because it is an "initiation story," Dorothy represents each one of us, so it becomes our story too. As we grow into becoming adults, we're trying to discover what we're here for, what we're really good at, and what we can give to the world. Now in order to be able to do that, we have to become very strong and learn to use our own wits. We need to learn what the resources for help and guidance are, and we need to discover and claim our personal power. When I say "personal power," do you feel that you have personal power?

When her house landed in Oz, suddenly the familiar was gone, and Dorothy was alone with her dog, Toto. She needed help to find her way back home to Kansas. The wonderful, magical thing was that new companions showed up to help her get to the wizard in the city of Oz. When you remember that you are observing an "initiation story," you begin to note that the characters of the Scarecrow, Tinman, and Lion represent Dorothy's inner qualities that must be developed for her to arrive "home." *(Sing)* "A brain, a heart, the 'noive'" were all qualities she needed, too. It was their companionship and their working together to overcome all obstacles that also helped Dorothy find her way home.

Just like Dorothy opening the door of her house and stepping into the magical world of Munchkin land, we've all shown up here together! Away from our everyday life, we can take a look at our lives differently, we can jump into something brand new and try it on for size *(put on a mask)*, we can create new things that will deeply show us something wonderful about who we are and what is important to us *(show a doll, a pouch)*. We can't wait to share them with you and have you share whatever you want to with this Circle of daughters.

We're all daughters, aren't we? Remember how important it was for Dorothy to get back to her Auntie Em? She needed her Auntie Em to be there for her when she was scared and not sure of herself. But, aha! One of the dilemmas of growing up is that each girl must distance herself from the person who has been the most important caregiver and guide in her life. We daughters and mothers must do this paradoxical thing. We daughters push away, and we mothers must cut ties so that our daughters can fly.

The initiation stories represent this in similar ways—the daughter is usually an orphan whose mother has died. This is true in Dorothy's case and in a much older story we will hear tomorrow night, "Vasalisa the Wise." The story opens with Vasalisa receiving a gift from her dying mother. These stories are symbolic of how a mother's guidance must be replaced by something internal, though it can be built on our mother's teaching and love.

In *The Wizard of Oz*, Dorothy is separated from Auntie Em, but she sees Auntie Em reflected in the witch's crystal ball calling her name. It is a crucial, motivating image to help her escape.

When we leave the safety of home and our mother, we begin looking for guidance and power outside ourselves that actually mirrors back what's already inside us—that shows us our own power. Remember Glinda? The good witch of the North? People and experiences like Glinda show up in our lives in many times and places, showing us love and truth in ways that expand what our parents can give us.

So, what about power? Is power good? Can it be evil and destructive? Should you seek power? Should you avoid it? Is love power or something else? Are all people who offer guidance good? What happens if we don't realize we don't have to give our power to others? Initiation stories always introduce us to both "the light side of the force and the dark side of the force" as Luke Skywalker learned in *Star Wars.* In *The Wizard of Oz*, we find Glinda, the good witch of the North, who guides Dorothy, and the wicked witch of the East, who imprisons her. In "Vasalisa, the Wise," we find the stepmother and stepsisters who demean and abuse her, and the Baba Yaga who helps her find her power in the burning light of truth.

The archetypes of the Four-fold Way are personifications of inner qualities like the Tinman, Scarecrow, and Lion, but much wiser, and we find their positive attributes and their shadow side. In Bible stories, familiar and not-so-familiar, we find Jesus blessed by God in the form of a descending dove, and we find Jesus tempted by Satan while in the desert for forty days. We find Jesus talking to the woman at the well who had used her gifts of beauty and attraction in ways that betrayed her true inner self, but Jesus held up to her the mirror of love and restored her to a right use of her personal power.

Our time together this weekend is to help us remember, really know, that all we need when we go out into the world is already within us. But we do need assistance to become "awake" to it, to develop it in positive ways, and to use it to co-create our work with God in the world. Jesus was very clear to his disciples at the last supper recorded in John 14, that though he was "going away," he would not leave them "as orphans," but God would send the Holy Spirit to dwell in them and guide them and remind them of all he had said to them, just as God was in Jesus to guide him. This is the same time that he also makes it clear to all of his followers that they are to be companions to each other. "I give you a new commandment, that you love one another. Just as I have loved you, you also should love one another" (Jn. 13:34).

That's what this weekend is all about. We're not alone! We are those companions for each other. Because the Creator has given many ways to learn, this weekend offers learning through story, song, drama, art, dance, poetry, worship, and nature. There is also time set aside for you younger ones to celebrate your time of passage from childhood to womanhood, and time for you older ones to celebrate new awareness of calling and direction in your life.

Come, let our Daughters Arise!
DONNA HUMPHREYS AND CLAUDIA WALKER

2. WHY ARE YOU HERE? A LITANY

Grandmother Crone enters with a large basket and asks:

Why Are You Here, My Daughters?

We respond:

We're here because we have been told we are made in the image of God. We need each other to reconcile that image with how women are seen in society and culture.

We're here because we have a deep hunger to give our gifts and be accepted for all that we are.

We mothers, grandmothers, and women friends have been searching the ancient archaeology for the feminine spiritual gifts. We have been reclaiming our full image from the wisdom of our Christian and cultural heritages. We are here to make Circle around the Holy Fire, share our potsherds, and together fashion a new holy container—a new grail full with love for our daughters.

Passing the basket around the Circle, Grandmother Crone asks:

What do you wish to ask?

Taking turns we say:

We came to ask, "What does it mean to have the River of Life flowing through my body?"

We came to ask, "Why does this river begin to flow long before I will use it?"

We came to ask, "What does it mean to have personal power? How is it different from the power of sexual attraction?'"

We came to ask, "How did Mary recognize the angel as God's messenger, and how did she have the confidence to accept?"

We came to ask, "How will I know the voice of God?"

We came to ask, "What does it mean that Jesus had a human body, just as I do?"

We came to ask, "How is the fire Vasalisa received from Baba Yaga like the fire of Moses' burning bush?"

We came to ponder mysteries, "Who am I really? What is my work here? What am I longing for?"

We're here to ask, "What are the skills to prepare for the journey of womanhood and how can we weave a strong living Circle in which to teach and learn?"

DONNA HUMPHREYS

3. WHY WE USE THESE RESOURCES

When our Circle of Stones writing group was asked by our Methodist Conference's Commission on the Status and Role of Women to help write a ritual of passage for girls entering womanhood, we were excited, yet immediately challenged to the core! None of us had had any experience of such a passage in our own lives. We didn't want to write something that had not evolved out of our own experience or our daughters' experiences, so we decided we needed to spend time together, to live apart for a time and learn how to honor this important passage. Some of us would like to do this seasonally, at the fall and spring equinox and summer and winter solstice times, because these rhythmic changes signal ways to live more in harmony with ourselves and with our natural home. But for now, we meet in the summertime, when blue skies and warm sunshine beckon us out-doors to revel!

Because we are from a faith community, a Christian one, we seek to align the values of the Gospel with how we live, and so we use the Bible as a reference and guide. We do this from a feminist perspective using women theologians like Miriam Therese Winter's works (*WomanPrayer*, *WomanSong*, and others) to assist us in understanding and often entering into the stories Jesus told, and the lives of the women who encountered him. This way of working uses a style of interpretation and discernment called "midrash." It's an ancient Hebrew discipline, and by using midrash, a story may be retold from a different perspective from the one in the original account. It may be told in the first person or from the point of view of another character in the story. Biblical scholarship on midrash by theologians is important, yet it is out of the intuitive, contemplative realm that the story is relived.

Stories from folklore, our collective ancient stories, are important to us too. Clarissa Pinkola Estés work, *Women Who Run with the Wolves: Myths and Stories of the Wild Woman Archetype*, has become a treasure trove of insight for us. From a master storyteller's point of view and with expertise as a Jungian analyst, Pinkola Estés breathes fresh life into these stories and thereby helps us to understand the necessary tasks and skills we must learn to be healthy and whole women.

Our process is an organic one, growing each time we gather to sing, tell stories, and be together. Another resource we have come to use is anthro-pologist Angeles Arrien's work, *The Four-fold Way*. One of the members of our writing Circle came across this book in a singing lesson! Her teacher, responding to the desire of her pupil to sing out of the core of her being, told her about the principles of the Four-fold Way: showing up and being present, telling the truth, listening to what has heart and meaning, and being open to outcome. This led to the group's study of Arrien's learn-ings from indigenous people. The group has experienced this structure as a helpful way to frame our questions and life learnings.

Each year new resources come to us. The bibliography keeps growing. The cutting edge for us is to be true to the young girls' needs and experi-ences. This is always a challenge because our needs are different from theirs, and their lives are not the same as the ones we lived at their age. Yet just being together and listening to whatever they want to share with us is so very precious to all of us. We need all our ages together. They need us and we need them. We know we are creating a legacy of honoring our-selves, we who are made in God's image.

CLAUDIA WALKER

In our Daughters Arise! retreats, we have used several different introductions to the practice of Circle. Choose what best serves your retreat setting, or use these as a springboard for your own introduction. The important thing is that the foundational practice of Circle is introduced to the participants and that they agree to its principles. Following are three texts we have used. We always try not to read these texts, but rather to be so well acquainted with the material that we can speak it to the retreat participants.

A reminder: In this guidebook, we use a capital "C" in "Circle" when we refer to an intentional gathering, following the guidelines of Circle that we describe here; circle with a small "c" is just an arrangement of bodies or other objects in a circular shape.

CREATING CIRCLE—1

"Take Off Your Shoes"

A man named Moses was watching over his father-in-law Jethro's sheep. He was deep in the dry wilderness in the land of Midian. Moses was a good man, but had gotten himself into deep trouble . . . at least here in the desert no one could find him. In his wandering he came near a mountain called Horeb; some had called it a holy place. As he neared, he was amazed to see a beautiful bush. It was so lovely it almost took his breath away . . . it seemed to be on fire . . . he could not take his eyes off it. As he stood silent in wonder, a voice said to him "Moses, this is a Holy moment, this is my Holy creation, take off your sandals and receive me. Pay attention, I am here." And Moses talked with God. —Exodus 3:1–5 (paraphrased)

You are here. You have chosen to be present in this space and with these journeying daughters. You might have been any of dozens of other places, answering other calls on your time and talents, but you have come here; you have shown up. *(This is the way of the Warrior/Leader.)*

You probably do not have much information about what will happen this weekend. Perhaps someone you trust has encouraged you to come; perhaps it was something you read. Maybe someone you know has been here before. Even if this is not your first Daughters Arise! retreat, it is a different time, other women here, a different you. You are here, waiting to see what this time will be. *(This is the way of the Teacher.)*

Stop for a moment, breathe in deeply the air of this place. Close your eyes and listen and, with your eyes closed, smell the scent of sea and fir. When you open your eyes, look up through the trees and watch heaven drift overhead.

> *Slip silently into space, simply for itself . . .*
> *You need gather no leaves for preservation,*
> *nor twigs to build proof or witness*
> *Come simply to be.*

This place—God's creation, this time—God's day—are holy. God's revelation awaits only our attention. *(This is the way of the Healer.)*

We will be doing many things this weekend, but what we most want to share with you is the importance of process. We come together around the joy of welcoming girls into the journey of becoming women and to learn together the wisdom we all need for that journey. The ground of what we seek to remember and to create with you is in the shape of a Circle—a way of understanding and of being together that has been nearly lost in millennia of disuse.

Look around the circle we have formed. You have probably met in a circle before, but this weekend we will learn more about being together in the shape of a circle. Can you imagine early humankind warming themselves around a fire? Can you imagine how much safer they felt, each counting on the others? Can you imagine how the same warm fire lit each of their faces, how familiar and valuable each one might have been?

We have no wild beasts threatening our peaceful time here, only a peculiar menagerie of gentle creatures. Our nighttime campfires will be filled with songs and s'mores. But the Circle is no less life-giving to us, for in Circle, with the flame of the Holy at the center, we will remember a very old way of being together—of being daughters on a journey. We will learn to see each other through the sacred center, with eyes that see each of us as God does, precious daughters, faithful sisters. We will learn that in Circle we become one body; each part is precious, each part unique and necessary. In Circle, we share the responsibility for the life of the Circle. Leadership moves easily from one to another as each person's gifts are offered and received. In our usual lives, we all experience power outside of ourselves, power over us—whether it's parents, school, government, church, or peers. But in Circle, we learn how to find power within us, power flowing through us.

In the Circle, no one is any closer to God than anyone else, and no one is alone. In the center of the Circle we will build our altar. On the altar belong images that remind us of the Holy. Some are symbols of God we have known most of our lives, symbols of faith. Others may be souvenirs of our journey, bits of creation, treasures of our souls. In effect, we will lay pieces of ourselves on the altar, sharing our truth in love. *(This is the way of the Visionary.)*

In Circle, all are needed and wanted, all belong and each is different. When we get to the campfire, notice the ring of stone—each one is different. No one is just like another; some are larger, some smaller, some broken by earth's deep pressures, some rounded by flooding waters. But remove any one of them and the circle is incomplete. Like the ancient glaciers that brought these rocks to this land, we come from many places, many different experiences, and many expressions of faith. In our Circle this weekend, we will honor God, and we will honor each other. We ask your consent to proceed this way and trust that the Holy One will breathe with all we do, bringing forth what we have not even imagined.

CIRCLE GUIDELINES

Speak only when you are led to speak. It is the invitation and intention of the Circle that all shall be heard. But remember also that silence is a gift to the Circle and that some of us need silence before being able to speak. Silence is not empty; it is holy.

When you speak, imagine that you are laying some sacred part of yourself on the altar in the center; you are **giving of yourself in sacred trust.** When someone else speaks, honor the same for her.

Whoever is speaking has everyone's attention. An equal gift to the Circle is the loving, attentive receiving of others' gifts and offerings.

Speak not in reaction to someone else, but for yourself, from your own heart. **Speak your own truth:** your feelings are valid.

Try to speak succinctly without rambling, honoring the time so that others may speak.

Intend in your speaking and in your listening **that love will be known,** that your truth will be told in love, and that the realm of God will be made manifest within us.

We will ask for a volunteer at each Circle to be a "Keeper of the Circle." The Keeper, while still sitting in Circle, will keep her attention on the life of the Circle. Is it functioning within our guidelines? Is the process offtrack? Sometimes the Keeper need only ring the bell. We will all be quiet for a few moments and realign ourselves with the center. When the Keeper rings the bell again, we will continue. Sometimes she will need to say what she is observing. There may be a time when the Keeper, or someone else, goes to sit or stand behind one who is speaking difficult words or expressing deep emotions. This presence is intended to give her loving support. Anyone who senses such a need may respond. If you are led to place a comforting hand on her shoulder or back, ask for her permission before doing so.

Do we all agree to be in Circle together?

SALLY WINDECKER

CREATING CIRCLE—2

What, above all, we Stones hope to witness to this weekend is relationship, a way of being together. We gather around the hope, the need, to discover a way to welcome girls into the journey of becoming women. Like my understanding of salvation, it is not an event, though events signal its reality. It is a journey, a journey of discovery and of remembering.

The ground of what we seek to remember and to create lies in the shape of a circle, a shape of understanding and being that has been nearly lost in millennia of disuse. The Circle mirrors the communal shape our soul was created for and in which our journey of becoming woman can best take place. We will build Circle here with you, will teach you what we have come to

know of it, ask your agreement to proceed this way, and trust that the Holy One will breathe with all we do, bringing forth what we have not yet even imagined. That is our experience and our witness. Remember for a moment Jesus' witness about our relationship to each other (Lk. 22:24–27, Jn. 13:12–17). When the disciples asked, "Who is the greatest?" Jesus taught that no one is greater because all are beloved children.

I am convinced that the shape of the soul is a circle. Circles have been important, even sacred, in human experience since people first gathered around a fire to warm themselves against strange and cold nights. Circles lie deep within what makes us human, within our traditions. A circle is as ancient as the shape of our solar system, and as new as the shiny gold bands on newlyweds' fingers.

Tonight we will tell stories—stories of women becoming. In the stories, you may notice that the women, half-formed, debilitated, frightened, timid, or even—as Jairus' daughter—dead, are trying to find wholeness in cultures and contexts that impose and organize themselves in layers of power. These contexts assume that power lies outside the soul, not within. We will experience, in the Circle we create, that power is internal—within each of us and at the center of the Circle and of creation.

When we sit in Circle, acknowledging the Sacred to be our center, seeing each other through the light of that Holy One, feeling the balance and flow of need and gift, question and answer, around the Circle, each one of us responsive and responsible, we will experience power and grace. What we need will come to us, what we are to do will be made clearer as the path we are to follow. "God knows we need all these things."

In the Circle, God is present at our center. Our vision of each other passes through the center, through what is Holy. No one is any closer to the center than anyone else, and no one sits alone. In the center are symbols that remind us of our experience of what is holy: the flame of the Holy Spirit, the rock of our faith, the water of rebirth. As we build our altar for this sacred time together, we will lay on it objects of our own faith—experience, need, and hope—laying in effect, ourselves on the altar.

At the campfire tonight, notice the circle of stones surrounding the fire. No one stone is just like another, some are larger, some smaller, some covered with moss, some cracked by earth's deep pressures, some rounded in the tumble of water. They are different compositions, different colors, but without any one of them the circle is not whole. Like the ancient glaciers that brought them here, we come from many places, many experiences, many expressions of faith. In our Circles this weekend, we will honor God, and we will honor each other, in our community and in our diversity.

In Circle, leadership is fluid—it rises or wanes in each of us according to need, according to gift, each in its own season. Like leadership, responsibility is shared by all, as need and capacity request. We experience Circle as an expression of the Body of Christ; all gifts are received in the Circle in its workings, both for our being together and for the work that we do.

(Continue here with "Circle Guidelines" and "Keeper of the Circle" from previous pages 128 and 129.)

SALLY WINDECKER

A PRACTICE OF CIRCLE: OUR "CHECK-IN" TIME

(See also "Balance Input with Process Time," Journey Pouch, page 88.)

Who has a need or concern to share?

Along with caring for one another, it is right and good to take care of ourselves, to ask for what we need. On a women's retreat last winter, I was struck by the importance, the magic, of beginning our work each day with the opportunity to express a special need or concern.

One woman, Joyce, shared her concern about her son being on a winter mountain climb and her fear of avalanche; she lightened her burden of worry by sharing it with the group.

Clare's camera had ceased working, and she expressed disappointment and sadness in not being able to photograph her experiences; perhaps someone had a disposable camera to spare? Jan's face brightened with relief as she admitted her dislike of taking pictures and offered the use of her extensive equipment. Who could have imagined this satisfactory outcome?

Perhaps some of you have something on your heart that you need to express in order to be more fully present. Who has a need you want us to be aware of, or a concern to share?

KITTY ADAMS

Story

To walk into story is to walk into grace—the place of honor and forgiveness, of truth and reconciliation. Story is not only about life; deep story *is* life. Story lays down no laws. It ascribes no demerit; it does not stand in judgment and bars no exits. It asks no qualification and bestows no credential. It draws no lines saying "this far and no farther." It builds no boxes to separate or exclude. Story spins out the mystery of creation and of our place in it. It tells of the inherent truth in experience and wisdom. Story is the promise of growth, the memory of life, and the power of love acted out in *chronos* in the garb of eternity.

TELLING OUR OWN STORIES

A crucial component of storytelling is the telling of our own stories. We are often reluctant or do not know how to begin our stories, so the Daughters Arise! retreat has discovered a few good ways to get people started. The first two are invitations to think about names —especially our own. The second two suggest jumping into our own stories by remembering ourselves at earlier ages.

THE IMPORTANCE OF NAMES:
"You Have Called Me by Name" —1

(Introduction to small groups in which each woman and girl tells about her name.)

PRESENTER:
If we asked each other what we left behind to come to this retreat, we would have as many stories as we have women and girls here. Some left chaos, some left pain. Maybe you left boredom or fun or work. But we invite you now to leave behind what is behind and to hold on to what you brought with you. One thing we each brought is our name—and our name is usually what we first offer to someone we are meeting. Names can sometimes create confusion.

I have a friend whose name is pronounced "Kahren," spelled "K-a-r-e-n." More than once, when she has spelled and pronounced her name for someone, the person has said:

"Oh, you call yourself 'Kahren.'"

She smiles and says yes, sometimes explaining that in Norwegian there is no "a" as it sounds in the word "care." She perhaps would like to say, "Oh, and you call yourself 'Jane.'" After all, it is our parents who call us whatever our names are. And yet, my name becomes what I call myself. In France, if someone would ask my name, I would say, *Je m'appelle Gloria* —I call myself Gloria.

My parents called me "Gloria" because they liked the name. In my teen years, I didn't like my name much. In movies, it seemed to me that someone named "Gloria" was usually a wild, wicked woman—remember Elizabeth Taylor in *Butterfield 8*? Or a woman who was a rich snob. I guess that came from Gloria Vanderbilt. I didn't like either image and really wished my parents had named me something else. But as I began to sing in church choirs, something wonderful happened. I heard my name in a whole new way.

When the voices of the choir swirled around me, *Gloria in excelsis Deo*, my head knew the words weren't about me, but my heart filled with joy that my name was used to sing, "Glory to God." I am very fond of Christmastime!

My friend Nada ("a" as in the word "way") had a joker for a father. Someone had suggested the name "Nada," to her mother at a baby shower. Her mother and father both liked the name. But when her dad, the funny Norwegian, told the story, over and over, during her childhood, he said, "When she was born, I took one look at her and said, 'Nay—Da!'" Said in this way, "Na—Da" is the equivalent of *Ufda!* or "Oh, No!" A few years later, Nada, who grew up in Southern California, was devastated to learn that her name in Spanish means "nothing"—"nada." How do you live with a name that means "Oh, No!" or "nothing"? During her growing up years, Nada's name made her feel negative about herself. But in her mid-twenties, she consciously decided that she as a person was OK—and that she could change her name or like it. Somewhere in the process, she learned to love her name—and she now tells its story, but with her own ending. When it came time to name her own firstborn, she chose the name "Desta," which means "happiness" in the Ethiopian language.

Now it's your turn:

(Presenter shows and reads aloud questions on tag board.)

- Tell about your first, middle, or last name.
- Were you named after someone?
- Do you like or dislike your name? Why?
- Have you ever changed one of your names? How did that feel?

I invite you to form a group of two or three people who are not related to you. Using the questions here, share some stories or information about your name. You will have about five minutes to talk.

(Presenter also joins a small group. Presenter calls all back to the complete group after five to seven minutes.)

PRESENTER: What we learn from each other is that the names we call ourselves or that others call us in some way become part of our identity and affect deeply our feelings, both positive and negative, about ourselves.

GLORIA KOLL

"You Have Called Me by Name"—2

(Presenter begins by passing around a little bronze otter.)

I dearly love this little animal. It is a creation of artist Georgia Gerber who lives on Whidbey Island and whose *Boy and Dog* statue looks out on the water from Langley—and whose life-size pig waits patiently in Seattle's Pike Place market. Our twenty-something kids knew that their dad and I have longed for a Georgia Gerber of our own. We couldn't afford a big one, but last Christmas, our kids, Karen and Rob, gave us this little one.

Until recently, this little creature had no name. Then, at a folk concert, I found just the right one. A singer whose songs flashed back to the '60s, full of peace and justice, unplugged guitar and Irish harp—this singer had dropped his birth name and taken another: "Otter Dreaming," he called himself. So, borrowed from the folksinger, this little mammal, warm in the hand, now has a name—Otter Dreaming.

In Washington, D.C., there stands a black wall engraved with fifty thousand names—names of those killed in Vietnam. A traveling memorial wall came to Whidbey Island, and my husband Bill, who served in the Navy during that time, took paper and chalk and rubbed from the wall the names of fallen friends. In his hands he held the names, calling back in memory the men he had known.

Some names are passed down in families. Karen is my middle name and my daughter's first name. But long before, it was the name of my *farmor*, my father's mother. My grandmother in Norway was named Karen, pronounced "Kahren," but, after crossing the ocean, she changed the pronunciation to the familiar "Karen." Relatives in Norway told us that "Kahren" is a very old name in the family. Pointing to an ancient cottage, my second cousin said, "That is where the first 'Kahren' lived."

Other names are the subject of dark mystery. Married for a year and holding a one-month-old baby, my aunt landed on her sister's doorstep. Her husband had disappeared. Matt, who was the baby in her arms, has lived over forty years with a last name he knows little about—a name that connects him to no one.

Some names have clear meanings: Joy, Grace, Ruby, Pearl, Daisy, Rose. Others have meanings that need searching out: Claudia, Linda, Katherine, Donna.

Now it is your turn. I invite you to pair with another person who did not come here with you. Tell a story or share what you know about your first, middle, or last name—or a nickname. Here are some questions to get you started. You will have about five minutes to talk.

(*Participants choose from questions to be printed in large letters on poster board. These should be read aloud by presenter before the sharing starts.*)

• Tell about your first, middle, or last name.

• Were you named after someone?

• Do you like or dislike your name? Why?

• Have you ever changed one of your names? How did that feel?

After the paired sharing, the group reassembles. Those who would like to may share their stories with the entire group.

GLORIA KOLL

"THE YOUNG GIRL WITHIN"
Personal Stories of Being 7–10 Years Old

PRESENTER:
We are every age we have ever been.

At the core of our identity is a distinct, vital, authentic self that is first articulated in childhood. For most women, this "young girl within" is bright and able, confident in her abilities, and comfortable in her body. Remembering her can help us recognize our strengths and passions. A preadolescent girl usually knows who she is and what she is about.

At this time, I invite you to go back in time to who you were at age 7—8—9—10. Close your eyes. . . . What is your name? What do you look like? Who is in your family? Where do you live? What do you like to do? What do you want to be? How do you feel about school, church, your parents, boys? Do you have a best friend? A pet? What do you like to do on Saturdays?

You will have the opportunity to introduce the young girl within you. As we go around the Circle, introduce yourself as the girl you were then. For instance "My name is Kitty; I am 8 years old. . . ." Speak as though you *are* that eight-year-old. You may pass if you like, and we will go around a second time.

(*Another presenter may begin the sharing of "the young girl within" to model for other participants: "My name is Sharon Bradley. I am eight years old. We just moved to a farm in Oregon. I love riding horses as fast as I can. But I'm afraid of the pigs. . . . "*)

KITTY ADAMS

"THE YOUNG GIRL WITHIN"
Personal Stories of Being 11–17 Years Old

This morning Kitty led us to a time of childhood. But there was a time in our girlhood after that—a time of change in our bodies, in our families, in our friendships, in school.

I invite you to go back to that time—when you were 12 or 13 or 14 or 15 or 16 or 17. If you are now one of those ages, you are already there— or, if you like, you can go back a year or two.

Let's take our minds back to that earlier time.

Did you go to a junior high, middle school, or high school?

Picture it: Was it big and overpowering—or small and safe?

Did you have friends? Who were they? girls? boys?

Had anything changed in your friendships?

Where did you live? on a farm? in the city?

What was the closest store?

Who in your family was most important to you?

Who were the people in your life who made you feel strong?

Were there people who chipped away at you?

After a time of silence, I invite you to introduce yourself to this Circle as the girl you were then, telling us your name, your age, and something about yourself.

GLORIA KOLL

Presenting Midrash

For anyone who loves stories, as I do, the Bible is a wonderful book. One problem, though, for women, is that it is a book written down by men (who were the only ones allowed to write in those days) and the stories are mostly about men. In almost every story, men have power—and some misuse it; but women have no power—so they use their wits, their friends, and their faith to survive. There are, after all, plenty of women in the Bible—you just have to seek them out.

There is a wonderful way of retelling Bible stories done by Jewish scholars. It's called *midrash*—and this is how it's done:

You find a story in the Bible that you like, and then you imagine what that story would be like told from another point of view—or in another place—or in another time. Like—what if Jesus had been born in India? Would he have ridden into the capitol city on an elephant? Or what if Noah's flood happened on Puget Sound? Would the ark have landed on Mount Rainier? What if Eve had written down the story of the Garden of Eden?

If your brain is now moving to the exotic rhythms of midrash, we are ready for our stories, some from the Hebrew Bible, the scripture that Christians call the Old Testament, and some from the New Testament. Finally, we will hear a midrash set sometime in the future. First, the story of Ruth and Naomi:

GLORIA KOLL

EXAMPLES OF MIDRASH

RUTH AND NAOMI

For these longer scripture passages, we have used the older Revised Standard Version of the Bible because of copyright restrictions on the New Revised Standard Version. However, for its more inclusive language and more recent scholarship, we prefer the NRSV.

A deletion of biblical text is indicated by ellipses (. . .). See the Bible for the complete version.

A summary of Ruth 1:1–7: A famine has driven a Bethlehem couple, Elimelech and Naomi, and their two sons to Moab. After Elimelech dies, Naomi's sons marry Moabite women, Ruth and Orpah, and they all live in Moab for ten years. Then both of Naomi's sons die, and the three women are left as widows. They begin to walk back to Judah, where, they have heard, there is now food.

Ruth 1:8–22: But Naomi said to her two daughters-in-law, "Go, return each of you to her mother's house. May the Lord deal kindly with you." . . . And they said to her, "No, we will return with you to your people." But Naomi said, "Turn back my daughters, why will you go with me? Have I yet sons in my womb that they may become your husbands?" . . . Then they lifted up their voices and wept again; And Orpah kissed her mother-in-law, but Ruth clung to her. . . .

Ruth said, "Entreat me not to leave you . . . for where you go I will go, and where you lodge I will lodge; your people shall be my people, and your God my God; where you die I will die, and there will I be buried." . . . So Naomi returned, and Ruth . . . and they came to Bethlehem at the beginning of barley harvest.

Ruth 2: Now Naomi had a kinsman of her husband's, a man of wealth . . . whose name was Boaz. And Ruth the Moabitess said to Naomi, "Let me go to the field and glean." . . . Then Boaz said to his servant who was in charge of the reapers "Whose maiden is this?"

A summary of the remainder of chapter 2: Boaz is told of the family connection and is impressed that Ruth left her own people to remain with and care for Naomi. He eats with her and tells his servants to let her glean freely and to leave extra bundles of grain for her. Ruth tells Naomi of this, and Naomi advises Ruth to continue gleaning in this safe place.

Ruth 3: Then Naomi her mother-in-law said to her, "My daughter, should I not seek a home for you? . . . Is not Boaz our kinsman, with whose maidens you were? See, he is winnowing barley tonight at the threshing floor. Wash therefore and anoint yourself, and put on your best clothes. . . . When he lies down, observe the place where he lies; then go and uncover his feet and lie down; and he will tell you what to do." And she replied, "All that you say I will do."

A summary of the remainder of chapters 3 and 4: Boaz is at first shocked and then deeply touched when he wakes to find Ruth lying at his feet. She reminds him that he is next of kin. He blesses her and promises to go through the legalities needed to help her. He sends her home with a generous gift of barley. Naomi counsels her to wait for the outcome, knowing that Boaz will take action. Boaz, with ten elders witnessing, informs an even closer relative of Ruth's father-in-law that he has family lands available to buy; and that Ruth, as the widow of the former landowner, comes with the land. The closer relative declines the land and Ruth.

Ruth 4:9–17: Then Boaz said to the elders and all the people, "You are witnesses this day that I have bought from the hand of Naomi all that belonged to Elimelech . . . also Ruth the Moabitess, the widow of Mahlon, I have bought to be my wife, to perpetuate the name of the dead in his inheritance." . . . So Boaz took Ruth and she became his wife. . . . She bore a son. Then the women said to Naomi . . . "He shall be to you a restorer of life and a nourisher of your old age; for your daughter-in-law who loves you, who is more to you than seven sons, has borne him." Then Naomi took the child and laid him in her bosom and became his nurse. And the women of the neighborhood gave him a name, saying, "A son has been born to Naomi." They named him Obed; he was the father of Jesse, the father of David.

"Naomi and Ruth": Midrash

Characters: Naomi is an older woman; her shoulders are no longer straight, her walk is slow, and her age shows in her weary face and sad demeanor. She and her husband Elimelech traveled years before to Moab needing to escape the famine in Judah.

Ruth is a young, strong Moabite woman of lighter step and loving mien. She married Naomi's son Mahlon. She loves Naomi and remembers the loving, faithful mother-in-law Naomi was before the loss of her husband and two sons.

Orpah is Naomi's other daughter-in-law. She also loves Naomi, but is more reserved than Ruth.

Boaz is Naomi's kinsman.

Also speaking are a narrator and a servant.

NARRATOR: The early autumn sun seemed heavy on the shoulders of the three women. They walked slowly eastward, toward Judah, native land of the eldest woman. Their steps were heavy and slow and the faces of even the younger women were as worn as the dusty, treeless land they walked. The older woman broke the heavy silence.

(Circling some distance outside the fire circle, Naomi is walking heavily, carrying a large basket filled with personal things—a blanket, an earthen jar, another robe. Ruth and Orpah follow somewhat behind her, also circling outside the campfire.)

NAOMI *(looking back at the two women):* Why do you keep following me? My sons, your husbands are dead. Their father, dead, too. Even if he were alive, do you think this old womb could somehow ripen with another son? Do you imagine to wait for that impossible son to grow so you can marry him and regain a name and protection?

ORPAH: Naomi, let us go with you back to your town of Bethlehem. You are all we have now. Our husbands are dead; fate left us no children. We have nothing.

NAOMI *(nearly in tears):* Go back, I tell you. Leave me!

RUTH: Naomi, don't be hard on Orpah. She loves you, as I do, and doesn't want to leave you.

NAOMI: I don't mean to be harsh, but my soul is tired and angry. I just think you would have a safer time of it if you returned to your own family. Perhaps someone would take pity on you. Perhaps you would find another husband. I don't know what chance I have back in Bethlehem other than to glean with other widows and poor people. Surely you don't want to join me in that tenuous existence. And you women are Moabites—unlike the warm welcome we have received here in Moab, there would be little tolerance for you in Judah.

ORPAH: It is a difficult decision, Naomi, but perhaps you are right. It frightens me to imagine life in your country. Maybe in my own land I might fare better. But, Naomi, it breaks my heart to leave you. Ruth, will you come with me?

RUTH: No, Orpah, I cannot leave Naomi. She has loved me well. In her abiding faith I am learning of a loving God, though I must admit God seems far from us now. I will follow Naomi to Bethlehem.

NAOMI: No, Ruth! Go with your sister-in-law. Stay in your own land, among your own people!

RUTH: Naomi, I beg you, don't ask me to leave you; don't turn me away. I have made up my mind. You have loved me well; we must face what comes, together. Now that the world rejects us, we must care for each other. I want to come with you to your land; I want to worship your God; I want your home to be my home. I want to make you and your people, my people. And may God grant us peace together.

RUTH *(turning to Orpah):* Go, now, Orpah. Oh, I will miss you. May there be for you a blessing from the heart of God.

(Orpah nears Naomi, tears filling her eyes. They look at each other in love and sorrow. Naomi reaches out to Orpah, hugs her long, then gently pushes her away. Ruth and Orpah cling to each other, then Ruth says:)

RUTH: Go with God, Orpah. Shalom.

(Orpah exits. Ruth walks with Naomi now, and they enter inside the fire circle.)

NAOMI: O, I am weary. Home seems so strange to me after all these years. I wish people wouldn't fuss about us. I even wish they wouldn't call me Naomi. That name means "pleasant," but I don't feel pleasant; I feel bitter. They should call me "mara," for I am bitter and angry with God. God has forsaken me, or is punishing me for something. This is my home, but with no husband and no son, I have no place here.

RUTH: Hush, now, Naomi. Life has brought us many sorrows, your husband and sons are dead, my husband died and we had no sons. But look, it seems the famine is gone from your land—the fields are ripe with grain. And we have each other; I know something good will come for us. You have taught me about faith: together we must hold on to hope now. We must find the shelter in each other that the world refuses us. Let me go and glean after the reapers in the barley fields. Perhaps they will be generous and let a bit extra fall to the ground.

NAOMI: Well, we must have something to eat. Boaz is my dead husband's relative; perhaps he will be kind to you, widow of his kin.

NARRATOR: Ruth goes to glean in Boaz's field. Later Boaz arrives to see how the harvest is coming.

BOAZ *(asking of his reapers)*: Who is that woman gleaning after you? To whom does she belong?

SERVANT: She is the Moabite woman, widow of your kinsman; she's Naomi's daughter-in-law. She asked if she could glean behind the reapers and has been at it all day without even resting.

BOAZ *(to Ruth)*: My daughter, glean only in my fields. Stay close to my women; I have ordered that no one is to bother you. If you get thirsty, my servants will give you water.

RUTH: Why are you treating me, a foreigner, so kindly?

BOAZ: I have been told of your kindness to Naomi since the death of your husband. I know you left your family and your native land to come here with her. May God bless you and hide you in the shelter of God's wings.

RUTH: Even though I am a stranger, you have been a comfort to me. I will try to deserve your kindness and generosity. Thank you.

NARRATOR: Ruth returned to Naomi at dusk with a basket full of grain.

NAOMI: How did you find so much barley?

RUTH: Your husband's kin, Boaz, was more than kind. He welcomed me, allowed me to glean with his servants. He said I could drink the water his servants had drawn and even shared lunch with me!

NAOMI: Blessed is the man who took notice of you. God has not forgotten either the living or the dead! Glean only from his field until the harvest is done. You will be safe there, but not in other fields.

NARRATOR: So Ruth gleaned close to the women of Boaz all through barley and wheat season, bringing home to Naomi the fruits of her work.

NAOMI: Ruth, because Boaz is my husband's kin, he has the right to restore your name and family that were lost when Mahlon died. I have been thinking about a way that Boaz might become your husband. As kind as he has been, until you are married and have a son, you cannot be redeemed from namelessness and neither your security nor mine can be counted on. Tonight, they will be winnowing the wheat on the threshing floor; they will not return home, but sleep there to continue the work in the morning. Wash and anoint yourself and put on your best clothes. Go to the threshing floor and hide there until Boaz has eaten and drunk his fill. When he lies down to sleep, crawl under the blanket at his feet and lie there until he wakes.

NARRATOR: Ruth did as Naomi had instructed her. Around midnight, Boaz woke up, startled.

BOAZ: Who is there? Who are you, woman?

RUTH: Boaz, it is I, Ruth, Naomi's daughter-in-law. Since you are my husband's next of kin, I have come that you might spread your cloak of protection over me.

BOAZ: You surely are a brave and loving woman. You have remained faithful to Naomi, and now you seek me out, rather than the handsome, younger men. You have asked for my protection, but it is I whose life would be warmed by your love. But you have an even closer relative than I. If he is unwilling to exercise his prior right, then I will act as your next-of-kin and do what you have asked of me. Stay this night, and if he does not claim his right, then as God lives, I will take you home with me.

NARRATOR: The next day Boaz went to the man who was next in line for Elimelech's land, asking him if he wanted to exercise his right to claim the land. He reminded the man that along with the land came the responsibility to redeem, that is marry, Ruth. The other man renounced his claim to the land saying he was not able to take on the responsibility of marrying Ruth. So Boaz said to the company that had gathered round:

BOAZ: Today you are all witnesses that I have acquired from the hand of Naomi all that belonged to Elimelech, including Ruth, the Moabite wife of Naomi's son. She will become my wife so that the dead man's name will continue, and the son can inherit the land.

NARRATOR: Then the people said, "We are witnesses. And may God bless you with children who will bestow a name in Bethlehem." And Boaz married Ruth; and he loved her. In due time she bore a son and everyone said to Naomi, "Blessed be God who has again looked with favor upon all you have done. May the child be a blessing to you, a restoration to you of life and happiness in your old age! And may the child be renowned in Israel."

NARRATOR: Ruth gave the baby to Naomi to nurse and to love.

RUTH: This is your baby, too, Naomi. Care for him as you did your own. We are family now, with safety and security. I see my Naomi's old smile return and it blesses me.

NARRATOR: And from the two women who had nothing but each other, one who thought God had forgotten her, and another a faithful stranger in a foreign land; and by the kindness their friendship invoked in another, a baby was born, a baby whose inheritance would change the world. For, you see, Ruth's baby was named Obed, and Obed was the father of Jesse, and Jesse was the father of David. And from the house of David came Jesus of Nazareth.

SALLY WINDECKER

MARY AND MARTHA

Here follows a rather mischievous midrash of Martha and Mary. First, the story as it is told in Luke 10:38–42 (RSV).

Now as they went on their way, [Jesus] entered a village; and a woman named Martha received him into her house. She had a sister called Mary who sat at the Lord's feet and listened to his teaching. But Martha was distracted with much serving; and she went to him and asked, "Lord, do you not care that my sister has left me to serve alone? Tell her then to help me." But [Jesus] answered, "Martha, Martha, you are anxious and troubled by many things; one thing is needful. Mary has chosen the good portion, which shall not be taken from her."

"MARTHA AND MARY": MIDRASH

My sister Martha says there are only two ways to be with a man: one is at the dinner table and the other is in bed. In either case, she says, it is the woman's duty to serve the man. That, she says, is what a man wants from a woman, and that is God's plan. My sister Martha says many things. In fact, she talks nonstop. When we were kids, the rest of us used to call her "Martha the Mouth."

I'm so different. I'm different from Martha and from every other woman I know. Usually, I'd rather listen to the men talking than to the women. Women in my town talk about cooking and babies. Men talk about politics and religion! I love to hear their ideas. I have ideas of my own, although, of course, being a woman, I'm not allowed to say a word.

A teacher named Jesus came to our house last week. Now there is a man with a mind! No question was too difficult for him. He tossed out wild ideas about God and people. I was right with him, sitting on a pillow beside him, listening to every word. I could grasp his ideas, and he encouraged me with his eyes. Sometimes he put a question right to me, even though the other men would have spit at me if I had answered. Every one of them gets up each morning and says, "I thank you, God, for not making me a woman." But Jesus looked right at me when he made a difficult point, sort of like he was saying, "Just between you and me, I know you're the only one in this room who's smart enough to understand this part."

"Martha the Mouth" was rushing around, muttering to herself, slapping plates on the table, tromping through the living room like a Roman soldier. Finally, she interrupted Jesus mid-sentence to say, "Lord"— "Lord," she called him. She is *so* respectful, even when she's being totally rude. "Lord!" she said again, and he looked at her, sort of raising up one eyebrow in a question mark like rabbis can do. Martha planted her big sandals right in front of Jesus and put her hands on those wide hips. "Lord, doesn't it bother you that my sister Mary has dumped all the work on me and is just lounging here at your feet?" She flashed a righteous look at me that said, what kind of woman do you think you are, sitting on your butt, talking with the men!

Jesus has a gentle way of correcting people when he knows they're making an honest mistake. "Martha," he said her name so softly. "Martha, Martha, you worry so much about everything. Food is good—and yours is especially good. But even better than the most delicious food is feeding each other with ideas. Mary has chosen that; I'm not going to take that away from her. Sit down for a while. I'll peel the potatoes after we talk." And Martha sat down, right by me. "Martha the Mouth" became "Martha the Attentive One." Each time Jesus said something completely new and amazing, Martha would squeeze my hand or I would give her a little nudge, like, don't forget that, we'll talk about it later.

Martha and I have called a few of our women friends together. We're going to start a writing group to write and talk about Jesus' ideas—and our own ideas, too. When we gather all the ideas and stories together, we'll put them in a book. We'll call it "The New Testament!"

GLORIA KOLL

THE BLEEDING WOMAN AND JAIRUS'S DAUGHTER

Mark 5:21–43 (RSV): And when Jesus had crossed again in the boat to the other side, a great crowd gathered about him; and he was beside the sea. Then came one of the rulers of the synagogue, Jairus by name; and seeing him, he fell at his feet and besought him saying, "My little daughter is at the point of death. Come and lay your hands on her, so that she may live." And he went with him.

And a great crowd followed him and thronged about him. And there was a woman who had had a flow of blood for twelve years, and who had suffered much under many physicians, and had spent all that she had, and was no better but rather grew worse. She had heard the reports about Jesus, and came up behind him in the crowd and touched his garment. For she said, "If I touch even his garments, I shall be made well," And immediately the hemorrhage ceased; and she felt in her body that she was healed of her disease. And Jesus, perceiving in himself that power had gone forth from him, immediately turned about in the crowd, and said, "Who touched my garments?" And his disciples said to him, "You see the crowd pressing around you, and yet you say, 'Who touched me?'" And he looked around to see who had done it. But the woman, knowing what had been done to her came in fear and trembling and fell down before him and told him the whole truth. And he said to her, "Daughter, your faith has made you well; go in peace, and be healed of your disease."

While he was still speaking, there came from the ruler's house some who said, "Your daughter is dead. Why trouble the teacher any further?" But ignoring what they said, Jesus said to the ruler of the synagogue, "Do not fear, only believe." And he allowed no one to follow him except Peter and James and John the brother of James. When they came to the house of the ruler of the synagogue, he saw a tumult, and people weeping and wailing loudly. And when he had entered, he said to them, "Why do you make a tumult and weep? The child is not dead but sleeping." And they laughed at him. But he put them all outside, and took the child's father and mother and those who were with him, and went in where the child was. Taking her by the hand he said to her, "Tal'itha cumi"; which means, "Little girl, I say to you arise." And immediately the girl got up and walked, for she was twelve years old. And immediately they were overcome with amazement. And he strictly charged them that no one should know this, and told them to give her something to eat.

"THE BLEEDING WOMAN AND JAIRUS'S DAUGHTER": MIDRASH

Woman: I have nothing to lose. For twelve long years I have lived alone—cast away from my husband's household and family. I live and breathe, eat what I can, sleep some, but it is a living death. I am ignored, feared, even worse, it's as though I don't even exist. I was nearly nothing before the continual bleeding began. Now, even what I was is gone.

Why is my bleeding such a sin? Why is every woman's monthly bleeding so abhorrent, so unclean? What are the men afraid of? What have we done? Why did God create us to mature and give birth in blood and water? The scriptures say that God looked on all creation and said it was good! Then why are our natural ways so hated? And why have I bled so long? It is as though my life seeps away day by day. The doctors have been able to do nothing for me. They really would rather not bother themselves with me for fear of becoming unclean. Is this some kind of punishment? For what? Just for being a woman?

I have listened to the conversations of those who pass through the gates I am condemned to sit beside, begging whatever pittance the judging eyes can spare me. Lately, I have heard many talk of a prophet who heals, someone sent, they say, from God. Crowds follow him. They speak of the power in his words. They say he talks with women and shares meals in the homes of tax collectors; that he blesses children and heals lepers and demoniacs. He is supposed to be coming this way soon. I can't believe, can't even imagine he'd talk to me. Dream on, woman, its no use. What would any man have to say to you?

But what if I just touched his robe as he passed through the gate? No one would even notice and if he is the prophet they say he is, maybe I could be healed and he would never need to know or be bothered. Maybe I'm losing my mind. But then, I have absolutely nothing else to lose.

What a crowd surrounds him! He draws so many near. His helpers are trying to keep the crowds from pressing him too closely . . . if I reach just a little farther . . .

Jesus: Who touched me? I felt someone touch me.

Apostle: Master, hundreds push in around you. It could have been anyone—it could have been dozens!

Jesus: Someone touched me—I felt someone touch me; power went out from me.

Woman *(aside):* I've been found out—how could he tell? I only touched his robe! Well, it's done now, I'll have to confess . . .

What's happened?! As I stand, I feel no warm, sticky oozing down my leg; I am dry!! I am not bleeding! Could it have been the prophet? Did he bring God's love to heal even me?

Woman *(to Jesus):* Pssst . . . Sir, I'm the one who touched your robe. Please forgive me for presuming so. I really did not want to bother you, but, you see, I've been dead so long. I only hoped . . . if you're all they say you are, I could be healed and . . .

Jesus: Shhh, good woman. Don't be afraid. You have done nothing wrong. You are not unclean; you are whole. Because of your tiny, persistent hope, and because of the power of love that sent me, you are made whole. This world's bondage can never finally overcome the power of love. Go, and live in the light, child of God.

Woman: I can't take my eyes off him. He sees so deeply into me and I feel so full, so free. I am drawn after him, just like all these others . . . just to be near . . .

He's going into that wealthy man's house—he seems to move so freely wherever he goes. This man Jairus has asked Jesus to heal his twelve-year-old daughter . . . Ah, but he's too late; she is already dead. Well, then what are we waiting around for? But the father persists even though they tease him for his hope.

It's strange . . . Jesus brought me back from a kind of death, could he bring the girl to life? Perhaps she had just begun her first bleeding—why, she was just born when my hemorrhaging began. Now she would have to begin hiding herself in shame for seven days every month. Jesus didn't even think twice about becoming unclean when I touched his robe . . .

The child lives! She was brought back to life, too! Could it be, this Holy One loves women as much as men? . . . wants women to be whole, too? Could the God he says sent him think that the woman-half of creation is good, too? Might this young girl-becoming-woman live her life in some kind of hope?

For the first time in my life, I feel the power of hope, the strength of my own knowing, of recognition and acceptance, of having been seen and heard. Maybe it's the same for the girl, too, and for others this world disdains. That truly would be a miracle! I must watch now, to see what happens to this prophet—this Good Nazarene.

SALLY WINDECKER

MARY MAGDALENE

John 20:11–18 (RSV) *(paragraphing added):* But Mary stood weeping outside the tomb, and as she wept she stooped to look into the tomb; and she saw two angels in white, sitting where the body of Jesus had lain, one at the head and one at the feet. They said to her, "Woman, why are you weeping?"

She said to them, "Because they have taken away my Lord, and I do not know where they have laid him." Saying this, she turned around and saw Jesus standing, but she did not know that it was Jesus.

Jesus said to her, "Woman, why are you weeping? Whom do you seek?"

Supposing him to be the gardener, she said to him, "Sir, if you have carried him away, tell me where you have laid him, and I will take him away." Jesus said to her, "Mary." She turned and said to him in Hebrew, "Rabboni!" (which means Teacher).

Jesus said to her, "Do not hold me, for I have not yet ascended to the Father; but go to my brethren and say to them, I am ascending to my Father and your Father, to my God and your God." Mary Magdalene went and said to the disciples, "I have seen the Lord"; and she told them that he had said these things to her.

"MARY MAGDALENE": MIDRASH

My name is Mary Magdalene. I am here to share with you my story. When I was young, I was alone—without family, friends, or a husband. I did not have the means to receive shelter or food. Being a woman of many resources, I used my beauty and intelligence to attract men. I was enticing, and the men were quite stupid. Men had all the power; women were not heard. Women despised me because I did have powers over men.

I was able to survive, yet I was a very unhappy woman. I was lonely, abused, and emotionally wounded.

Then, unexpectedly, I met Jesus the teacher. He was unlike any man I'd known. He looked at me, and he saw the beauty in my heart. He knew my very soul. Jesus was the first man that didn't try to use me. He valued women. I was completely undone. I had not known love, let alone unconditional love.

I followed Jesus and the other disciples. It was not a custom of the time for devout Jews to speak with women, but Jesus accepted me as an equal and engaged me in conversation. To my great surprise, I became friends with women. My life gradually changed as I became more devoted to Jesus. I learned to receive love and to give love.

Then came that horrific day, the authorities arrested Jesus. He was unmercifully killed. How could this be? I felt the light had gone out of my life.

Some of the women and I went to his tomb. A white illuminated angel rolled away the stone protecting the tomb. The soldiers guarding the tomb were disabled with fear. The angel showed us the vacant tomb and told us he had risen. I was overwhelmed by fear. Yet a swelling joy took over my emotions.

Suddenly, we heard his beautiful voice say, "Rejoice!" Mary and I fell to our knees, and I knew that it was our Lord. I embraced with tenderness his beloved feet. I recalled memories of washing his well-traveled feet. Melancholy, like a flood, came over me as I remembered the liberating day he forgave all my previous sins. His voice dispelled all grief and lifted my soul to joyful celebration.

Later, after he bodily left this earth, his spirit as presence has remained with me in my heart. I am empowered with many gifts of the spirit. I have known the one great truth because he lived among us—that love is the most potent healing force available. His first lesson to me was to love me unconditionally, then for me to accept this love though it was difficult for me to understand. I struggled with great resistance; over time I began to trust his forgiveness. I learned that I could forgive, and that there was a healer within me. As I prayed, I began to share this good news teaching younger women and their daughters that in God's eyes we are all one.

Now, I am brave as a warrior to face the future. I can trust myself to the difficult task of living courageously without paralyzing fear.

Ah. I remember those early days when I was on fire with his love!

(Begin singing, "I Don't Know How To Love Him," from Jesus Christ Superstar)

LINDA WHITE WADSWORTH

PARABLE OF THE TALENTS

Matthew 25:14–28 (RSV) *(paragraphing added):* [Jesus said]"For it will be as when a man going on a journey called his servants and entrusted to them his property; to one he gave five talents, to another two, to another one, each according to his ability. Then he went away. He who had received the five talents went at once and traded with them; and he made five talents more. So too, he who had the two talents made two talents more. But he who had received the one talent went and dug in the ground and hid his master's money.

Now after a long time the master of those servants came and settled accounts with them. And he who had received the five talents came forward, bringing five talents more, saying, 'Master, you delivered to me five talents; here I have made five talents more.' His master said to him, 'Well done, good and faithful servant; you have been faithful over a little, I will set you over much; enter into the joy of your master.' And he also who had the two talents came forward, saying, 'Master, you delivered to me two talents; here I have made two talents more.' His master said to him, 'Well done, good and faithful servant; you have been faithful over a little, I will set you over much; enter into the joy of your master.'

He also who had received the one talent came forward, saying, 'Master I knew you to be a hard man, reaping where you did not sow and gathering where you did not winnow; so I was afraid and I went and hid your talent in the ground. Here you have what is yours.' But his master answered him, 'You wicked and slothful servant! You knew that I reap where I have not sowed and gather where I have not winnowed? Then you ought to have invested my money with the bankers, and at my coming I should have received what was my own with interest. So take the talent from him, and give it to him who has the ten talents.'"

"A New Parable of the Talents": Midrash

A wealthy landowner was preparing for a long journey. Wanting to provide for the three women who were tenants, the landowner called Ruth in and said to her,

"Ruth, I'm lending you ten acres of my best farmland—use it while I am gone."

Sending for Sarah, and telling her of the journey, the landowner handed her a large burlap sack, filled to the top and sewn shut.

"Sarah, this is seed from my highest-yielding wheat field. Use it well while I am gone."

Then the landowner summoned Rebecca and, while she stood trembling, handed her a well-used hoe saying,

"This is for your use while I am gone. Take care of it well."

Each woman returned to her house wondering what she should do with her bequest. Ruth pondered how she could use the land. Ten acres was too much for one old woman, and she had long ago sold her gardening tools for food. Sarah thought to grind her seed into flour to bake coarse bread, for she had no land to plant it in, and she was hungry. Rebecca considered the hoe she had been given and puzzled, for she had no land, and she had no garden, and she didn't know much about growing things. She had only a small, dark room, and she often sat there alone and afraid.

Ruth, the eldest, sat in stillness for a time, seeking guidance. The word within led her to seek her friend Sarah to counsel with her. When she told Sarah of the gift of land and learned of Sarah's gift of seed, the way was clear. They sought out the shy woman, Rebecca, who timidly told of the hoe she had been given, and the task was confirmed.

Together, they worked the soil and planted, tended, and harvested the wheat. The bountiful yield was too much for their own needs, and they were able to save seed for the next planting, grind flour for bread, and give seed away. Each season yielded more wheat. The women were able to sell wheat, to hire workers, and to feed the people who were hungry.

Upon returning, the landowner found a community of people working and fed and money in the bank from the harvest profits.

"Well done, good and faithful servants. With the gifts you were given, your lives and others have been blessed. You have been faithful to the way of love."

Sally Windecker

David and Bathsheba

2 Samuel 11:2–5 (RSV) *(paraphrase or summary in parentheses)*: It happened late one afternoon when David [the King] arose from his couch and was walking about the roof of the king's house, that he saw from the roof a woman bathing; and the woman was very beautiful. David sent and inquired about the woman. And one said, "This is Bathsheba, daughter of Eliam, the wife of Uriah the Hittite (who is out fighting your war.)

(Now she was purifying herself from her menstrual period.) So David sent messengers and took her, and she came to him and he lay with her. Then she returned to her house. And the woman conceived; and she sent and told David, "I am (pregnant.)"

(David brought Uriah back from the battle and tried to get him to go to bed with his wife Bathsheba, so that Uriah would believe she was carrying his baby. But Uriah was such a loyal soldier that he insisted on remaining on duty by the king's door.)

2 Samuel 11:14: In the morning David wrote a letter to Joab and sent it by the hand of Uriah. In the letter he wrote, "Set Uriah in the forefront of the hardest fighting, and then draw back from him that he may be struck down and die."

2 Samuel 11:26: When the wife of Uriah heard that Uriah her husband was dead, she made lamentation for her husband. And when the (seven days) of mourning was over; David sent and brought her to his house, and she became his wife and bore him a son. But the thing that David had done displeased (Yahweh.)

GLORIA KOLL

"BATHSHEBA FERNANDEZ": MIDRASH

Summer

The baby pool glittered in the afternoon sunlight, reflecting in miniature the diving and splashing in the big pool beside it. Water heaved over the edge of the main swimming pool onto the sunbathing teenaged girls as male adolescents crashed against the water's surface. The baby pool, separated from the high waves by a strip of concrete, held a circle of smooth, safe water for the mothers and their little ones. Only miniscule bubbles disturbed the surface of this shallow pool. Bathsheba coaxed three-year-old Marietta, "It's fun. Look, Mommy's putting her face into the water. Blow bubbles. Good girl! We'll show Daddy when he comes home!"

Both mother and daughter were clad in one-piece suits, appropriate attire under the government's new directive, "Poolside Dress Code for Women and Girls." Marietta splattered away in comfort in her stretchy cotton suit, but Bathsheba straightened and tugged the shiny Lycra creeping up underneath and pulling down against the stays of her push-up top. Nothing else available, she thought. Not many choices in the stores anymore. Not many choices.

At a clang from the poolside bell, Bathsheba's eyes focused on the clubhouse doorway. The smiling club manager held the door for a man she immediately recognized. The Leader's face graced the walls of all public buildings: schools, post offices, and churches, next to the flag/cross symbol of his ruling Christian Patriot party. As the Leader came through the club door, each person in the pool swam quickly to the side. Those sitting beside the pool stood. Everyone smiled and applauded appreciatively as the Leader, his guard dog trotting at his side, strode to a poolside lounge chair.

Grey-blond, tall, massive, an ex-football player striving to keep his athletic body, Leader David stopped whenever possible at local gyms and pools to work out—and to keep in touch with those he ruled. Those God ruled through him. His people had learned to respect his privacy. The country club members returned to swimming and sunbathing, carefully leaving an unoccupied area of the pool and sundeck for Leader David, for his personal trainer, and for David's attentive, obedient German shepherd.

A glass of carrot juice arrived at David's table, and three striped towels appeared on his bench. At David's nod, the red-haired, freckled-faced trainer, Garth, squirted tanning oil on David's wide shoulders and rubbed the oil in with a firm massage. David's clear, benevolent eyes moved around the pool and stopped at a pretty pair, Bathsheba and Marietta, blowing bubbles into the baby pool. "That's what it's all about," he thought. "That's what I'm working so hard to protect."

At that moment, Marietta, forgetting to blow bubbles, inhaled a mouthful of water, coughed, and sputtered. Bathsheba stood, tugged at her suit, first at the bottom and then at the bodice, and glanced up self-consciously. Her eyes met those of the Leader, and she looked quickly away. She lifted her little daughter into her arms and wiped the water from Marietta's tiny nose and mouth. "You're OK, sweetie. You're a good little swimmer."

Today, as on each Tuesday, Bathsheba shared a picnic lunch with the other mothers and toddlers on the grass beside the pool. Mothers' groups were encouraged by the Christian Patriot party as a way to strengthen the family and the nation. The women sat in a circle on the lawn, while the little ones stepped and tumbled on the soft, green grass in the middle. As the mothers finished their sandwiches, a man approached the group and knelt directly behind Bathsheba. His freckled nose and mouth moved up behind her left ear. "You are required to come," he said softly. "The Leader has ordered it."

Bathsheba stilled even her breath for a moment, and it seemed to her she felt each woman in the circle stop breathing. "I have a little girl," she said.

The man smirked, and his orange freckles wiggled on his upper lip. "You would like to send her instead, maybe?"

"Give me one minute here. I will come." Her voice was controlled and steady. As the man withdrew, Bathsheba reached for her purse. She slipped her Visa card from its cover and pressed it into the hand of the young woman next to her. Then she wrote carefully on a slip of paper and placed that on top of the credit card. She looked directly into the eyes of her friend.

"Marietta's grandmother lives in Illinois," she said. "This is the address. She'll be safe there." Bathsheba's friend drew Marietta into her lap and nodded silently. Among these women, in these dark times, a subtle movement, a quiet nod, contracted a firm and faithful promise. Bathsheba rose and walked, smiling, to Leader David.

Winter

Steam from David's hot coffee clouded the window glass, obscuring his view of the frozen lake. In the misty glass, he drew a circle and, within the circle, two large eyes and the curve of a smile.

"So what is it about this one?" Garth, always lacking in imagination, seemed puzzled at his Leader's passion for this woman. "She's married to a Mexican, for God's sake."

Leader David spoke slowly and clearly. "Bathsheba's pregnant. Her husband is an ultra-loyal border patrol type. Trying to prove what a good American he is, even with his Latino blood. He won't come home until his two-year term is up."

Both men were silent then, weighing the possibilities. Abortion clinics were closed now, thank God, but that did narrow the possible choices. Scandal must be avoided. The Leader's public image held God's chosen country together. Sometimes difficult decisions had to be made for the good of this great land. Strong men had to be willing to make those decisions.

David spoke. "Use him in the next major preemptive border strike. Send him in the first wave. Have him hold off his little brown Mexican brothers while our men retreat. After he's dead, we'll give him the Medal of Honor."

A Psalm of Bathsheba

"Oh God, my God, you who sit and weep with women, hear my cry! My beloved husband is dead. I wept for him. My sweet daughter is far from me. I wept for her. I submit at his whim to a man who has the power of life and death over me and mine. The first sweet baby born of this foul union died in my arms. I had no more tears to shed, and I watched in silence as this man David cried. I will never love him. Do not ask me to, for I cannot. But I love this new baby here at my breast. I have called him Solomon because he is born of hard wisdom. This child is your gift to me, your balm for my pain, your answer to my cries. You hold me in your soft bosom and you comfort me. You give me rest. I sleep in your embrace and trust in your care. May your day of peace and justice come! Amen."

GLORIA KOLL

ADAM AND EVE

Genesis 3:1–19 (RSV): Now the serpent was more subtle than any other wild creature that the Lord God had made. He said to the woman, "Did God say, 'You shall not eat of any tree of the garden'?" And the woman said to the serpent, "We may eat of the fruit of the trees of the garden; but God said, 'You shall not eat of the fruit of the tree which is in the midst of the garden, neither shall you touch it, lest you die.'" But the serpent said to the woman, "You will not die. For God knows that when you eat of it your eyes will be opened, and you will be like God, knowing good and evil." So when the woman saw that the tree was good for food, and that it was a delight to the eyes, and that the tree was to be desired to make one wise, she took of its fruit and ate; and she also gave some to her husband, and he ate. Then the eyes of both were opened, and they knew that they were naked; and they sewed fig leaves together and made themselves aprons.

And they heard the sound of the Lord God walking in the garden in the cool of the day, and the man and his wife hid themselves from the presence of the Lord God among the trees of the garden. But the Lord God called to the man, and said to him, "Where are you?" And he said, "I heard the sound of thee in the garden, and I was afraid, because I was naked; and I hid myself." He said, "Who told you that you were naked? Have you eaten of the tree of which I commanded you not to eat?" The man said, "The woman whom thou gavest to be with me, she gave me the fruit of the tree, and I ate." Then the Lord God said to the women, "What is this that you have done?" The woman said, "The serpent beguiled me, and I ate." The Lord God said to the serpent,

"Because you have done this, cursed are you above all cattle,
  and above all wild animals; upon your belly you shall go,
    and dust you shall eat all the days of your life.
I will put enmity between you and the woman,
  and between your seed and her seed;
he shall bruise your head, and you shall bruise his heel."
To the woman he said,
"I will greatly multiply your pain in childbearing;
in pain you shall bring forth children,
yet your desire shall be for your husband, and he shall rule over you."
And to Adam he said
  "Because you have listened to the voice of your wife
and have eaten of the tree of which I commanded you, 'You shall not eat of it,'
cursed is the ground because of you; in toil you shall eat of it
  all the days of your life;
thorns and thistles it shall bring forth to you;
  and you shall eat the plants of the field.
In the sweat of your face you shall eat bread till you return to the ground,
    for out of it you were taken;
you are dust and to dust you shall return."

"Eve and Adam": A Midrash

Note: This script is in simplest note form, and is expected to be added to and ad-libbed in order to fill it out.

Setting: E. D. N. 2,000; President Garth Oswald Dewey (G.O.D.) presiding.

World: "Woms" and "manwoms" instead of women and men. Manwoms stay home with the kids and do housework while woms go off hunting and fighting for the village. Hence, the roles of everyday life are opposite of what they are now.

Scene 1: Adam the manwom is looking at himself in a freestanding mirror. He is clad in an apron and plaid "logger's" shirt. An expression of disapproval is on his face. Much like a woman would look at herself in a mirror and wish she were thinner, he is wishing he had more weight on him. This is because women naturally have more fat than men; and in our world, women are constantly wishing they had the fat ratio that men, the more dominant sex, naturally have. Since in this world, the women, or woms, are more dominant, the manwoms are constantly trying to gain weight so as to be the same as the woms.

Adam:	I'm much too skinny, I need to gain more weight. Just look at those spindly chicken legs . . .
Eve:	Honey, I'm home. Look at this big fish I caught! It must be at least a forty-pounder! Work was so tough today. How are the kids?
Adam:	Today was rough. Little Eve Jr. kept me so busy I never had a moment to myself. I've been on my feet all day, slaving in front of the fire, my arches have fallen, I thought you'd never get home . . .
	(He is interrupted by Little Eve Jr.)
Eve Jr.:	Daddy, when's dinner gonna be ready? I'm starving! Oh Mommy, I missed you!
Eve:	I missed you too, kiddo.
	(She gives Evie a pat on the head while Evie hugs her knees.)
Adam:	I'm going to go take a walk, could you watch Little Evie for me, please?
	(Eve nods, not listening at all to what Adam just asked.)
Adam:	I can't take this anymore. I made her favorite dinner and she didn't even thank me. She never even calls me her little macho man anymore. Maybe it's my fault. Maybe she thinks I'm too skinny. What can I do?

(He is lost in his own turmoil and doesn't even notice the "Dealer" in a long trench coat standing in the street, until . . .)

Dealer: Hey, pst . . . pst . . . Yah, you; come over here. I wanna show you something. Take a look at this. *(He shows Adam a bottle of Power Pills hidden inside his coat.)* This will solve all your problems.

Adam: Are those . . . Power Pills? President G.O.D. says we're not to go near that stuff. I mean, what would my wom say?

Dealer: What will she say? She'll love you for it! This will make you a whole new manwom. Just one little pill will bring you knowledge and power. Just between you and me, how do you think G.O.D. got so smart?

Adam: Gee, I never thought of that. Will this put the spark back in our marriage?

Dealer: Will it ever! This is just the thing you need; it will solve all your marital problems.

Adam: How much does it cost?

Dealer: Well, my friend—it just happens to be your lucky day. I'll sell it to you for half price. But you can't tell anybody. This is our little secret. And, because we're friends, anytime you need anything, you just call me.

(He hands Adam a business card with "The Serpent" written in large letters on it.)

Narrator: Later that night in the house of Eve and Adam.

Eve *(to Little Evie Jr.):* Time for bed kiddo.

(Eve gives her a little nudge in the direction of her bedroom. Evie Jr. exits offstage.)

Adam: I met this manwom today while I was on my walk. He gave me this. *(He shows the Power Pills to Eve.)* It will give you power like G.O.D. I mean, how do you think G.O.D. got so smart? This could be the spark our marriage needs . . .

Narrator: Due to the graphic nature of the following sequence of events, the following clip has been edited to protect the innocent.

Messenger: Open up in the name of Garth Oswald Dewey!

(Adam opens the door. The Messenger unrolls a scroll.)

Messenger: Eve and Adam. Stop. Your presence is requested at Dewey Hall. Stop. Come immediately. Stop. Signed G.O.D. Stop. Garth Oswald Dewey. Stop.

Adam: Oh No! G.O.D. must have found out!

Eve: Don't worry, I'll protect you.

              (They exit, following the Messenger around the stage until they reach G.O.D.—preferably played by a small, young girl.)

G.O.D.:   So, you have something to tell me? . . .

Narrator: And so, Eve and Adam were punished. Eve, who was accustomed to being the head of the family, the decision-maker, the provider; and Adam, who was accustomed to staying home and nurturing the children; would henceforth have their roles reversed. But inside each of us, we, the women, know the truth.

WRITTEN AND PERFORMED BY GIRLS AT ONE OF THE RETREATS

In this section, we include some of the ceremonies, services, proclamations of the Word (sermons), prayers, litanies, and poems that we have discovered or that have been written by our retreat facilitators. We offer them for your blessing.

WORSHIP

Gathering in circle (conch and drum)

Creating altar (Sally)

Gathering song (Claudia)

Inviting all into God's presence (Gloria)

> The spirit of God
> is a life that bestows life,
> root of the world-tree
> and wind in its boughs.
> Scrubbing out sins,
> she rubs oil into wounds.
> She is glistening life
> alluring all praise,
> all-awakening,
> all-resurrecting—Hildegard of Bingen.[1]

Confessing our pain:

All or voices: My mind is confused and battered about.
My eyes hurt with seeing.
I talk too much.
I hit the wrong notes
   and come in
   at the wrong cues.
My bones ache.
Take me away, River, take me away.
I want to be cold, and swift, and clear.
I want to be brown and green with life.
Swirl foam around my dripping hair.
Lift me over the rocks.
Turn me around and around.
Fill my mouth with aspen leaves,
   And I will spit them out.
Take me away, River, take me away. —Gloria Koll

Song: "My Lord, What a Morning" (Claudia)
1. My Lord, what a morning.

   My Lord, what a morning.

   My Lord, what a morning—

   When the stars began to fall—

2. When the sun began to shine—

3. When my heart began to sing—Traditional African American spiritual[2]

Asking for healing:

(Gloria)
We ask forgiveness
of one another,
woman to woman,
sister to sister.

(Amy)
We ask forgiveness
of one another,
as children of God,
as friend to friend.

(Donna)
Too many times
have we failed to stand
together
in solidarity.
Too many times
have we judged one another,
condemning those things
we did not understand.

(Sally)
For limiting, labeling, and consequently
oppressing each other.
We ask forgiveness, O loving God
　　　　　　　　　—Miriam Therese Winter[3]

Responding with gratitude: (Gloria)
Confident of the forgiving spirit of God,
And the generous hearts of friends,
We receive with joy the grace-filled gift of renewed life.

Song: "Hallelujah" [4] (Claudia)

Proclaiming God's Word: (Donna)
John 15:5–17; Philippians 4:8,9

Blessing the Bread and Wine: (Gloria)
"Jesus—
descendant of Israel's liberator Miriam,
born of Mother Mary,
recognized by Prophet Anna,
and anointed by an unnamed woman—

this Jesus broke the bread
(server breaks bread) and poured the wine
(server pours wine)
and gave it to them, saying, 'Eat and drink.
Do this in remembrance of me.'"

Inviting all to come:
"You may dip the bread into the wine or
grape juice before eating it. Serve your neighbor with words: 'A gift of God.'
All are welcome. Please join in the meal."
(Bread and wine are passed.)

Song: "Eat This Bread" [5] (Claudia)

Prayer: (Sally)
Come, O Holy Spirit,
O Sanctifying Spirit,
fill our hearts,
fill our lives
with the feel of your fiery Presence,
so that all that we do,
all that we are,
comes from you within us.
Anoint us now,
so that from this day
we are your disciples only,
committed to carrying out faithfully
your mission in the world,
now and always. Amen.
　　　　　　　　　—Miriam Therese Winter[6]

(Sally instructs in anointing ceremony. Each marks the next forehead with oil)

Anointing Psalm: (Donna, Amy)

Anoint me with the oil of integrity, O God, and the seal of your sanctifying Spirit.

Voice 1:　Anoint my head so that all of my thoughts come forth from the will of your being to fill me with grace and peace.

Voice 2:　Anoint my eyes so that I might see your Presence and Providence clearly.

Voice 1:	Anoint my ears that I might hear the cry of the poor all around me and the whisper of your word.
Voice 2:	Anoint my lips that I might proclaim the Good News of your mission and the meaning of Jesus the Christ.
Voice 1:	Anoint my hands to hold and heal the many lives that are broken, that I may do good, do what I must to bring hope into hopelessness.
Voice 2:	Anoint my feet to walk in your ways, to run and never grow weary, to stand up for justice unafraid.
Voice 1:	Anoint my heart with warmth and compassion and a genuine generosity toward all who are in need.
Voice 2:	Anoint the whole of me, O Holy One, that I too may be holy.
Voice 1:	Anoint my spirit for mission, that I might reach out and into the heart of the whole hurting world.
Voice 2:	Anoint my soul for ministry, that I might have the courage to respond with the whole of my being to the daily demands of grace. Anoint me with the oil of integrity, O God, and the seal of your sanctifying Spirit.—Miriam Therese Winter[7]

Blessing us on our way
Song: "Bless Us God" (Claudia)
Song: "Hallelujah! (Claudia)

GLORIA KOLL

PROCLAIMING THE WORD
JESUS PROMISES THE HOLY SPIRIT

As anyone who has grappled with the grammar of a language, our own or another, comes to realize, each language has its own overtones both in its nouns and in using pronouns to replace nouns. French, for example, uses *il* (he), or *elle* (she), to replace such non-gender words as chair or table. In biblical Hebrew and Greek, nouns and pronouns are gender specific, too. To someone learning French, Spanish, Hebrew, or Greek, it seems that every book, tree, and car has been assigned a sex!

In the following proclamation, the author has included the womanly half of humanity in Jesus' invitation (as we believe was his intention) by changing words that are gender specific in English. Please compare this version with the cited texts in the New International Version of the Bible and with other translations. You will see for example, that the Hebrew word for the Holy Spirit is *ruah*, a feminine noun. Better still, if you have studied the ancient languages of the Bible, compare those early texts with this and other paraphrases and translations.

Sermon Based on John 14:12–14 (NIV)
Presenter:

At their last supper together, Jesus predicts his betrayal, Peter's denial, and his coming death in terms of going away. "I am going to a place you cannot go." He begins with the words recorded in John 13:33.

My children, I will be with you only a little while longer . . . A new command I give you: Love one another. As I have loved you, so you must love one another.

Jesus Comforts His Disciples (Jn. 14:12)

I tell you the truth, anyone who has faith in me will do what I have been doing. [You] will do even greater things than these, because I am going to [God], and I will do whatever you ask in my name, so that the Son may bring glory to the [parent]. You may ask me for anything in my name, and I will do it.

Jesus Promises the Holy Spirit (Jn. 14:15)

If you love me, you will obey what I command. And I will ask the Father/[Mother], and [God] will give you another Counselor to be with you forever—the Spirit of truth. The world cannot accept [her], because it neither sees [her] nor knows [her]. But you know [her], for [she] lives with you and is in you. I will not leave you as orphans; I will come to you. Before long, the world will not see me anymore, but you will see me. Because I live, you also will live. On that day you will realize that I am in [God], and you are in me, and I am in you. Whoever has my commands and obeys them, that is the one who loves me. [She] who loves me will be loved by my parent, [God], and I too will love [her] and show myself to [her].

So, dear daughters, daughters of every age, this is what you need for your journey—though we may go far away from our mothers or the physical presence of Jesus, no matter how long, no matter how perilous, no matter how deep and dark the forest, no matter how strong the evil one who tries to capture you and steal your power, or tempt you to wrong use of your power,
—you have the resource within you to guide you safely

—to stand by your heart, to stand in the heart of God, to reflect the light of love, to anoint others with healing love and recognition

—to speak the truth, not in judgment of others, but that truth will reveal what is needed to align with God's will

—to show up for your calling and use your power for good

—to teach others with openness to the outcome, not in an effort to control, but to affirm and nurture God's call to each individual.

DONNA HUMPHREYS

REFLECTIONS ON THE STORY OF THE BLEEDING WOMAN

Luke 8:40–55 and Mark 5:21–43. The story of the woman with the flow of blood is placed in the center of the story of Jairus's daughter. How are these two stories related? Does the woman's wound flow from the same loss of Self that the adolescent daughter is experiencing? Might their brokenness stem from the fact of being female in a patriarchal society that devalues what women do naturally and instinctively?

Jairus is desperate because his only daughter is dying and his love is not enough to save her. At twelve years old, she is losing her life. I painfully remember my own sense of loss at that age: loss of confidence, of being comfortable in my body, the loss of my self-worth, of knowing how to be who I was, what I wanted. My authentic Self was dying.

Jean Shinoda Bolen, in *Crossing to Avalon*, perceives that "Whereas preadolescent girls speak their minds easily and can be exuberant, assertive, and able to compete with boys, adolescent girls typically lose their self-esteem and refrain from self-expression."[8] Jairus's daughter did not express what was happening to her nor could she ask for help on her own behalf.

In *Reviving Ophelia: Saving the Selves of Adolescent Girls*, Mary Pipher describes how American girls are increasingly vulnerable to demeaning messages from television, music, magazines, and movies from the "girl-poisoning" culture in which they live. Girls are portrayed as sex objects and on the receiving end of violence. Despite the advances of feminism, girls are told to be pleasing instead of smart or competent, and their creative spirit and natural impulses are stifled, which ultimately destroys their self-esteem. Yet girls often blame themselves or their families for this loss of spirit. Destructive behaviors such as drug use and eating disorders are dramatically rising among adolescent girls; their rate of suicide went up 240% from 1980 to 1992. Our daughters, too, are dying.[9]

Now entering the story is an unnamed woman who has been bleeding for a very long time. Although she has repeatedly sought help, the wound in her body cannot be healed by doctors. She bleeds from being cut off from vital aspects of herself. Nothing in her society recognizes or affirms her value; she is unendingly unclean just for being born female. The first words uttered at my birth, as told to me by my mother recently, were "Ah, too bad," by the nurse. "Too bad. It's a girl."

I can imagine the bleeding woman's alienation from community and from her own depths. Even worse, her condition is considered her fault, her failing. Sounds like my own sense of not being good enough, of feeling all alone, of forgetting what I know, and blaming myself for it.

Our woundedness as women, of being unworthy by gender, of being cut off from our sacred worth and soul's knowing, is a spiritual wound that needs spiritual healing. In Bolen's words, "It is the soul that knows something is meaningful, that recognizes what it loves and that it is loved, that is nourished by what we do when what we do comes from our own depths."[10]

The bleeding woman's life force, her creative potential is draining out of her; her life-supporting capacities are being wasted. Yet from deep within her being she realizes the necessity and possibility of regeneration and healing, and that she is in a place of choosing. Quietly, she "came up behind him, and touched the fringe of his garment" (Lk. 8:44).

In a similar condition, I reached out to the Circle of Stones writing group and dared reveal my Self, my secret longings and pain. The sanctuary of the Circle, receiving me as I am, nourishes my soul. I am learning to listen to my body, give voice to my story, and the hemorrhaging has stopped! Similarly, the unnamed woman's seeking is incomplete until she "touches" the sacred and "immediately her flow of blood ceased." She knows "in her body" that she has been healed. By asking "Who?"—Jesus invites her to bring forth what she knows, to tell the truth of her own life. By calling her "Daughter" —Jesus declares to all her inherent worthiness as a precious child of God.

In spite of society's attempts to minimize her, the woman holds on to the belief that she matters, and opens herself to the healing touch of a nurturing, affirming (mothering) God, God's Grace, which makes her whole.

Now the story returns to Jairus's daughter with the news that she has died. Jesus says, "Do not fear, only believe and she will be well." Perhaps "she" refers to the wounded inner child of the older woman as well as Jairus's daughter. Someone else's love and belief in us can really help, especially in dark times. In *Sex in the Forbidden Zone*, Peter Rutter writes: "A father who does not want his daughter to turn into a victim will take time to listen to her and to show interest in how she sees things . . . asking about her world. . . . [She will learn] to use her own strength inside and outside of the home . . . know that who she is matters to the world."[11]

"How can Woman help her daughters know the Feminine Self?" asks Judith Duerk in *I Sit Listening to the Wind* ("Know Your Self . . . Yourself").[12] In *Reviving Ophelia*, Mary Pipher summarizes with: "most importantly ask, 'Who are you?'" and she offers a process that a girl can use for the rest of her life, which includes centering in a quiet space, self-defining questions, journal writing, the ability to separate thinking from feeling, time travel, and the discovery of the joys of altruism.[13]

Jesus goes to the daughter, takes her by the hand, says "Arise," and her spirit returns. He then instructs the people to *feed* her—God is aware of her spiritual hunger, her hunger for self-worth, and her need for a nourishing community. With the hemorrhaging woman, Jesus wants to know who touched him. These personal acknowledgments remind me of how my chaos was transformed into overflowing love and vitality (my spirit returned) when in a visualization I asked for direction, and the face of God appeared looking directly at me as if I mattered, and smiled!

It is not maleness that saves a girl, as fairy tales and patriarchal society would have us believe, (Jairus could not save his daughter even though he was an important man in the community). What keeps us in pain isn't what someone has done, but "what I think about me." It is in choosing to seek wholeness and being received as a worthy individual that we are reunited with our sacred worth and our soul's knowing, and restored to the fullness of our lives. As Duerk says,

> How might your life have been different . . . if as a young woman there had been a place for you when you had feelings of darkness . . . and there had been another woman, somewhat older, to be with you in your darkness, to be with you until you spoke, spoke out your pain and anger and sorrow, until you understood the sense of your feelings and how they reflected your own nature. . . . How might your life be different if deep within you when things seem very, very bad you could imagine that you are sitting in the lap of the Great Mother . . . held tightly . . . embraced at last . . . and you could hear Her saying to you, "I love you and I need you to bring forth your self.[14]

KITTY ADAMS

"MARY'S STORY"

I want to close our time together this weekend recalling the story of Mary, the young woman-girl who would become the mother of Jesus. Her story is told in Luke, mostly in skeleton framework: just enough of the story from Luke's perspective to tell how the circumstances of Jesus' birth fulfilled scripture and to confirm Jesus' divinity. But, to capture a reality for what this meant to the young maiden Mary, we must engage the story to bring flesh and the breath of life to its bones.

Mary was on the same threshold between girlhood and womanhood as many of you are. We know from Luke's account that she was engaged to be married to a man named Joseph; this tells us that she was physically capable of childbearing. An average age for this in her time and culture could have been as young as thirteen to sixteen years old.

As you listen and visualize Mary's story, I invite you to recognize some of the personal spiritual qualities we have been talking about this weekend, which Mary reveals in her interaction with the messenger and the message from God. I invite you to listen to themes about care and worthiness in God's invitation to human beings for relationship and interaction. The story of the visitation of the angel to Mary should always be told as it is written—with the parallel story of the miraculous birth of John the Baptist. The parallel stories give two opportunities to learn how God reaches out to humans to cooperate in God's work in the world and what happens, given the variety of responses from each person.

Mary's story begins with God's preparation of a loving, earthly support system for Mary before God sends the angel to reveal to her the calling from God. This is how it happens: The angel named Gabriel first appears to Zechariah, a priest of the temple. The angel tells Zechariah that his wife, Elizabeth, will bear a child, even though she is past childbearing age. (This child will become John the Baptist.) Now, Zechariah and Elizabeth are Mary's relatives—kinfolk by birth or marriage. They are also described as kindred people by their spiritual training and devotion to God.

Six months later, (just enough time that Elizabeth's pregnancy will be physically visible to anyone who sees her), the angel, Gabriel, appears to Mary. We are so accustomed to hearing this story at Christmas that it has become commonplace and domesticated. But I want you to recapture how wild an experience this was—uncommon—untamed. In that time and culture, young unmarried maidens did not go about alone or even engage in conversation outside their family circle. They would not have been addressed by important personages, so it would have been startling enough just to have been addressed by name alone, not to mention being addressed by a heavenly personage.

The angel said to her, "Greetings, you who are highly favored. The Lord is with you." Mary was greatly troubled at his words and wondered what kind of a greeting this might be. But the angel said to her, "Do not be afraid, Mary, you have found favor with God" (Lk. 1:28–30 NIV).

Then Gabriel goes on to tell her that she is being invited to carry and give birth to a very special child. The greeting from the angel reveals to us that Mary already has an openness to God's presence which is pleasing to God. Mary displays the attitude of love that overcomes her fear of the angel and enables her to pay attention to the angel's message. Love is the human resource of the Way of the Healer. Mary does not ask for proof—something in her has been nurtured enough to discern that this is a messenger from God even though she is troubled by the content and meaning of the message.

Startled and concerned as she is, she displays the Way of the Visionary; she tells the truth about the incredible nature of the message and its implications. "How will this be," Mary asks the angel, "since I am a virgin?" (Lk. 1:34 NIV). I find it absolutely amazing that Mary was not overwhelmed and simply silent and awed before a visitor from God. But she is an intelligent, wise-for-her-years, young woman. She has been pledged to become Joseph's wife but is still a virgin. She knows that to come to the marriage pregnant would certainly appear to be a betrayal of the promises made and, in her society, would be the same as committing adultery. We know from the story of Mary of Magdalene that adultery could be punished by being stoned to death. So, this encounter is not a scene from a Walt Disney movie; this is a life-defining moment with unforeseen consequences for a young teenager! Can Mary trust her intuitive knowing? Can she use her intellect and wisdom developed thus far? Can she risk trusting? Will she agree?

God, in the voice of the angel, honors her question. Gabriel explains to Mary, "The Holy Spirit will come upon you, and the power of the Most High will overshadow you. So the holy one to be born will be called the Son of God" (Lk. 1:35 NIV). This is still not a very specific or usual explanation; I'm not sure how reassuring that would have seemed to Mary. But Gabriel continues and then reveals to Mary that she will have a companion in this journey of the miraculous, a beloved kinswoman, Elizabeth. "Even Elizabeth your relative is going to have a child in her old age, and she who was said to be barren is in her sixth month. For nothing is impossible with God" (Lk. 1:36–37 NIV). God knows that when the visible presence and power of the angel departs, this young person will need "someone with skin on" to affirm the reality of the spiritual encounter and to give support for the path she has chosen.

This is the turning point. Mary, in the power of her free will, walks the Way of the Warrior/Leader and is present—"shows up"— for what God is calling her to do. "I am the Lord's servant. May it be to me as you have said" (Lk. 1:38 NIV). Or in the familiar words of the King James version, "'Behold the handmaid of the Lord; be it unto me according to thy word.' And the angel departed from her." Mary now is in the attitude of the Way of the Teacher. She knows that what will come is now in God's hands; she is an active, willing participant, but is open to the outcome.

There are two powerful contrasts here with the parallel story of Zechariah's encounter with Gabriel. First is the theme that it is God who chooses who is worthy to be called for God's service, not the artificial structures that humans design. In Mary's culture, a vision or visitation, though not a regular occurrence, might be expected to be granted to a dedicated, venerable priest due to his position and role. Only men were allowed to study and discuss the scripture, only men were allowed to be rabbis and priests, and only men of a certain patriarchal bloodline were allowed to serve in the temple and burn incense. Gabriel reveals to Zechariah that the child carried by Elizabeth—a child born to a recognized religious leader in the community—is being born for a role even more important than that of a priest, a role to prepare the way for one who is greater.

Then God chooses to reveal and trust the incarnate divine message of God's love through a young maiden, one without status or role, one without power or voice in her society. God discloses in this act that all persons are worthy co-creators for God's loving work: class, status, age, sex, superstructures, and divisions of human's creating are not barriers or qualifiers recognized by the Divine.

The pivotal qualifier that finds favor with God is this: Who recognizes the voice of God? In both visitations, Zechariah and Mary are startled when Gabriel appears. Luke says Mary was "greatly troubled and wondered what kind of greeting this might be;" (1:29) Zechariah was startled and "gripped with fear" (1:12). Remember how Mary's question was honored by Gabriel? Contrast that with the interaction when Zechariah asks the angel; "How can I be sure of this? I am an old man and my wife is well along in years" (1:18). Zechariah doesn't just ask how; he's asking for proof that this message is from God. Gabriel is ticked. An angel shouldn't have to prove anything to a priest. The angel answered, "I am Gabriel. I stand in the presence of God, and I have been sent to speak to you and to tell you this good news" (1:19) Then the angel continues with this great twist of irony, "And now you will be silent and not able to speak until the day this happens, because you did not believe my words, which will come true at their proper time" (1:20). It's as though the angel is saying, if you're going to say dumb things, you'll be struck dumb for awhile to let you think about it.

The second theme about worthiness is that the divine revelation is fully incarnated-in-flesh through the body of a woman, shattering forever the false teaching that spirit and the sacred reside only in the intellect, shattering forever the false teaching that women's bodies are profane, unclean, or temptation for sin. (The Jewish tradition taught that women were unclean during their menstrual flow, even disallowed from attending worship service.)

Mary's story confirms irrevocably that it is God who decides what and who is worthy; confirms that all God created, even our bodies and bodily processes, all is good and sacred. I believe this is another reason for Zechariah's involuntary silence. Had Zechariah been able to come out of the temple and verbally witness to his en-

counter with Gabriel, all the attention would have been on him, the role and gender he represented, and the revelation would have relied solely on the spoken word. The priest's silence meant that God's promise would reveal itself in the undeniable swelling of a woman's body and come into the world whole—incarnate divinity in the flesh containing the divine, the wholeness, the completeness of soul, spirit, intellect, bone, sinew, muscle, organ, miraculous breath of life.

After Mary's acceptance of God's calling, Mary got ready and hurried to a town in the hill country of Judea where she entered Zechariah's home and greeted Elizabeth (Lk. 1:39–40 NIV). When Elizabeth heard Mary's greeting, the baby leaped in her womb and Elizabeth was filled with the Holy Spirit. In a loud voice she exclaimed: "Blessed are you among women, and blessed is the child you will bear! But why am I so favored, that the mother of my Lord should come to me? Blessed is she who has believed that what the Lord has said to her will be accomplished" (Lk. 1:41–45 NIV).

Mary upon hearing this confirmation of all that the angel said, sings the song of the Visionary, her Magnificat. (Claudia sings her Magnificat.)

The third theme in Mary's story about worthiness is who has the right to "name us" in the sense of defining who we are, in the sense of contributing the likeness our name and face will reflect and in the sense of what status or worthiness will derive from that. In these two parallel stories, Gabriel gives the name of each baby to the mothers. In patriarchal Jewish tradition, the male baby was circumcised and named on his eighth day. The father chose a name to continue and honor the male lineage of the family, and the father publicly announced the name at the time of the circumcision ceremony. But look at the story of speechless Zechariah. "On the eighth day they came to circumcise the child and they were going to name him after his father, Zechariah, but his mother spoke up and said, "No! He is to be called John" (Lk. 1:59–60 NIV). By God's action through Gabriel, Elizabeth is empowered and granted the privilege of announcing the name. The divine Creator alone gives life, "knits us in our mother's womb," declares parentage of those created in God's image. The only lineage important to God is spiritual lineage.

Lest you think this story deals harshly with the men and honors and elevates only women, listen to the "rest of the story." Once Zechariah breaks the patriarchal tradition and publicly confirms Elizabeth's pronouncement by writing, "His name is John," (Lk. 1:63 NIV) Zechariah's speech is returned to him. He, too, is gifted with a song of the Visionary, his own Magnificat, a song of thanksgiving and praise for the birth of John who will prepare the way for Jesus and will become the companion and the midwife of the spirit for Jesus as Elizabeth has been for Mary.

Surely, I tell you, daughters, there will be a time when the Holy Spirit will come to you, and the power of the Most High will wish to overshadow you to create in you the gift you will bring to the world. For the story of Mary is also a metaphor, a mythic archetype, of God's call and invitation to each of us. The creative work will be as unique as each of you. It may be a gift of compassion like that of Mother Teresa; it may be a gift of peace, such as creating a thousand paper cranes; it may be a gift of artistry, painting, music, dance, poetry; it may be the gift of understanding through study, teaching, research, journalism; it may be the gift of the prophetic. The gestation time will be different, but when the time is fulfilled, God will give you the name of this gift for the world.

Your work now is to feed your soul as Vasalisa fed the doll her mother gave her, to learn to sort what gives life from what destroys life, to tune your whole body through singing, dance, storytelling, and silence, to seek out the company of the Elizabeths in your life and to daily bring yourself into the presence of God, so that when the messenger of the Lord comes to you, you will recognize God's voice. You will know, like Mary, to ask questions and, like Vasalisa, sometimes not to ask.

Our work as mothers and grandmothers is to become like Elizabeth, expecting God's work even in our later years, fruitful ourselves, and available for affirming the work of the Holy Spirit in our daughters. May it be so. Amen.

DONNA HUMPHREYS

THE GIRLS' CEREMONY

Each year, using their own ideas, along with suggestions from two women chosen by them to help, our girls have asked for some or all of the following elements in their ceremony. (Attendants—girls who have experienced the ceremony in previous years—may also help and advise.) The Girls' Ceremony is the last event of the retreat, just before the festive noon meal celebrating their passage. You will include symbols and traditions dear to you. Here are some that have significance for us:

- **Adorning for celebration**—colorful skirts, scarves, meaningful jewelry, or other mementos

- **Anointing with oil**—a Judeo-Christian tradition of touching oil to the forehead of each girl, making a meaningful symbol such as a cross or a circle

- **Smudging**—an American Indian tradition of wafting the smoke of small, lit, sage bundles around each girl as a symbol of cleansing and new beginnings

- **Singing of songs** such as "Mother and God" and "Come Forth"

- **Giving the Grandmother gift and blessing of the girls by the women.** The women form an arch near the tipi door and sing to welcome the girls. The girls come through the arch, one by one. Next, the women form a circle around the girls. After the girls are encircled, the Grandmother steps forward, holding a basket containing seashells, each on a silk cord. The Grandmother asks the first girl. "Who are you my daughter?" The girl speaks her name. The Grandmother asks, "What do you wish, my daughter?" The girl replies, "I would like a blessing."

The Grandmother places a seashell on a cord around the girl's neck and says, "We joyfully receive you into the company of women, daughters of the Divine—warrior/leaders, visionaries, healers, teachers. We invite you now to join the Circle. Remember, even when we are not here, this Circle exists and you are never alone." After the last girl is given her seashell necklace and words from the Grandmother, the women sing "Mother and God" (page 222) or "You Are Not Alone" (page 236).

Each girl goes to a woman in the Circle for words of blessing. She then moves on to the next woman in the Circle, until every girl has received a blessing from every woman. If there are attendants, they may provide quiet music during the blessing.

- **Playing games** such as "Mend and Weave"
- **Celebrating** with noise, music, dance, and movement activities. Serendipitous circumstances can be slipped into the celebration. One year, a young presenter taught us Irish step dancing on the grass. Just after another ceremony, a strong, warm wind blew through the tall fir trees and along the bluff. Girls and women ran with it, scarves and skirts flying.

"HAIL, VALIANT WOMEN!"—A LITANY

Author Renita Weem tells us:

> Whereas one woman can be overlooked, several women cannot be ignored. The women disciples knew this, even if Matthew, Mark, Luke, and John did not. Perhaps this is why the women always traveled together, thereby forcing history to remember them as a group—as "sister." They stayed together because there is strength and visibility when women band together. They were a community of women among an outfit of men, not apologetic for their numbers, but empowered by their shared vision.[15]

We are joined into the sisterhood of valiant women in the Bible and in the rest of history: Women who were Warriors/Leaders, Teachers, Healers, and Visionaries. Women like us. Let us remember and praise the biblical women on whose shoulders we stand.

Each announcement of praise will end with the phrase, "We remember and honor you." You are invited to respond: "Hail, Valiant Women!"

We regard Warriors/Leaders—Miriam, who with her brothers led the children of Israel out of the slavery of Egypt; and Deborah, who exhorted a fearful commander and led 10,000 men into victorious battle. O Warrior/Leaders, Miriam and Deborah, we remember and honor you!

HAIL, VALIANT WOMEN!

We regard Teacher—Mary, mother of Jesus, invited by God to be co-creator of new life. She spoke to the angel asking, "How can this be?" Then, in the sweet territory of silence, she listened. In trust, she let go of her fears and birthed Divine Presence into the world. O Teacher Mary, we remember and honor you!

HAIL, VALIANT WOMEN!

We regard Healers—Naomi and Ruth. Ruth, who, against all advice, refused to leave her mother-in-law. With Naomi's wisdom and counsel, and Ruth's grace, hard work, and cleverness, they mended both of their broken lives. O Healers, Naomi and Ruth, we remember and honor you!

HAIL, VALIANT WOMEN!

We regard a Visionary—the Cannanite woman, pushy, in-your-face, never giving up, she yelled at Jesus, and knelt before him, too. "My daughter has a demon," she said. "Help me. I will take even crumbs from the table to make my daughter well." And Jesus answered, "Woman, great is your faith! Let it be done for you as you wish" (Mt. 15:21–28 paraphrased). O Visionary Cannanite woman, we remember and honor you!

HAIL, VALIANT WOMEN!

LITANY OF REMEMBERING

Where are the voices of our Mothers?

Listen, valiant women, and hear the stories.

The angel Gabriel came to Mary and said,

"Greetings, favored one. The Lord is with you. Do not be afraid, Mary, you have found favor with God. The Holy Spirit will come to you with the power of God and the child held within and born of you will be holy, the child of God."

Mary replied, "Here I am, the servant of the Lord."

Hail, valiant woman, woman of God . . .

Mary hurried to a town in the Judean hills to visit her cousin Elizabeth. When Elizabeth saw Mary she cried out with joy,

"Blessed are you among women and blessed is the fruit of your womb. As soon as I heard the sound of your greeting, the child in my womb leaped for joy. Blessed is she who believed that there would be a fulfillment of the promise."

Hail, valiant women, women of knowing . . .

On the first day of the week, at early dawn, Mary, the mother of James, Mary Magdalene, and Joanna came to the tomb, taking the spices they had prepared. They were perplexed to find the stone rolled away from the tomb and the body of Jesus gone. They saw two dazzling angels, who asked them,

"Why do you look for the living among the dead? He is not here; he is alive. Remember how he told you that he would be handed over and crucified, but on the third day he would rise again?"

Then they remembered his words, and returning from the tomb told all this to the eleven and to all the rest.

Hail, valiant women, women of remembering . . .

There was also a prophet, Anna, the daughter of Phanuel of the tribe of Asher. She was of a great age, having lived with her husband seven years after her marriage, then as a widow to the age of eighty-four. She never left the temple but worshiped there with fasting and prayer night and day. When Mary and Joseph brought the baby Jesus to the temple to be circumcised, Anna came and began to praise God and to speak about the child to all who were looking for the redemption of Jerusalem.

Hail, valiant women, faithful women . . .
Hear the voices of the women and be glad.

SALLY WINDECKER (PARAPHRASING LUKE 1; 2; AND 24 IN THE LITURGI-
CAL STYLE OF MIRIAM THERESE WINTER IN *WomanPrayer, WomanSong*

A LITANY FOR OPENING

AND IT WAS GOOD . . .

Voice 1:   The love of God dreamed light into the darkness . . .
        and creation was born.

          God created earth—
        bearing—blossoming—bringing forth.

Voice 2:   We have been brought forth from the hands of our loving
        Mother God,

          from the same matter as the cedar and the salmon.

          With all earth's bounty, we come from one ecstatic breath
        of creation.

          Daughters of God . . .

All: *. . . imagine the love!*

Voice 3:   *Find a fragrant rose . . . dive into its deep, sweet center,*
        Daughters of God, and . . .

All: *. . . imagine the love!*

Voice 4:   From that creative breath came all the generations of earth—
        limpet and lion, root and rhizome, feather and fin.

          Gigantic, joyous burst from the soul of the Creator,
        passionate, intimate, fertile,
        birthed in water and blood.

Voice 3:   *Listen to the sigh of sea feathering foam against the sandy*
        shore, Daughters of God, and . . .

All: *. . . imagine the love!*

Voice 5:   Earth labored and we were born—female and male.

          In the garden, the human and the heron,
        the snail and the sockeye, fern and thistle—

          The families of life above, within, and on the earth,
        all kinds, *all* forms, *all* faces—

Voice 3:   *Push your hand deep into the loamy soil,*
        and feel the sand of your bones, Daughters of God, and . . .

All: *. . . imagine the love!*

Voice 1:   And we are created in the image of love,

          We too are the Daughters of the Word: "Good God!"

          Look at us, Daughters of God, and . . .

All: *. . . imagine the love!*

LITANY (REPRISE) NEAR CLOSING

AND IT WAS GOOD . . . (FULL TEXT)

Voice 1:   We have been brought forth from the hands of our loving Mother God

        from the same matter as the cedar and the salmon.

    Our molecules of life spin from the same stuff

      as the redtail and the rose.

    With all earth's bounty, we come from one ecstatic breath of creation.

Voice 2:   *Stand on the edge of the wind—bear the breath of God in your face, Daughters of God, and . . .*

All: *. . . imagine the love!*

Voice 1:   Tell us again the story of such love . . .

Voice 3:   The Word of God went out upon all that was chaos and spoke form.

    The love of God dreamed light into the darkness . . .

      and creation was born.

    From the solitary effort of love came the host of life.

    Gathering carbon and hydrogen and light

      into secret, rounded form, God created earth—

    bearing—blossoming—bringing forth.

Voice 2:   *Find a fragrant rose . . . dive into its deep, sweet center, Daughters of God, and . . .*

All: *. . . imagine the love!*

Voice 4:   From that creative breath issued the Mother of Life—

      the God-created womb of the generations of earth—

        limpet and lion, root and rhizome, feather and fin.

    Gigantic, joyous burst from the soul of the Creator,

      passionate, intimate, fertile

      birthed in water and blood.

Voice 2:   Listen to the sigh of sea feathering foam against the sandy shore, Daughters of God, and . . .

All: *. . . imagine the love!*

Voice 5:   In the very image of love, from the same substance,

      earth labored and we were born—

        female and male—

    Clothed in frailty and freedom, in pain and perfect joy:

      life aware of love.

Voice 2:	*Push your hand deep into the loamy soil and feel the sand of your bones Daughters of God, and . . .*
All:	*. . . imagine the love!*
Voice 6:	In the garden, the human and the heron,
	the snail and the sockeye, fern and thistle—
	The families of life above, within, and on the earth,
	all kinds, *all* forms, *all* faces—
	every being birthed in the profusion of bliss.
Voice 1:	And we are created in the image of love,
	We, too, are the Daughters of the Word: "Good God!"
	Look at us Daughters of God, and . . .
All:	*. . . imagine the love!*

SALLY WINDECKER

A PARTING LITANY

If the words of my faith had honored women's ways; if my own inner voice of the Holy had been encouraged; if ancient holy women had been remembered . . .

How might I be different?

If deep within me, when life was dark and hopeless, I could find the Mother God who would wipe my tears and calm my fears . . .

How might I be different?

If when I was little, my own truth was honored so that I didn't forget its voice now that I am older . . .

How might I be different?

What if each year, when I was growing up, there had been a Circle of women and girls who honored women's ways, encouraged my own inner voice of the Holy, and remembered the stories of ancient holy women . . .

How might I be different?

On Whidbey Island, in the waning summer, girls and women gathered in a beautiful place . . .

We have been changed.

We sang, we danced, we worshiped, we made masks and pouches . . .

We have been changed.

You told me your story; I told you mine . . .

We have been changed.

We bless each one here, today and each day after; we will remember.

We have all been changed.

SALLY WINDECKER, IN THE STYLE OF JUDITH DUERK IN *Circle of Stones*

SONG: "REUNION"

Reunion of body and soul
Communion beyond all we know
Remembering who we are
Opening for us to begin
Surrounded by family and friends
Remembering who we are

Like a reed in the wind let in
All the love coming to you
Like a river in spring let out
All the love flowing through you

Follow the way to your heart
Compassionate fire of the heart
Remembering who you are
Ocean of silence within
Surrender it all to the friend
Remembering who you are[16]

SUSAN OSBORN

TIPI PRAYER

O Spirit God, O Invisible Silent One,
    Do you flow on the wind?
    Do you sleep like Bear in wintertime?
    Are you as close as my breath . . . distant as the stars?
      Do you hide like camouflaged Deer moving through the shadowed thicket?

Where are you, Spirit God?
    Has my busy-ness kept me from noticing you?
    Has my affluence convinced me I need you less?
    Has fatigue tempted me not to care?
Will you be there waiting for me when I finally have time for you?

Let's meet at the tipi . . . this spring after the soil dries a bit.
We'll spread the sweet oat straw down softly and bank the
      rocks against the fire pit.
    We'll bring out the rough blankets and build a fire.
    We'll flicker in the shifting glow and shadow.
    We'll lie against the earth and let her rhythm pulse life back into us.
    We'll watch the stars winking through the smoke hole.
    We'll breathe deeply as the cedar-scented air flows upward with our thoughts into
    the vertical draft . . .

Let's do it soon while the frogs are still in full voice around the pond.

I'll face the door to the east so the moon can climb right up over the poles and look in.
You'll need to remind me how to tie a clove hitch and
    I'll need to whittle a few new lacing pins.
It's been two years since we met in the tipi and I'll be a bit rusty.
    I'll bring the flute and the bead basket.
    I'll hang the herbs on the door-pole.
    I'll bring the heavy wood for the night fire.
Let's preserve the memory of wild freedom.

Will you come if I make things ready?
    If I show up, will you bless me?

MAUREEN ROWLEY

CORTEZ ISLAND

Nula nula nu-la, nula nula nu-la . . .

Woman: I came here to be fed, I came here to be filled.

Where is the peace, where is the rest I crave?

Nula nula nula . . . nu-la nu-la, nula nula nuuu-laaa

Ocean: Watch me, I am changing . . . Watch me, I am rearranging the world.

I see you . . . I see you.

I flow, I spin, I move, I open, I close, I swallow, I spit.

You are full of my life. I cover you the way the tide covers the rocks.

I cradle you, I expose you, I embrace you, I ignore you.

In your dreams you slip into my great cold expanse,

like a seal, like an otter in the dark, in the wet.

There is where you are graceful and free.

There you are fed from my abundance.

But this wet world is not for you now.

I've called you to walk the dry earth, to live in the world of Man . . .

to see, to feel, to witness this dry realm.

You must learn to breathe the dry air, to carry your weight heavily over the dry rocks,

to walk in the parched loveless places for a season of strengthening.

And to you I give the gift of salted tears to moisten your journey

and to remind you of the great depth of the water place.

Breathe through your longing . . . it will always be with you.

Breathe through the flowing of the waters.

MAUREEN ROWLEY

"SOUL-EXPANDING NAMES FOR GOD"

Having trouble stretching your God vocabulary beyond what you were raised with? These cut-and-paste, soul-expanding names can help. Simply clip the God-name that touches your heart and paste it on top of the over-used God-name you had written in your meditation or prayer. The minds and imaginations of your listeners and you will grow as you contemplate new and expanded visions of God.

Creator

Loving God

Divine One

God of Compassion

God of Joy and Dancing

Winter God, God of hidden face (1)

God of thawing moments, melt my frozen life (1)

You keep us waiting. You, The God of all time (1)

You keep us looking. You, The God of all space (1)

Healer of our every ill (2)

Restorer of the Dawn (1)

God of Flesh and Blood

We are in our Middle-Time of Trying—Despairing—Becoming—Christ is the Completer (3)

Oh God, vast and mysterious as the cosmos, immediate, and all-embracing as life (4)

God of Surprises

Liberator

Clap your hands; Shout for Joy: God is real! God is here! (Psalm 49)

Eternal Wellspring of Peace

God of the Oppressed

Mother and Father of us all

You Who Empower

Source of all Life

Life-Giving Spirit

O God, scatterer of ignorance and darkness (5)

Weaver God—weave mercy in the warp of it and love throughout (6)

Mother of Exiles, Shelter of the Homeless (6)

GLORIA KOLL AND
(1) MACRINA WIEDERKEHR, OSB
(2) MARTY HAUGEN
(3) LONA FOWLER
(4) PIERRE TEILHARD DE CHARDIN
(5) YOJHT VEDA
(6) PAT KOZAK AND JANET SCHAFFRAN

GOSPEL PASSAGES ABOUT WOMEN

Mark

1:29–31	Healing of Peter's mother-in-law
5:21–43	Jairus's daughter and woman with flow of blood
6:17–29	Herodias and her daughter
7:24–30	Syrophoenician woman
12:41–44	Poor widow
14:3–9	Woman who anoints Jesus' head
15:40–41	Women disciples of Jesus
16:1–8	Women at the tomb
16:9–11	Mary Magdalene and risen Jesus

Matthew

1:1–17	Women in Jesus' lineage
1:18—2:23	Birth stories (focus on Joseph)
9:18–26	Jairus's daughter and woman with flow of blood
13:54–58	Jesus' sisters
14:21	Women present at multiplication of the loaves
20:20–23	Mother of Zebedee's sons
27:19	Pilate's wife
27:55–61	Women at the cross
28:1–10	Women commissioned at the tomb

Luke

1:1–80	Elizabeth and Mary
2:1–33	Birth stories (focus on Mary)
2:36–39	Anna the prophet
7:11–17	Widow at Nain
7:36–50	Woman who anoints Jesus' feet
8:1–3	Women disciples of Jesus
8:40–55	Jairus's daughter and woman with flow of blood
10:38–42	Martha and Mary
11:27–28	Blessed are they who hear God's word
12:52–53	Reference to division of families, includes women
13:10–17	Healing of bent over woman
24:1–10	Women at the tomb

John

2:1–12	Jesus' mother at wedding in Cana
4:4–41	Samaritan woman at the well
8:1–11	Woman caught in adultery
11:1–44	Martha and Mary at death of their brother
12:1–8	Anointing at Bethany
20:1–28	Mary Magdalene commissioned at the tomb

COMPILED BY ANNETTE ANDREWS LUX

On the following pages are the presentations we have made in various years to introduce and explain the Four-fold Way[17] and the archetypes. Whether you use these presentations or write your own, learn them well enough to speak rather than read them.

Four Elements Medicine Wheel Prayer
Turtle Island West Coast[18]

O Great Spirit of the North,
Invisible Spirit of the Air,
And of the fresh, cool winds,
O vast and boundless Grandfather Sky,
Your living breath animates all life,
Yours is the power of clarity and strength,
Power to hear the inner sounds,
To sweep out the old patterns,
And to bring change and challenge,
The ecstasy of movement and the dance.

We pray that we may be aligned with you,
So that your power may flow through us,
And be expressed by us,
For the good of this planet,
And all living beings upon it.

O Great Spirit of the West,
Spirit of the Great Waters,
Of rain, rivers, lakes and springs,
O Grandmother Ocean,
Deep matrix, womb of all life,
Power to dissolve boundaries,
To release holdings,
Power to taste and to feel,
To cleanse and to heal,
Great blissful darkness of peace.

We pray that we may be aligned with you,
So that your powers may flow through us,
And be expressed by us
For the good of this planet,
And all living beings upon it.

O Great Spirit of the East,
Radiance of the rising Sun,
Spirit of new beginnings.
O Grandfather Fire,
Great nuclear fire—of the Sun.
Power of life-energy, vital spark,
Power to see far, and to
Imagine with boldness.
Power to purify our senses,
Our Hearts and our minds.

We pray that we may be aligned with you,
So that your powers may flow through us,
And be expressed by us,
For the good of this planet Earth,
And all living beings upon it.

O Great Spirit of the South,
Protector of the fruitful land,
And of all green and growing things,
The noble trees and grasses,
Grandmother Earth, Soul of Nature,
Great power of the receptive,
Of nurturance and endurance,
Power to grow and bring forth
Flowers of the field,
Fruits of the garden.

We pray that we may be aligned with you,
So that your powers may flow through us,
And be expressed by us,
For the good of this planet Earth,
And all living beings upon it.

INTRODUCTION CEREMONY TO THE FOUR-FOLD WAY

(Instruct that when Grandmother Crone says, "O, Holy Creator," all are to respond with, "We thank you.")

Wise Grandmother Crone appears in her wig and jacket, perhaps an old woman mask . . . she is the magician/peddler . . . she carries a basket of four instruments: bell, drum, sticks, rattle.

Crone: Hello, my daughters. Do not be afraid. Though I don't look familiar to you, something inside you knows who I am. I am, "She Who Has Gone Before and Knows the Way." I am here to teach you the oneness of all God's creation. The way to wholeness is represented by four paths: The Warrior/Leader, the Visionary, the Healer, and the Teacher. Learning to follow these paths, we come into wholeness as daughters of God. It is a journey of a lifetime! We will welcome our guides by calling to the four directions.

Crone turns to the North:

O Great Spirit, friends and relations, and creatures of the North,

Invisible Spirit of the

fresh, cool winds,

O boundless Grandfather Sky,

Your living breath animates all life.

Yours is the power of clarity,

And the power to hear the inner sounds,

In the ecstasy of the dance

You sweep out the old patterns,

bring change and challenge.

O Holy Creator . . .

All respond together: We thank you.

Crone turns to the East:

O Great Spirit, friends and relations, and creatures of the East,

Radiance of the rising sun,

Spirit of new beginnings,

O Grandfather Fire, vital spark,

Power to imagine with boldness,

Power to purify our senses,

Our hearts and our minds.

O Holy Creator . . .

All respond together: We thank you.

Crone turns to the South:

O Great Spirit, friends and relations, creatures of the South,

Protector of Grandmother Earth

And all green and growing things,

> Great power of the receptive,
> Of nurturance and endurance,
> Power to grow and bring forth trees and grasses
> Flowers of the field
> Fruits of the garden . . .
> O Holy Creator . . .

All respond together: We thank you.

Crone turns to the West:

> O Great Spirit, friends and relations, and creatures of the West,
> Spirit of the Great Waters
> Of rain, rivers, lakes, and springs,
> O Grandmother Ocean,
> Womb of all life,
> Power to taste and feel,
> Cleanse and to heal,
> Great blissful darkness of peace.
> O Holy Creator . . .

All respond together: We thank you.

Crone leads a song.

Crone begins to shake the rattle: Help me to call in the **Warrior/Leader**, whose way is to *show up and be present.* Let each one of us call her with the rattle. She shakes the rattle then begins passing it around the Circle.

Circling, Crone explains: The rattle is an ancient instrument that makes the sound of the rain, cleansing, as the rain does, and purifying, and calling the soul to come and be present.

Warrior/Leader enters wearing her mask. She takes the rattle and begins shaking it as she dances slowly around the circle, blessing each one as she shakes it above each head. She finishes in the **North** and hands the rattle back to Crone. She gestures as Crone speaks for her:

Crone (speaking for the Warrior/Leader): "I am inside all of you. I have learned to come and be present, showing honor and respect for all living things. I have learned to set clear limits and boundaries, and to lead and to speak when needed. I have learned to use my personal power responsibly."

Warrior takes her place sitting in the Circle in the North.

*The Crone begins **drumming**.*

Crone: Help me to call in the **Healer** whose way is to *pay attention to what has heart and meaning.* All of you, *drum* the Healer to our Circle. *She passes the drum around the Circle.*

Crone: the drum represents the universal heartbeat. When we allow it, the drumbeat helps to open the heart. A great African drummer and teacher once said; "We say that rhythm is the soul of life because the whole universe revolves around rhythm, and when we get out of rhythm, that's when we get into trouble. For this reason, the drum, next to the human voice, is our most important instrument."[19]

The Healer appears in the **South** (wearing mask) and takes the drum to the center of the Circle. As she is drumming, she gestures to each one in the Circle. She ends, giving the drum back to Crone and gestures as Crone speaks for her.

Crone (speaking for Healer):

"I am in each one of you. I have learned that the power of love is the most potent healing force available to us. When I stand by my heart, I am able to honor my core, my most essential self. I extend the arms of Love through gratitude, recognition, and acceptance."

Healer takes her place in the Circle in the South.

Crone rings the bell: Help me to ring in the **Visionary**. We use the bell, whose sound calls us back to remembering our true purpose and calling.

The Visionary comes to her position outside the Circle in the **East**, taking tiny bells of her own and gently ringing them in each woman's ears, she circles back, returns the bell to Crone and gestures as Crone speaks for her.

Crone: I am in each one of you. I have learned to make the truth visible, *speaking what is true without blame or judgment.* On this path, you will know your creative purpose and life dream. You will learn to act from your authentic self, honoring your intuition, insight, and vision.

The Visionary take her place in the Circle in the East.

Crone (playing the sticks): Now we call the **Teacher**. The instrument we use reminds us of the bones of our ancestors.

The Teacher appears from the **West**. She takes the sticks and, moving to the center of the Circle, gestures them skyward, circling them 'round and 'round as if calling to the ancestors. Teacher takes her place in the Circle in the West.

Crone (speaking for Teacher): I am as one of you. I am open to outcome, yet remain unattached to outcome. I teach trust, understanding the need for detachment. I have acquired wisdom. I know the meaning of the teaching from the Tao Te Ching: "True mastery can be gained by letting things go their own way. It can't be gained by interfering."[20]

Crone: We, daughters of the Creator, seekers of the Way, give thanks for the Wisdom and the teaching of the Warrior/Leader, the Visionary, the Healer, and the Teacher. We give thanks for the joy of unfolding life, for the infinite variety of God's care and love, and for creating us to learn and to grow.

Crone: Stand now and sing with me, "We Are One in the Circle . . ."

CLAUDIA WALKER

THE WAY OF THE WARRIOR/LEADER

Wise Grandmother Crone begins shaking a rattle to call in the Warrior/Leader. The Warrior/Leader enters and shakes a rattle around the Circle, calling out positive Warrior/Leader qualities:

Shows up . . . Disciplined . . .

Sets boundaries . . . Presence . . .

Honors . . . Right action . . .

Respects . . . Takes a second look . . .

Courageous . . . Responsible . . .

She circles again, announcing misuse (shadow side) of the Warrior/Leader:

Rebellion . . . Criticism . . .

Fear of accountability . . . Harsh judgment . . .

Hiding . . . Giving in to fear . . .

Giving away power . . .

Quiet pause

The Warrior/Leader is the Archetype of Leadership.

We come into our leadership skills by being courageous and staying in our power rather than giving into our fears and giving our power away.

By showing up and choosing to be present rather than hiding.

By extending honor and respect to others rather than criticizing and judging.

By being responsible and accountable rather than rebellious and unaccountable.

By being present to the Holy Spirit moving us rather than driven by our egos.

Mary, the mother of Jesus, showed her leadership skills by being fully present in the face of the angel Gabriel and accepting the responsibility God asked of her. Even Dorothy of *The Wizard of Oz* showed her Warrior/Leader side when she become the leader of the group and extended honor and respect to her companions.

Standing Meditation: teach posture of presence.

Reflect silently on leadership skills that you have or are now developing. *(Pause.)*

Recall a situation where you gave your power away. Was there a particular person or situation that ignited your lack of courage? *(Pause.)*

Reflect on a situation where you stood up for yourself. *(Pause.)*

Now let us affirm together aloud, "I can stand on my own two feet." *(Group repeats.)*

"I can take a stand." *(Group repeats.)*

"I know what I cannot stand." *(Group repeats.)*

Remember, whenever you are fully visible and know where you stand, you experience what it means to be in your power.

The reader performs a chant and an exit verse.

DANA CONSUELO SMITH

THE WAY OF THE WARRIOR/ LEADER

"Warrior Song," by Cynthia Crossen, Journey Pouch, page 215.

"I am here to remind you of the Warrior/ Leader in each of you!" In an indigenous society, as described in the book *The Four-fold Way* by Angeles Arrien, the Warrior/Leader is represented by a winged creature whose direction is north and whose element is air. Hers is a standing meditation; she shows presence; she shows up. Her healing salve is dancing; her instrument is the rattle, and her season is winter.

In our contemporary Western society, we think of a Warrior as an effective leader in any field of endeavor. Becoming effective as an individual or a leader requires developing the inner Warrior. Today I speak of that inner Warrior. What gives you inner strength and courage for leadership? First of all, you have shown up and are physically present. But, are you mentally, emotionally, and spiritually present as well? It is easy to drift off then think, "What is she talking about?"

Every human being can embody the power of presence. Walt Whitman recognized this power when he wrote in *Leaves of Grass*, "We convince by our presence."[21] Some people have such powerful presence that we identify them as charismatic, magnetic personalities. When we "show up" energetically with all four intelligences—mental, emotional, spiritual, and physical—we express the power of presence.

Another important aspect of the Warrior/ Leader is the ability to extend honor and respect. When respect and honor are not given, there can be serious repercussions. Chief Sitting Bull described what happens when respect is not extended and when words and actions are not credible: "What treaty that the whites have kept has the red man broken? Not one. What treaty that the white man . . . made with us have they kept? Not one."[22] Children recognize the importance of keeping trust by honoring contracts when they cry, "But you broke your promise!" Can any of you remember uttering that? Or remember how hurt you felt?

In our modern culture, if a corporation demonstrates a lack of respect and honor, its employees feel that a valuable trust has been broken. The corporation may experience a backlash if it violates this common trust: respect for the employees. *(Here the leader shared a story from her own experience—the courage required for her and her coworker flight attendants to strike against their employer, a major airline, and the empowerment that resulted by their demand for respect and consideration.)*

Empowerment is a human resource like no other. When we do not accept "This can't be done!" we are freed from patterns of self-diminishment. We feel brave and courageous. Empowerment overcomes fear. We flight attendants were empowered when we were willing to risk the jobs we loved for the higher principle of restoring honor and respect.

Mary, the mother of Jesus was indeed a model of the Warrior/Leader. Mary, though afraid when the angel appeared to her, found courage to take on the most amazing responsibility in the most extraordinary manner. She made herself present and available to God; then she found additional courage by going to her cousin Elizabeth, a wise, older woman. The two women listened to the Holy Spirit and were strengthened each by the other in the bond of friendship. Together, they became Warriors for the amazing journey that lay ahead.

In a like manner, we are empowered by mothers, grandmothers, family, and friends here today. *(Leader introduces a friend who shares her own story of empowerment and courage in facing a nearly fatal accident and a painful divorce. She concluded with the apt quote: "People are like tea bags. You find out how strong they are when you put them in hot water.")*

Another important characteristic of the Warrior/Leader is her ability to set limits and boundaries. We need to understand the importance of and difference between yes and no. If we say yes when we mean no, we lose personal power and become victims. You will in your life, no matter what your age, experience being down, depressed—that "can't get out of bed" feeling—

because of a relationship, a disappointment, a loss, or a debilitating health issue. But when you have found personal power, it will strengthen and enable you to cope and overcome.

I hope you will remember this Warrior/Leader presentation—the Warrior song, the rattle, the stories, and her characteristics. And remember, too, a loving God as your friend, companion, and confidant. No individual replaces that love and consistency. It will bring you up when you are down and make you a warrior, strong with love, strength, forgiveness, and, most of all, a receiver of grace! God's grace will help you reinvent your dreams to achieve and restore your sense of honor. Each of you is a Warrior/Leader. You will leave here with the pouches you will make containing symbols of memories to make you strong. You will hear the voices of your mother, grandmothers, ancestors, and friends.

Let's take the "Warrior Song"—these copies are made to roll up in your pouches. There is ribbon being passed around. Let's sing the song twice. Feel free to move and dance and shake your rattle!

TAKEN FROM A RETREAT PRESENTATION BY
LINDA WHITE WADSWORTH

THE WAY OF THE HEALER

I represent the Healer in each one of you. My way is to pay attention to what has heart and meaning because I have learned that the power of love is the most potent healing force available to us.

When I "stand by my heart," that is, have the courage to speak and act according to what has heart and meaning, then I am able to honor my most essential self and the most essential selves of others. I am able to discern what is needed and extend the arms of love through gratitude, recognition, and acceptance.

I wish now to tell you my story of the Way of the Healer recorded in the Holy Bible in both Mark 14:3–9 and Mathew 26:6–13. When I say "my story," I mean I will tell the story as the woman who anointed Jesus' head with oil.

(She places a shawl or scarf on her head or shoulders to indicate moving into the role of the woman.)

"Two days before the feast of the Passover, Jesus was having dinner in Bethany at the house of Simon the leper. There was a great deal of tension in the air. The Pharisees and priests had become increasingly angry with Jesus. At first, I was surprised by this; I heard in Jesus' teachings and stories an echo of the early prophets who talked of life guided by attitudes of the heart, 'love justice, show mercy, and walk humbly with God'; these were the requirements of holy life pleasing to God. But the Pharisees teach that we are holy because we keep the specific religious laws and rituals that have been taught from interpretation of the scripture. When Jesus told them that the 'Sabbath was made for man, not man for the Sabbath,' they believed Jesus was disrespecting and undermining the law that God gave to Moses. Jesus tried to help them understand that the law is like a tutor for people until God's teachings dwell in their hearts; then they could trust their hearts' guidance. This inner life is more important than outward form and behavior, which can even hide what is in a person's heart.

"The Pharisees were also dismayed by Jesus' associating with people who broke the laws. What is to be done about such people whose hearts have hardened and who live without meaning? The Pharisees' answer was to avoid and shun such people, both to protect others from their bad influence and as just consequence for dishonoring the community of the faithful. Jesus, too, saw their brokenness, but he had a different response.

"Jesus showed love by looking to a person's heart; he saw them whole with eyes of love and acceptance. In the presence of friends and enemies alike, Jesus would show them honor by his presence, would give recognition of their true worth.

"Jesus spoke to their hearts and called each to pay attention to what had heart and meaning. Matthew was one of these. He was a despised tax collector for the Romans until the day Jesus said, 'Follow me.' Jesus was criticized for openly going to Matthew's home for dinner. But hear what happened: Matthew became one of Jesus' disciples and later recorded the stories of Jesus, even recorded my story. Matthew changed so much after that day that one could say his calling forth into a new life was almost as dramatic as Lazarus being called forth from the tomb.

"As I remembered these encounters, the image that began to come to mind was that of anointing. In the customs of my people, anointing is a sacred act of pouring or smoothing on a fragrant oil as an act of dedication or consecration for a special role. It is also used in preparation for burial to consecrate the body of a loved one. In the stories of my people, the most sacred anointing is that of a leader, usually a king, who would lead the people to fulfill their covenant with God. Messiah means 'the anointed one.' The anointed one is 'to save the people' by restoring their purpose in the living out of this covenant. In those months of Jesus' teaching and healing, the word 'Messiah' was being whispered among the crowd. But my people, including the disciples, believe the Messiah would come to restore a Jewish Kingdom and replace the Romans as political leader as well as a religious leader.

"But, I began to discern that Jesus was fulfilling the prophecies in a different way. I began to think how like anointing his actions were for these individual people he had restored. By recognizing and acknowledging the value of their essential, highest selves, he was saving them, healing any brokenheartedness, so that each could be consecrated and anointed to the special meaning for his or her own life. Jesus, the Anointed One, was not a teacher of laws; Jesus was a teacher of the way of love, the way of the Healer, and he was anointing us to consecrated lives guided by the very Heart of God.

"A great swelling of gratitude filled me and I knew I must show Jesus I understood the fullness of his gift, the immensity of his calling. But I had no words, no way of explaining. And truly, I had no voice in the company of disciples. But I knew that something had to be done to ac-knowledge his holy calling and office. Then I thought of a symbol of highest honor usually reserved for anointing of kings and great prophets—the oil called spikenard. It is sold in fine alabaster vases from Egypt and is so rare it would cost a whole year's wages. But the cost was so little in comparison to this gift of Jesus.

"I hurried to the house where Jesus was having dinner in Bethany. The house of Simon the leper (another soul judged 'unclean' by the Pharisees). I entered and moved toward Jesus, broke the neck of the alabaster vase; the rich perfume of the spikenard filled the room. Lovingly, with my heart beating strong and full, I poured the pure and costly ointment over Jesus' head; I anointed my teacher, the Messiah!

"I was unprepared for the response from the others in the room, including some of the disciples. They were outraged and indignant. They did not understand my holy act. 'For what purpose is this waste?' they roared. 'Ointment like this could have been sold for more than three hundred denarii, and the money given to the poor.' Their anger rolled over me, but Jesus said, **'Let her alone. Why do you trouble her? This beautiful thing she has done for me. As for the poor, you can do good to them whenever you wish. The poor you will always have with you. You will not always have me. She has done what was in her power to do. She anointed my body for burial. Truly, I assure you, wherever throughout the whole world this Gospel is proclaimed, what she has done will be told in memory of her.'**[23]

"All fell silent. I know beyond any doubt that the heart of God had been moving my heart and it was for good. I had stood by my heart and fulfilled its leading. Far beyond what even my mind had discerned, God had used me to give longed-for recognition to the Messiah. Jesus knew that I had discerned by the Holy Spirit who he was and the sacred role to which he was consecrated. My act of proclamation and acceptance before the witnesses in that room two days before Passover gave Jesus healing comfort though seeing his own death in the fulfillment of that role.

"My intent had been to anoint him to the life of healing that he was showing us. But Jesus knew it was for the anointing of his body for burial. I learned that day that they were a part of the same circle of eternity—to be anointed to fulfill the heart's destiny is to complete our birth and it is also to be anointed to be ready to die without regret and enter our resurrected life.[24]

"What if I hadn't listened to my heart? What if I had feared judgment and disapproval by the disciples and Simon? What if I had been frozen to inaction by needing to know for certain if it was the right thing to do? What if I had just stayed home, withdrawn and bitter that the disciples did not invite me to share my insights? What if I had waited for some sign or permission of authority to act on the spiritual wisdom my heart already knew? How close I came to not fulfilling my heart's destiny and faithfully doing my part in God's great plan of love.

"Thank you for receiving my story. It has been healing to recall and tell it to you. I often return to Jesus' words when I am troubled, misunderstood, confused, fearful. They comfort me and strengthen me, so that I remember to stand by my heart and act on its guidance."

(As Healer archetype, she removes scarf or shawl.) Jesus has left special words of comfort for each of you. John 14 tells of the promise of the Holy Spirit and how it dwells in each one of us. Recall these words from verse 25: "These things I have spoken to you, while I am still with you. But the Comforter, the Holy Spirit, whom [God] will send in my name, [she] will teach you all things, and bring to your remembrance all that I have said to you." ("Comforter" in King James translation means "one called alongside to help;" "Counselor" in RSV.)

Now, I will teach a meditation for strengthening your heart.

Cradling work

This form of meditation is done lying down. *(Everyone lies down.)* It is found in many spiritual traditions and is used to reopen oneself to the many aspects of love. This form of lying down meditation is called "cradling work, and it is a practice to stay connected to the [best] in one's own nature."[25] Philippians 4:8 gives us a way to think about this meditation. "Finally, whatever is honorable, whatever is just, whatever is pure, whatever is lovely, whatever is gracious, if there is any excellence, if there is anything worthy of praise, think about these things" (RSV).

"In cradling meditation, we lie on our back and place both hands over our heart (in many cultures, as in our own, hands symbolize healing).[26] The lying posture is the most healing posture that the body can assume. The body equates this posture with rest and the nourishment that comes from receiving and giving love. It is the posture of surrender and openness."[27]

Your back is protected by the earth and reminds you of the interconnectedness that supports and binds all things together. The earth is the great nourisher and regenerator of all physical life, which is why so many refer to nature as "mother nature." The earth is the garden given us by God for our dwelling place. The Way of the Healer is associated with the direction of the South and the season of spring when new life and healing are so visible.

With our hands warming our hearts, with this life-sustaining earth cradling our backs like a mother, we are free to look upward and call Divine love to our whole body for any healing and wisdom needed. We will take a few minutes to relax and be aware of this surety, this abundance. *(Pause.)*

To strengthen your heart, you must now acknowledge the gifts you have been given. I will ask you to acknowledge certain things. Then, I will ask you to share this with the person lying nearest to you. Find that partner right now. *(Still lying down.)*

Acknowledge your strengths and talents. The skills, the ability to do, or the talent for doing a special thing. There are obvious ones affirmed in our culture, such as artistic or athletic ability.

Other abilities and talents include putting people at ease, showing care, discerning needs, analyzing of complex issues, solving scientific puzzles, knowing what is needed for a trip, motivating people to accomplish something together like a choir or play. Share this with your partner.[28]

(*For each sharing allow three to five minutes.*)

Acknowledge what character qualities you like about yourself—your moral nature—special ways in which any person feels, thinks, and acts, such as being compassionate, cheerful, resilient, patient, honest, not giving up easily, taking care of things, can be counted on, keeping a confidence, caring about justice. Share this with your partner.

Acknowledge the contributions that you have made and are making. This means giving help or support along with others. Have you taught something? Have you danced or laughed or sung as your heart has moved you? Have you noticed birds singing, flowers blooming? Have you painted, played an instrument, written a poem? Have you brought order to something, cooked a meal, arranged flowers, played with a brother or sister? Share this with your partner.

Acknowledge the love you have given. You have given recognition or affirmation to a person you have seen good in. You have thanked someone. You have helped; you have spoken up when someone needed backing. You have refused to be a part of hurtful teasing or put-downs. Share this with your partner.

Acknowledge the love you have received. Someone has given recognition or affirmation to you. Your family has provided the home and food, and opportunities for learning for you. You have received love from friends and people in your community, like pastors, teachers, Girl Scout leaders. You have received love from pets. Share this with your partner.

Finally, acknowledge that the Divine source of love, God, has chosen you and wishes to anoint you to fulfill the love placed in your heart.

No longer do I call you servants, for the servant does not know what the master is doing; but I have called you friends, for all that I have heard from my Father I have made known to you. You did not choose me, but I chose you and anointed you that you should go and bear fruit and that your fruit should abide; so that whatever you ask the Father in my name, he may give it to you. This I command you, to love one another. — John 15:16–17 (RSV)

Receive the anointing oil on your head as recognition that you have heard the words of love and anointing. Rest in the cradle of mother earth and know your oneness and yet uniqueness in God's creation. Amen, May it be so.

DONNA HUMPHREYS

THE WAY OF THE VISIONARY 1

Begin with the quote from Marianne Williamson: "Our deepest fear is not that we are inadequate. Our deepest fear is that we are powerful beyond measure. It is our light, not our darkness that frightens us. We ask ourselves, who am I to be brilliant, gorgeous, talented and fabulous? Actually, who are you not to be? You are a child of God. Your playing small doesn't serve the world. We were born to make manifest the Glory of God within us. It's not just in some of us; it's in everyone. And as we let our own Light shine, we . . . give other people permission to do the same."[29]

The Visionary asks that you make manifest the glory of God that is in you, that you bring forth your gifts and talents, working with God to fill that unique place in the world that is yours alone. Each one of you has the power of the Visionary within you. When you are true to your individual uniqueness, it is a blessing for the world and an honoring of self.

Remember our ancestor Mary? Gabriel came to her saying, "O highly favored one, God has plans for you to bear a child and call him Jesus" (Lk. 1:28–31, paraphrased). As God worked within Mary, God works within you, has given you a special self that is yours alone. You, too, are highly favored and the Visionary asks you to come forward. Mary and God together brought forth Jesus. What gifts will you and God bring forth?

(Gloria sings.)

The Visionary tells us how to bring forth our gifted self. It is done by speaking the truth. When we speak our heart's truth, we are letting the world know who we are. It takes courage to do this, and an awareness of self. It is often very difficult. I know because it is very difficult for me. My reasons for not speaking the truth are not necessarily bad or wrong. They often stem from a basic human need. I keep silent because I want to be loved; I don't want to appear foolish, I want to keep the peace or not to offend. But the consequences of my silence are harmful because I begin to lose touch with myself. In trying to please others, I abandon who I am. Each time I deny my own feelings, for whatever reason, I move further away from who I really am, and in the extreme I can completely lose touch, no longer knowing what I want, who I am.

But when I speak and act my truth without blame or judgment, I give my gift of self to the world. It is all I really have to offer, but when I speak my truth, it makes me feel whole and it fills that unique spot that is mine alone.

(Claudia sings.)

As I was thinking about the Visionary asking us to bring forth our gifts, I was struck by the uniqueness of each of us, in both body and soul. How does our body contribute to our manifestation of the glory of God within us?

I was with my mother when she died. It was the most profound moment of my life. There is her body, housing her life, and suddenly her soul leaves. Her body remains, looking exactly the same as it did moments before, but that piece that made her my mother and that allowed her to offer her gifts, that piece that she shared with God, that piece that was life, is gone. It made me realize what temples our bodies are. They are holders of our souls. Without us inside them, they are meaningless. On the other hand, they help determine who that self inside us is. Think about your body. Has it helped shape who you are becoming within it? Are there talents you have developed because your body fits nicely with what you love?

We are about to take a silent walking meditation to the beach. As we experience the wonder of the natural world, take time to think about the glory of God that is within you, and how you can best share that with the world.

SUZANNE SCHLICKE

THE WAY OF THE VISIONARY 2

The way of the Visionary asks us: to tell the truth without blame or judgment, to honor who we are, and to learn to speak and act from our authentic selves. Each of us is a piece of the giant, intricate jigsaw puzzle of life; the whole needs each unique piece in order to be complete.

Most of us learned early on to hide our true natures. Out of our need for someone else's love, someone else's approval or acceptance, our need for maintaining balance or keeping the peace, we learned to avoid certain things or to perform what we thought others wanted to see. But if we do not express our own original ideas or listen to our own being, we will have betrayed ourselves. What we once needed to do to survive may now be a habit that no longer serves us. Each day we must choose. Sometimes it takes a great deal of courage to be who we are.

In the biblical story of the woman with the flow of blood (Mk. 5:25–34), when the woman touches Jesus' robe, Jesus calls her out of hiding and asks her to tell the truth of her own life, and her hemorrhaging stops.

Having a safe place where we can tell our stories and be heard and held, where our authentic selves are nurtured and encouraged to be expressed, seems crucial for recovering vitality.

For me, this has been my writing Circle. In story sharing, we are affirmed and connected when we hear ourselves reflected in another's words.

The way of the Visionary leads each back to her authentic self and helps her stay connected to her inner knowing. The Visionary uses prayer to touch the heart and spirit of others regardless of time and distance. The Visionary honors four ways of seeing: intuition, perception, insight, and vision. Paying attention to these is her way of honoring the sacred.

In my experience, being willing to speak our truth requires some sense of feeling valuable. One of my life's biggest challenges has been to believe that I *am* good enough, that I do matter, and have something worthwhile to offer. I had everything I thought I wanted (wonderful family, comfortable home, great friends) yet I often felt empty, alone, and sad. Had I abandoned that strong, resourceful child I remember being so long ago? What I still longed for was to be loved for who I am, really.

I had searched for years for answers outside myself and tried to fix what was "wrong" with me. How could I accept myself when I wasn't the way I wanted to be?

Three years ago, in a guided visualization, I pictured my chaos as things swirling around me, with myself all alone and motionless on a large ball, like the planet Saturn. When I asked my inner wisdom, "What can end my feelings of separation?" I suddenly saw God smiling at me as though I mattered; God seemed to be saying to me, "I love you just the way you are!" This filled my whole being with more radiant white light than I could hold, so that tears rolled down my cheeks, my cup runneth over! Then in the vision, this completely loving light radiated outwards and touched those around me. The swirling confusion had stopped, and I felt an incredible oneness with all. I felt plugged in to the Source of Life; I was so energized that for several days I hardly needed to sleep! A heavy burden had been lifted.

How can we empower the **Visionary** within us?

1. Walking meditation is a method for opening us to our creativity. Any physical activity (vacuuming, swimming) we choose for the purpose of listening to our internal processes will do. For fifteen minutes a day while moving: focus on an issue, let it go, then observe what is revealed. This encourages the unexpected. (We can do this tomorrow morning as we silently walk to the beach.)

2. Spend time alone in nature for the purpose of reflection and guidance. This reawakens us to our own life purpose. Nature is a profound reflection and teacher of our own inner nature. Listen to Job 12:7–8: "But ask the animals, and they will teach you; the birds of the air, and they will tell you; ask the plants of the earth, and they will teach you . . . " (Our time at the beach tomorrow can be for reflective listening.)

3. Singing feeds the essence of who we are and is healing. Sing every day. Rediscover the music of our own voices and experiment with sounds. Our most powerful song is the one we create. Last year when I picked up the challenge to write a lullaby, it first seemed impossible to get beyond songs already written by others. After several failed attempts, I remembered words that soothe my inner child's "infant" need to feel welcomed, cuddled, and loved. I sat in my rocking chair, cupped my arms as if holding baby Kitty, and started humming a tune as I rocked. The next day I tried it again and a similar sound came forth, and I wrote down the verses as I heard them whispered within me. Now, I sing this song when I need comforting. It has the power to relax my body and quiet my wailing soul.

4. Honor our dreams by recording them in a dream journal; listen to what they have to tell us. (Sunday morning will be a time to share these.)

5. Practice telling the truth every day, without blame or judgment, always considering timing, context, and body language.

6. Feed our intuition by listening to it and acting on its advice. Intuition is a direct messenger of our souls.

What can happen when we trust and let go of control seems magical! My daughter was getting married last summer, and I felt so inadequate trying to sum up the wisdom and love I wanted to share with her to honor this transition. I awoke early one morning with the vision of a Circle of women gathered under the large locust tree sheltering our home. I saw myself light a candle and slowly pour jasmine tea into awaiting cups before each woman shared her wisdom on a particular aspect of Jennifer's life; Donna would speak about family, Karen about friendship, and so on. The vision was accompanied by waves of creative energy throughout that day, supplying details to flesh out the ceremony, down to the closing prayer. Even the words I would speak and their accompanying symbols were made clear to me. I kept myself receptive as I moved through the day and wrote down what came forth from inside. Later, my writing Circle encouraged me to make it happen for real, and together we did, just as I had imagined. It was a dream come true! Besides strengthening my intuition, this wonder-filled experience taught me about the abundance available when we join together.

Dear sisters, we are embodied spirit. I encourage us all to honor ourselves and our Creator by listening to that still, small voice within, and bringing forth into the world our uniqueness to make our lives and the Circle whole. Each of our lives is precious and does matter!

The birthday candles we put in our pouches are to remind us of the way of the Visionary, to seek and express our truth. Let's let our lights shine! Sing the gospel song, "This Little Light of Mine, I'm Going to Let It Shine."

KITTY ADAMS

THE WAY OF THE TEACHER

Teacher Presentation Outline:
Make a sacred center with symbolic objects, surrounded by pairs of sticks representing bones of the ancestors to use later in # 6.

1. **Name qualities of Teacher** as facilitator moves around the Circle *(standing)*

2. **Centering.** Call in Circle energy by three deep breaths:

   to let go of past

   to become present to now

   to be open to what will come

3. **Way of the Teacher** *(sitting down)*

4. **Mary as example**

5. **Ancestor spirits**

6. **Breaking harmful patterns** *(striking sticks)* "You will be the one."

7. **Bringing forward the good, true, and beautiful** "You will be the one."

8. **What is being born in me?** Listening to inner voice

9. **Closing Song** "Be Still and Know that I Am God"[30]

Qualities of Teacher

Be open to outcome . . . not attached to outcome

Care deeply from an objective place

Be a fair witness and suspend judgment

Honor your heritage

bring forward the good, true, and beautiful

break the harmful patterns

Be flexible and fluid like Grandmother Ocean

Trust and let go

Be comfortable with uncertainty

Enter the silence . . . listen to your inner guidance

Wait and listen for wisdom when confused

The Way of the Teacher

The way of the Teacher is to sit in silence and listen to inner guidance.

The way of the Teacher is to be open to outcome, not attached to outcome, to be flexible and resilient like Grandmother Ocean and not rigid and stubborn with fear. Feel the difference in your body between flexible and rigid. When we are attached and have rigid expectations, we become controlling, inflexible, and lose our sense of humor. When we become channels for the living waters of God to flow through us into the world, we are Teachers.

To be open to outcome requires trust and being comfortable with uncertainty, with not knowing. To be open to all possibilities as life unfolds requires letting go of control.

We can practice trusting and letting go every time we say goodbye and when we go to sleep. Sometimes it is difficult for me to let go of the day; those things left undone or wished done differently repeat themselves in my mind and disturb my slumber until I let them go.

Detachment is different from unattachment, unconnectedness. To be detached from outcome means to care deeply from an objective place. We do this by:

calmly observing our reactions

being a fair witness and suspending judgment

accepting what is (this is definitely a task of mothers of adult children!)

When we are able to value our self-worth as much as we listen to the self-critic, we can tap into the resource of wisdom.

Mary

Who was Mary, to be chosen to be the mother of Jesus? She was only a young, inexperienced teenager with no power, no status, no voice, especially in those times, and probably had no desire to have a baby at that time in her life. Her fiancé might have rejected her, and two thousand years ago a woman could be stoned to death for being pregnant before marriage.

What would be your reaction, at any age, to an angel telling you, "Do not fear, but you will become pregnant by the Holy Spirit and the child you will bear will be the savior of the world"?

"No Way! Isn't possible! Why me? I can't. I don't want to. I don't have time. What will other people think?"

But God acknowledged Mary's worthiness and her abilities, by inviting her to be a co-creator of new life. In the sweet territory of silence, Mary was able to recognize divine presence, listen as witness to hear the message, and trust the guidance revealed to her. Her openness was evident when she only asked, "How? How will this happen?" Without knowing the consequences, Mary let go of her fears and quietly responded. "I am one with the will of God. Let it happen as you say."

What an amazing example of the way of the Teacher, of being open to outcome, of trust, and acceptance! As a willing participant, Mary became a vessel to receive and hold divine energy. Co-creating with God she brought a new possibility into the world.

Ancestors

The Four-fold Way is not about finding pleasure for today but for those who choose to leave a rich legacy for the future. The powers of Warrior/Leader, Teacher, Healer, and Visionary lie within each of us. As we learn to live them, we begin to heal our fragmented world and ourselves.

This is not any easy task, but help is deeply rooted within our own flesh and blood and memory. Our ancestors are a part of us whether or not we are conscious of them.

Mary, the mother of Jesus, is one of our ancestors. Her example helps to shape who we are and assures us that a woman's body is worthy of sheltering the sacred. This, too, is a house of the living God, holy ground.

When I am confused, it helps me to remember Mary's example of waiting for clarity before acting and of "pondering all these things in her heart," not in her mind. When I feel empty or worthless, I can think of Mary making herself receptive to co-create with spirit an unimagined possibility, the Messiah coming as a vulnerable babe. Mary is an inspiring example of letting go of fear to welcome new life.

Breaking Harmful Patterns

Let us remember others who have gone before us and honor them for bringing us here. Our ancestors are still with us, and stand behind us saying, "O, may this be the one who will bring forward the good, true, and beautiful in our family lineage; O, may this be the one who will break the harmful family patterns or harmful cultural patterns"[31]

Ancestors are like our bones that give definition and strength to our flesh; they can be present in our lives in a very real way. For example, if alcoholism has been a harmful family pattern, we have the opportunity to learn from the mistakes of our ancestors, and honor them by choosing to not extend that family pattern forward ourselves. We can listen to their guidance and call for their help by clicking sticks representing bones; the sound also affirms our commitment to break the harmful pattern.

Stand and pick up a pair of sticks that have been placed around the center.

Think of a harmful pattern you are willing to break. *(Pause.)*

As we go around the Circle, one by one, step forward and name that pattern, out loud or silently in your heart, then click your sticks together. After each one steps forward, speaking or in silence, to click her sticks, the rest click their sticks in support saying:

All: "You will be the one who will break the harmful pattern."

Bringing forward the Good, True, and Beautiful

Indigenous peoples believe that ancestor spirits literally stand behind us to support us in fulfilling our life purpose.

"O, may this be the one who will bring forward the good, true, and beautiful in our family lineage . . ."

In your family background and heritage, what are the qualities that have been carried forward that you can identify as being good, true, and beautiful?

As we go around the Circle again, one by one name a quality that you want to carry forward, and then the rest of us will encourage you with the words: "You will be the one."

Teacher stands with arms outstretched behind each person while each names the quality; then Teacher places her hands on the woman's shoulders to signal all saying, "You will be the one."

Let us thank our ancestors for what they've done to pave the way for us and for helping us.

All: "Now we are the ones."

What is being born in me?

Listening in the sweet territory of silence opens us to the still small voice within. Remember that we are all pregnant with possibility! Remember that with God anything is possible!

Close your eyes and listen to your heart's answer to these questions:

"How is God breaking into my life unexpectedly?"

"What am I being asked to surrender to, to say 'yes' to?"

"What choice is taking shape within me?"

"What is struggling to come to birth in me?"

"What is being born through me?"

Closing song: "Be Still and Know that I am God."[32]

KITTY ADAMS

CRiAFTS

Pouch-Making

Demonstrating pouch-making:

Pouch-making is as ancient, earthy, and female as the first mother kangaroo. Retreat pouches are created from scraps of ornate or plain fabric, chosen by each girl and woman from a collection of remnants. The craft demonstrator shows a premade pouch as a sample, and she encourages each sewer to choose thread, ornaments, and drawstrings following her own taste and whim. The craft person demonstrates simple stitching and embroidery techniques.

As girls and women begin their own needlework, those with more experience help ones trying their hand at this for the first time. Soon hand-stitched pouches emerge: roomy or snug, soft or rough, lavished with beads, or slapped together with humor. The work of imaginations and hands, they will hold small treasures from this retreat.

Supplies you will need:

Scissors

Fabric scraps—variety of size, texture, color, and pattern

Beads, buttons, braid, feathers, sequins, and other trim

Cord and ribbon for drawstrings

Needles, thread, embroidery floss, and yarn

Fabric paint

Alternatively, the craft demonstrator can pass out preassembled packets, each containing fabric scraps, needle, and thread. Trim can be in the packet or placed for selection on a cloth or table. If they want to choose their own colors and patterns, women and girls can trade their fabric for other fabric from a resource pile.

Making Masks

You will need plastered gauze—it comes in four-inch-wide rolls and can be found at most craft stores. Other supplies you will need to gather are old towels, large bowls, scissors, plastic wrap, and Vaseline. You will be able to make roughly two masks from a 180-inch roll of gauze.

The person whose mask is being made should lie down and be comfortable and warm. It will take about twenty minutes of lying still. We do our mask-making on the lawn, in the dappled sun, under an old maple tree.

1. Precut a pile of plaster gauze pieces in sizes ranging from about one inch square to about two inches by four inches.

2. Fill a large bowl with warm water.

3. Apply a layer of Vaseline around the perimeter of the whole face and under the chin, especially at the hairline, eyebrows, eyelids, eyelashes, and the upper lip. Then spread over the entire face.

4. Make a cap of plastic wrap, wrapping over the hairline and ears to the back of the neck.

5. Apply more Vaseline to the plastic wrap at face edge.

6. Select several of the longer strips of plaster gauze that you have cut and dip them in the warm water. Squeeze extra water back into the bowl. You want the strips to be damp but not dripping. Fold in half lengthwise.

7. Begin outlining the face with these folded strips just back of the hairline, keeping the folded edge away from the face. Outline in front of the ears and just under the chin. This will form a reinforced edge for the mask.

8. Cover the structural areas of the face with overlapping smaller, single thicknesses—along the eyebrows, the ridge of the nose, cheekbones, and chin.

9. Working in a circular pattern, from the outside of the face inward, begin layering on single dampened pieces of gauze, covering with overlapping pieces all the skin except the nostrils. When layering strips over the eyes, be certain there is adequate Vaseline on the eyelids and eyelashes, that the eyelashes lie flat and that the gauze pieces are not dripping wet.

10. After you have covered the entire face, repeat steps 8 and 9 for a second layer.

11. Let the mask dry until it's stiff to the touch. Test to see that there are no soft spots. To see if the mask is ready to remove, tap on it and listen for a hollow sound.

12. To remove the mask, have the person wiggle her face as you slowly pull the mask away from her face, starting at the perimeter.

13. Allow the mask to dry thoroughly.

14. On the inside of the mask, reinforce any weak or thin spots with more pieces of damp gauze. Wrap extra pieces over the edges of the mask to make a smooth finish.

AMY WINDECKER

CAMPFIRE: GAMES AND ACTIVITIES AROUND THE CAMPFIRE

Here are some ideas that have worked well for us:

First Night: A Fun Game

Example: When it's my turn, I make three statements about myself. ("I was born blond. I have eleven toes. My mother is a gypsy.") Two of them are true; one is not. After I make the three statements, the person to my left is asked to guess which statement is false. If she misses, anyone else can guess. *This is a good way to learn some fascinating facts about those participating. Be sure to give the women and girls some time to think up their statements. One of the retreat planners can be first, to model the game. Then take volunteers, as they are ready.*

Second Night: More Serious

Example: Tell about a turning point in your life. You may not have seen the happening or decision as significant, but, looking back, it is clear that it was life-changing. *Again, a planner may share first to encourage others—and remember to give a time of silence or music for thinking.*

Third Night: Use What You Have Made and Learned

Examples:
1. If there are Four-fold Way masks, several girls and women can circle the fire with them as others sing, drum, and tap rhythm instruments.

2. Girls present a play or midrash. They will have had help from a facilitator and time earlier in the day to prepare for this. These skits aim for fun and provide a fresh view of Bible stories.

3. The coordinator for campfire activities invites each one to bring something to campfire to share: a poem, a song, a thought, or something she's made.

CAMPFIRE: "VASALISA THE WISE"

From year-to year, planners look for new stories, songs, and activities to enliven the retreat. But the folktale "Vasalisa the Wise" glows in the flickering light of the campfire at every Daughters Arise! retreat. We have found the words and actions of this story so riveting we simply cannot do without it.

The version of the story we use is found in *Women Who Run with the Wolves* by Clarissa Pinkola Estés.[33] Needed for this simple but wonder-filled play is a dramatic reader who can be heard by all, and whose voice becomes sweet and trusting or evil and menacing, as each part requires. She sits with the audience, next to a person who shines a flashlight for her on the printed page.

Actors do not speak, but use their bodies and faces to portray the story as it is read. The area around the fire is their stage, at times the scene of a quiet encounter, but at other times a space wild with action. The audience sits a bit farther out, surrounding this theater-in-the-round.

After campfire gathering songs and a brief introduction, the story begins and the actors enter. Listed below are the characters with their costumes and props:

The dying mother: wrapped in a blanket that conceals a small doll for Vasalisa

Vasalisa: a simple red dress or skirt. Over this, an apron with a pocket for the doll, that is dressed in the same colors as Vasalisa

Stepmother and stepsisters: dresses or skirts, shawls

Baba Yaga: a dark cloak, black hat or wild wig
Props: small doll, broom

After the play, you may want to ask questions about the meaning of this story for a discussion around the fire or for women and girls to sleep and dream on. A discussion about "Vasalisa the Wise" and its meaning for girls' life adventures may also be held at a later time. In *Women Who Run with the Wolves*, Pinkola Estés discusses symbolism of this tale.[34] One year at our Daughters Arise! retreat, Grandmother Crone asked the following questions:

Our story wakes up many ideas and questions. We have a few; what are yours?
1. What was happening to Vasalisa?

2. Why does Vasalisa have to go to Baba Yaga?

3. Have you ever met someone like Baba Yaga?

4. Why does the mother have to die? What does she take with her?

5. Why doesn't Vasalisa complain to her father about the meanness of her stepmother and sisters?

6. Why does she do everything they want her to do?

7. What voices in the story are telling Vasalisa, "You're not good enough?"

8. Why are these voices in the story?

9. Why does the doll look like Vasalisa?

10. Why does Vasalisa feed the doll?

11. How does the doll know what to do?

12. Pretend you're Vasalisa; how do you feel as you set out on your journey?

13. How do you feel when you're coming back home with the fire?

14. Has someone ever given you a wise gift? Was it important to you?

15. Do you have a Baba Yaga in your life? Would you want one?

NATURE WALK

Reconnecting with nature's rhythms and textures is essential to the Daughters Arise! retreat. Look for a retreat site near forest, desert, shore, park, or other natural place. Consider scheduling your retreat during a full moon, or a meteor shower, perhaps during an equinox or a solstice. Set aside time during the retreat for women and girls to walk, sit, observe, and be in nature. Consider the timing of your walk. *(We scheduled our beach walk for a low tide.)* The walk itself gives the girls another welcome physical activity.

During the retreat sessions

We held as many activities and presentations outside as weather permitted. Women and girls sat on the deck or on the grass. Some took off shoes and felt the cool sod underfoot during dance and exercise. If a bird or animal entered our meeting space, it was welcomed and admired.

Just before the nature walk

Sally, our host, explained precautions that should be taken going down the steep wooden stairs to the beach and what appropriate manners would be for crossing (with advance permission) a neighbor's property. A walk in the nearby woods was offered as an alternative.

In Circle, girls and women anticipated what might be experienced on the beach walk. We were invited to bring back small, found treasures to place on the altar. We held the expectation of a spiritual gift from nature as well. Some wanted to take notebooks for writing or sketching. This was to be a silent walk. We would see others but would be in nature without human conversation. When we returned, those who wanted to share would be welcome to do so.

During the nature walk

Beginning the walk at intervals of a few minutes, women and girls walked in silence down a roadway and a path to a wooden stairway that led to the beach. At the beach, many took off their shoes and enjoyed bare feet in the sand. With the tide out, each walked in her own direction, some to the waves, others to streams and pools of the receding tide. Each looked for a place to accept nature's gifts to her. After an hour or so, we began our walk back to the farm, still in silence.

After the nature walk

Gathering again in Circle, women and girls placed items on the altar from their walk. Some chose to do this in silence and others spoke of the meaning or importance of the object. One year a woman created a small, simple sandbox, and moving sticks and shells about in the sand, she portrayed conflict in her life. Others read from their journals or talked of what they saw, heard, and felt at the beach. The Circle held the spoken or silent sharing of each with respect and love.

WALK AT EBEY'S LANDING

(Response to a nature walk.)

It is a glorious day, with mountains standing up proud showing off their new white coverings. Since the tide is high, I walk up along the bluff trail towards Perego's Lake and sit on a grassy knoll. The sea is calm and uncluttered, just a sailboat, a freighter, and a ferry off in the distance. In back of me a flutter of wings catches my attention. Several, plump, red-breasted robins playfully hop on the gnarled branches of the fir trees lining the bluff. I love these trees that are the first line of defense against the wind on the bluff. They're shorter than their counterparts a few yards behind and give you the impression of having their heels dug in and legs spread to hold their ground against the storms. Branches don't just grow out from the trunk; they twist and bend at awkward angles. Some branches are dead, the whitened, twisted grain of the wood a startling contrast to the green backdrop of their still living relatives.

I can't resist sitting on one of these curved way stations, and my hand strokes the grayish-white surface, worn smooth from its encounters with the elements. I muse to myself, "You trees who experience the most challenges and adversity are also the most interesting. I wonder if that's true of people?"

I lie back, head resting against the comforting trunk, as a child might lean back against a grandmother's bosom. Oh, to have bright sun—what a luxury. I'm soaking up every bit of sun I can. I tilt my head and open my mouth to let the rays permeate my insides as far as they can reach. Can they reach my stomach? What is the cause of the dull ache I've had for almost a month? I sit cradled in my tree nanny, looking out over the shimmering sunlight on the water. I can see why early peoples had an affinity for a sun god. Maybe my ailment is related to sun deprivation. I lie back, soaking up the silence, letting the sun reach down my throat.

I get up and walk a little farther along, then follow a deer trail that starts down the sheer face of the bluff. It peters out and I zigzag myself, a few steps angling down to the right, pivot, a few steps to the left, down the rest of the way. I wonder if one misstep would send me rolling all the way down, landing in a heap on the driftwood below.

The tide has just started to go out, so I can almost walk on the sliver of gravelly beach. Does this water have a mischievous personality? I walk along, and as soon as I turn my eyes away from the tide's edge, it seems the water is playing tag with my feet. I step up on logs, now a safe few inches from the water, my arms instinctively spread out for balance. Maybe this is a prescription, too—do you need more balance in your life, Karen? But who can be into analyzing when you have to concentrate on walking beach logs? Soon, I'm smiling. I feel like the years are dropping off in front of my field of vision. 45 falls off one side, 35 the other, 20, 16, 10. I'm 10 years old, carefree, jumping from log to log. (See also "The Young Girl Within," page 133.)

When I return that evening, I realize I've not been aware of the dull stomach pain all day. Was it the sun going in through my open mouth—or the magic of Ebey's Landing? Who knows—but I personally think the beach always has a way of opening me up to deeper wisdom to let healing take place.

KAREN ANDERSON

NOTES WRITTEN ON A BEACH WALK

I take off my walking shoes and sit on them because there is no big rock to sit on by the tiny tidal stream. I want to watch it rushing back to the Sound, carving a miniature Grand Canyon in the sand as it dapples along, quickly and quietly. The channel splits at my heel print, the lesser branch scooting sideways into the seaweed, and the main rivulet, about the span of a woman's hand across, pushes determinedly toward the Sound.

V-shaped lines of sunlight and water-shadow wriggle the length of my part of the rivulet. This shimmer of light and dark, this iridescent movement, checkers out wherever the stream meets resistance from a shell or a rock or a loop of seaweed. Without these little stream stoppers, the sand-bound canal would gush with all the charm of water from a hose. The resistant bits push and jostle the water, creating an unevenness that scatters the sun.

GLORIA KOLL

BRIDGE TO TIPI

Following are the full texts to our three parts of "Bridge to Tipi." in the Guidebook section, page 47.

1. MAUREEN SPEAKS OF POUCHES AND POWER

(The following story, written by a Circle of Stones member, portrays her experience coming into her strength as a woman and shows the in-

tegral importance of the work of our hands in synthesizing life experience.)

I want to speak about power, about holding, about listening, about waiting. Many young women make decisions that diminish the quality and potential of their lives. They do not understand the special power that is within them, and how to hold it.

Imagine a river flowing strongly through a fertile valley. It bubbles and bends. Its currents are crisp and deep. It's filled with fish, filled with life. The roots of trees gravitate to its fullness. Many growing things cluster along its edges and suckle to its bounty as the river sings the songs of eons, carrying the past into the future . . . holding, holding the balance. It sings of life, Life! . . . healthy, beautiful, strong . . . being all things it was meant to be.

Now imagine storms and rains for many days, filling the washes and draws that flow to this same river. Now it floods; jumping its banks, it covers the tender plants growing by its sides. It covers fields and farms and things that are not meant to live under water. The river that once brought life brings death and destruction.

This is the gift of power. As women, we have a special power or life within us. This is our gift. We make choices everyday that channel our personal energy. We must learn to identify our power and choose well.

When I was a young woman, I awoke from a strange spell to discover that I was a single parent of two very young children. It was a spell of darkness . . . a darkness of non-choice-making . . . a spell of not knowing my inner power.

I was very poor and quite gypsy-like as I struggled to make a life for my children. I had no power as this world defines it, but something was calling from within me, and I started upon the conscious journey to know my own soul. I discovered a deep satisfaction in making pouches. As I crocheted or hand-stitched or embroidered the bags, there was a deep work being done within me. I was very aware that this work was therapy for me. It was life-giving. I was creating a space within myself, a reservoir of my own power. Into these bags, I would put things that were symbolic of something important to me . . . a place, a memory, a color, an idea. I derived strength from the material objects as they were hidden away in "my" pouch.

At this time in my life, I had made a decision to be completely celibate. I knew I had a lot of work to do after five years of a terrible relationship with a man who did not honor me or the children before I could trust my judgment and decision-making ability in the man department. I knew deep within myself that the key to peace and success in my personal life depended on my being alone, learning to be completely, painfully, brutally alone. I had to learn to gather my power. I knew that any kind of sexual activity for me would disperse my power. I had work to do.

Years later, while observing my daughter's interest in little pouches, I began to wonder about their meaning. She would rummage through my old stuff and ask for this or that. She started collecting little boxes of various shapes and sizes. As I had, she would put little things in them . . . secret trinkets. I started to wonder about this inclination and whether or not it was common among young women everywhere.

A vivid dream spoke to me. In the dream, I was walking through the dusty streets of an old town in some unknown land. I saw two little American Indian girls, about eleven or twelve years old, who beckoned me to follow them. They were barefoot and raggedy-looking. Their clothing was of a dusty red-brown color. I followed them through what seemed like a crowded marketplace in a poor village. They led me to a street corner where two elderly American Indian women with long black and gray hair were standing. They were old and quite thin, with strong, sinewy muscles in their arms. One was holding a box in her two hands outstretched toward me as if she meant to give it to me. The look in her eyes as she gazed at me was the most striking thing about this dream. Her eyes were sharp and clear and looked right at me. Her eyes knew me . . . knew my thoughts.

She opened the box, still gazing intently into my face. I looked down and saw some things there . . . beads . . . gold coins on the top layer of the inside of the box. It was clear, however, that there was something more underneath, in an inner chamber.

I was a bit afraid of these women, but as I reached out to take the box I suddenly woke up . . . wide-awake and breathing hard, nearly sweating. There had been great power in that box and the dream had a deep impact on me. Here it was again—the box, the pouch, the small container, holding, hiding something . . . something secret, something of great importance and meaning and mystery, and yes, power. Something of Woman. The little girls knew about it, the old women knew about it. They meant to remind me, to share it with me, to let me in on their secret in this impoverished place. Their eyes were full of richness and knowing. Many possibilities tumble in as I think of this: The womb and the dark secrets it holds . . . the cup or chalice of blessing . . . the "witches" caldron . . . a seed as it waits until the moment of germination.

I am teaching my daughter how to hold her power—how to contain and channel the life-force-river that flows through the center of her being and her life. I will teach her about relationships and what it means to be attracted to a man—how to create a context of mature commitment in a relationship, to elevate it to a high and noble place. I want her to know the sexual encounter as a spiritual experience that brings health and life and strength instead of the erosion of heart and soul or the wasting of the fragile, tender new growth of leaf and bud waiting to come into its full beauty.

The bud gathers its power. The carbohydrate reserve flows from the roots to the bud. The bud swells and waits for the perfect, sunny, warm day. When all the elements of water, air, temperature are in place, the bud breaks and the blossom opens in all its glory, releasing its perfume, bringing life to the world. The plant knows its own timing. It knows what it needs to be all it was meant to be, and it holds its power and life force perfectly. It releases it perfectly.

I am teaching my daughter to value herself, honor her body, and care for it all in a context of choice-making and power . . . the power of Woman.

MAUREEN ROWLEY

2. OUR MIND, BODY, HEALTH, WISDOM CONNECTION

(Here, Paula is recalling the presentation she made to the girls and women at retreat.)

I brought to this group three "I"-concepts: Interconnectedness, Inner guidance, and Illness as healing concepts. These are all intense topics, but they are presented in a manner to start young women to think for themselves about health issues and how to honor their bodies.

Interconnectedness opens with the idea that menopausal women and our daughters in their early teens have a strong common bond. We are all experiencing hormonal changes in our bodies. In the young ones, their bodies are just beginning the process of being able to create life. It takes a couple of years for that switch to be made and for the hormones to settle into their new role. For the older women, a similar situation is taking place where we are shutting down this vital life energy, now ready to pour it out into the universe.

Especially for the daughters, I wanted to remind them how remarkable their bodies are. As they move into the menstrual-cycle years, they can start to become aware of three amazing concepts. The first is the constant rhythm within women's monthly cycles. We spend the two weeks past ovulation and before bleeding to search deeply within ourselves for what is important in our world. It is the time that PMS and other symptoms may occur. If we tend not to look at the messages our bodies are giving us through these symptoms and try to ignore them and mask them with medications, we will not be understanding and using our body's wisdom to help us with the deep issues of life. As we start to bleed and move toward ovulation, we are more outgoing, creative, energetic. It is important to realize this natural cycle and honor it and learn from it.

It has been observed that when women are living together closely, as in a college dorm, their periods can all be in synch. That means that they are so energetically and emotionally connected that their bodies will be on the same cycle together. They will ovulate at the same time and start their periods at the same time.

For women who are very tuned to nature, our bodies can naturally cycle with the changes of the moon. The normal tendency would be to ovulate at the full moon that coincides with the creative part of the cycle. As the moon is getting larger, so is our capacity to be open to the world. As the moon wanes, we go into our introspective time of contemplation and introspection, finishing with our bleeding at the new moon. As we "control" our cycles with birth control pills, for example, we are cut off from this opportunity to be in synch with the natural universe.

For the second "I"—inner guidance—we acknowledged that women have an intact inner guidance system in place ready to be activated and validated. This space is a gift from the Creator and is part of the Creator. Our job is to figure out how to access this place and honor it. This journey can be fun, surprising, intriguing, spontaneous. It can come in the form of dreams, prayers, meditation, a book, a friend, a movie, an animal, nature, a healer, an experience. The avenues are numerous. We need only to connect to that inner knowing which will help us to understand our role in this world and what we need to do about it.

The third "I"—illness—is looking at illness and our emotions as indicators of our own personal balance. When we acknowledge what our emotions do for us, we can then access the places where we are tender and need to spend some time. When we acknowledge an illness as an indication that we are out of balance, illness becomes a gift rather than a curse. It allows us to be open to looking into our lives at many levels for what it is that we are not authentically living out in our lives.

I am just mentioning these ideas that I presented at the weekend retreat. They are open for much discussion and exploration. My desire is that you may also take some time to think about these, too, as you journey with your daughters.[35]

PAULA PUGH

3. The Art of Holding and Releasing Our Daughters

Before the girls depart with their adult facilitators for the tipi, we present two wisdom pieces that come from the experiences of the presenters. We have discussed these in the Guidebook section, "How We Do It . . . Bridge to Tipi," page 47, and we have printed those two texts on the preceding pages. After the girls leave for "Tipi Time," the mothers and other women remain to share resources and support in a discussion about the gradual release of the daughters and young friends to their increasingly independent lives. We recognize the push and pull of the girls needing both closeness and growing independence. We speak of the skills we need in enabling our daughters to become strong, faithful young women.

Below is an introduction, an activity, and a list of key concepts with excerpts from resources with which we have started the discussion.

Introduction

Let's do a little experiment: What are the "memorable mom phrases" in your head, bits of wisdom that come to mind?

Gloria and Kitty have written wonderful pieces about "memorable mom phrases":

Mom in My Head

I have friends my age who still feel insecure because they were so put down by their mothers. My Mom, by taking us to concerts, helping with homework, giving us piano and voice lessons, aided our talents and nourished our spirits. She encouraged me to do whatever positive thing I wanted to try, even something others thought was a bit crazy—like going to Okinawa.

I am equally grateful that she had the guts to nix a couple of my boyfriends who would have made disastrous husbands. She used to say, "It's no trick getting married. The trick is finding someone worth marrying."

Of course, she loves the guys my sister Clarice and I married—who wouldn't? Though I have heard her say, "I know my sons-in-law aren't perfect. If they were perfect, they wouldn't have married my daughters!" What do you think, Clarice? Is that a compliment? To any of us?

Other sayings of Mom also flash around in my head when I need them: "Finish the job." (I hear this when I'm about to leave something undone.) "We're all going to be pretty surprised at who's in heaven." (This comes when I'm feeling judgmental about someone.) I usually listen to Mom-in-my-head—and my life runs more smoothly for it.

GLORIA KOLL

Losing Connection

Once there was a little girl who loved to daydream. She would sit by a window and let her mind carry her away to imaginary places. But her Mother shamed her for this, and admonished her to DO something, call a friend to play, stop wasting her time. Sometimes, the little girl was so absorbed in her own thoughts that she would not hear her Mother's demands and, at least twice, she was taken to the doctor to have her ears tested. Gradually, the little girl stopped going to those places in her imagination, and, gradually, she lost connection to her deepest Self.

Now, as I sit in my kitchen window seat, I catch glimpses of that little girl so absorbed in her own instinctual Self, and I feel the strength of her knowing and the possibilities of her imagination, and waves of sadness wash over me. How would things have been different if that little girl had continued to dream?

KITTY ADAMS

Activity

What are some "mom messages" that have made you feel capable?

What are some "mom messages" that have made you feel unsure of yourself?

We cannot emphasize enough how powerful our messages can be in the life of our daughters or young woman friends—messages that build strength or messages that build insecurity.

Some Key Concepts to assist in sending positive messages:

1. Recognize the essential role of encouragement.

2. Learn to really see your own child and avoid the "Ugly Duckling" syndrome.

3. Be aware of and avoid conflicting messages to girls about their success.

4. Acknowledge "necessary losses"—leaving childhood means leaving mother.

5. Understand and encourage the importance of creative "languages" of expression; and encourage the opportunity to express them and test against someone other than mother.

EXCERPTS FROM RESOURCES FOR DISCUSSING KEY CONCEPTS WITH MOTHERS AND OTHER WOMEN

These selections can be read by the planners in preparation. Using their own words as introduction, presenters may want to use some quotations as discussion starters.

1. Recognize the essential role of encouragement.

In an address to the Twelfth World Conference of the World Council for Gifted and Talented Children, Mihaly Csikszentmihalyi of the University of Chicago, remarked:

Talent is a developmental phenomenon that only reveals itself through time. Therefore, it needs care and cultivation to grow. . . . Care must include intrinsic and extrinsic motivation to sustain energy needed to grow.

Dr. Csikszentmihalyi continued:

"Talent is cheap," one often hears from people who ought to know. What they mean is that innate talent is not very useful unless nurtured over many years, and unless the talented person is motivated to develop his or her potential despite inevitable obstacles. My perspective is that talent is a developmental phenomenon that only reveals itself through time. This is in opposition to the view that "talent will out"' or the belief that talent is an all-or-nothing gift which inevitably will express itself.

Dr. Csikszentmihalyi talked of how enjoyment of an activity supports the development of talent, and of the important role of the family, schools, and mentors as they "help to provide the conditions in which the curiosity and interest of talented young people can best be cultivated."[36]

2. Learn to really see your own child and avoid the "Ugly Duckling" syndrome.

This means learning to recognize, acknowledge, accept, and nurture the actual gifts you see in your child, not projecting onto or molding her according to the requirements of culture. Clarissa Pinkola Estés discusses how to avoid being an "ambivalent" or "collapsed" mother in *Women Who Run with the Wolves:*[37]

Many women had parents who surveyed them as children and puzzled over how this small alien had managed to infiltrate the family.[38]

For a mother to happily raise a child who is slightly or largely different in psyche and soul needs from that of the mainstream culture, she must have a start on some heroic qualities herself. She must be able to steal these qualities if they are not allowed, shelter them, unleash them at the right time, and stand for herself and what she believes. There is almost no way

to make oneself ready for this, other than to take a deep draft of courage, and then act. Since time out of mind a considered act of heroism has been the cure for stultifying ambivalence.[39]

The way to cause a mother to collapse is to divide her emotionally. The most common way, time out of mind, has been to force her to choose between loving her child and fearing what harm the village will visit on her and the child if she does not comply with the rules.[40]

3. Be aware of and avoid conflicting messages to girls about their success.

a. Ambivalence of mothers towards daughters' success.

We may think that this time of danger for mother and child is long gone, that Pinkola Estés was writing of medieval or nineteenth century European social structures that created the danger of casting out or ostracizing of women who "step out of the beaten path." But in her research for her doctoral thesis, Alice Rowe—management consultant, educator, active Methodist laywoman, married to a Methodist pastor—found that this same fear of societal and family disapproval still causes mothers in contemporary American culture to be active in subverting, or at least to be ambivalent to, their daughters' success. In her book, *Where Have All the Smart Women Gone?* Rowe interviewed thirty-four women identified as gifted in school and shared their experiences of living psychologically in a section called "A Country Called Double Bind." Brenda recalled,

"My mother told me that she had lied in my baby book, because people wouldn't believe some of the things that I did by myself. I had a vocabulary of over 100 words by the time I was one-year-old. She told me stuff like that all the time while I was growing up, but she didn't dare tell others." Women have long bent to the cultural message that it is unfeminine to be bright.[41]

"Some women are taught that it is immodest to recognize or celebrate their abilities, and some become so uncomfortable with the dissonance created in their families by their success that they deny or avoid achievement. Many hide their abilities, in order not to alienate parents, friends, and significant others."[42]

These [cultural] expectations divide a girl against herself, driving the essential girl to an inner realm where she remains hidden—even from herself.[43]

b. Acknowledge and examine faith-based messages which are ambivalent.

"What lies at the root of Christianity's deep ambivalences toward women? How did women become identified with sin?" asks Rosemary Radford Ruether, professor of theology at Garrett Theological Seminary, member of the graduate faculty at Northwestern University, and visiting professor at the Graduate Theological Union in Berkeley. Ruether has written extensively on these questions over the past thirty years. Her latest book, *Women and Redemption*, delineates the theological history of the controversy regarding the claim central to Christianity that "in Christ there is no more male and female, but what does this mean in the Christian tradition?"[44]

An especially useful resource for this examination is a resource packet created by the World Council of Churches for "The Ecumenical Decade—Churches in Solidarity with Women (1988–1998)." This packet has newspaper articles, activities, Bible studies, writings by Christian women, lay and clergy, litanies, worship services, and a guidebook. Chapter nine in the guidebook is titled, "The Mind-Body Split" by Rev. Joy Bussert, a minister in the Evangelical Lutheran Church in America. Compassionately presented in nonacademic language, Bussert brings clarity to this dilemma of how mixed messages about women have arisen from the Christian social, political, and institutional tradition, not from the Gospels, nor from the words of Jesus.

4. Acknowledge "necessary losses"—leaving childhood means leaving mother.

Pinkola Estés discusses the necessary loss of the overprotective mother as prerequisite for a child to develop inner wisdom. She discusses the death of the "too-good mother" as the mythic representation of this process in *Women Who Run with the Wolves*. (See ch. 3, "Nosing Out the Facts: The Retrieval of Intuition as Initiation"—"The Doll in Her Pocket: Vasalisa the Wise.")

a. Discuss the anticipatory grief of both child and mother about this separation and the contradictory emotions and behavior it will create.

From Mary Pipher:

Mothers are likely to have the most difficult time with adolescent girls. Daughters provoke arguments as a way of connecting and distancing at the same time. They want their mothers to recognize their smallest changes and are angry when their mothers don't validate their every move. They struggle with their love for their mothers and their desire to be different from their mothers.[45]

And from Judith Viorst:

This freedom to choose is the burden and the gift that we receive when we leave childhood, the burden and the gift that we take with us when we come to childhood's end.

It is said that adolescents, in this letting-go stage of life, experience "an intensity of grief unknown in previous phases. . . ." It is then that we come to grasp the meaning of transience. And so we feel nostalgia for a past, a Golden Age, that never will return to us again. And, as we sigh over sunsets and summer's end and love gone astray and poems about "the land of lost content," we mourn—without knowing we mourn—a far graver ending; the renunciation of childhood.[46]

b. Discuss how to transcend the grief of loss of identity and control from the perspective of the mother. Discuss how letting go of the "divine right of mother" role can assist a mother to enter the new relationship with her daughter as "first beloved wise woman" in a widening Circle of wise women. These women will be loving colleagues to mentor your daughter as she tries her wings, increasingly making her own decisions.

5. **Understand and encourage the importance of creative "languages" of expression and encourage the opportunity to express them and test against someone other than mother.**

For an inspiring summary of what is needed to support the development or the "saving" of a girl's growing awareness of self, see chapter 25, "A Fence at the Top of the Hill," in Pipher's *Reviving Ophelia:*

Many women tell stories about what saved them from the precipice. One girl was saved by her love of books, by long summer afternoons when she read for hours. Another was saved by thinking of faraway places and people. One was saved by her love of music, another by her love of horses. Girls can be saved by a good school, a good teacher, or a meaningful activity.

In the past, many young women were saved by conversations and support from a beloved neighbor, a kindhearted aunt, or a nearby grandmother.[47]

This is the essence of what we mean by the art of holding and releasing our daughters. We need to always be there . . .
to hold them, giving love and encouragement;
to hold them when they need refuge—when they are tired, confused, wounded;
to hold with them the vision for their life which they are beginning to articulate and share with us.

At the same time we must continually strive . . .
to release them to their new awareness of their inner guidance by the Holy Spirit within;
to release them to know they will be different from us; to coach them in discernment and then;
to release them to finding new mentors and guides.

For leave us they must, and we must prepare to release them to their best selves and to Christ's guidance.

DONNA HUMPHREYS

Music Resources

This music resource has been compiled by Claudia Walker, with assistance from Clif Windecker, in computer transcription of musical notation of some of the songs. We are immensely grateful for their invaluable contribution. Claudia, our retreat music facilitator, has selected these songs and sources for their specific application to elements in the retreat. She has generously given permission to include several of her own compositions.

A lover of the sung word, Claudia is a lifelong Methodist and has been the music resource person for the Daughters Arise! retreat since its inception. The scope of her musical work in the community spans a seasonal women's singing circle, private voice work and composition, and music therapy with private clients and elders at two convalescent centers on Whidbey Island. Her witness to the transformational power of song brings her to the bedside of the dying and into the community to collectively reclaim the gift of this endangered oral tradition.

ALPHABETICAL SONG LIST

"And When I Rise" (Call and Response)

"Blessed Be the Earth"

"Blessing for Life, A"

"Call to the Mother"

"Chain of Life"

"Chant for Establishing the Breath"

"Child of God"

"Come Spirit"

"Daughter Come Forth"

"Follow the Voice"

"Follow Your Heart"

"Gathering Chant"

"Hallowed Ground"

"I Am a Warrior"

"I Greet You"

"I Was There to Hear Your Borning Cry"

"Let Your Beauty Sing"

"Lifegiver" (A paraphrase of the Lord's Prayer)

"Make Me Your Instrument"

"Mend and Weave"

"Mother and God"

"My Roots Go Down"

"Sing of a Blessing"

"Sister's Spiral"

"Spirit of Gentleness"

"Take Off Your Shoes"

"The Tiptoe Song"

"The Well"

"They'll Know We Are God's Children by Our Love"

"We Take a Little Friendship"

"What You Hold"

"Wild Holy Power"

"With a Love from Deep Within"

"Woman, Let Your Voice Be Heard"

"You Are a Rock"

"You Are Not Alone"

This list does not constitute permission to use except as follows: Songs may be photocopied for a one-time use during retreats on condition that the printed copies contain the name of the author or composer of the song along with the appropriate copyright notice. Copies must be recalled after use. All rights reserved.

To use a song for purposes other than a one-time retreat use, such as in a hymnal, a church bulletin, a worship service, or at a public event, permission must be obtained from each individual copyright holder.

SUGGESTED SONGS AND SOURCES

See the Annotated Bibliography for information about songbooks for songs from other sources than *Daughters Arise!*
(*Songs included in the Journey Pouch)

GREETING/OPENING SONGS

"Behold a Sacred Voice"	Marlena Fontenay, "Behold a Sacred Voice," *Circle of Song*, 14.
*"Hallowed Ground"	Gaielle Fleming. See page 214.
*"I Greet You"	Claudia Walker. See page 215.
*"Take Off Your Shoes"	Jim Manley. See page 228.
*"With a Love from Deep Within"	Claudia Walker. See page 233.

THEME SONGS

*"Call to the Mother"	Gaielle Fleming. See page 206.
*"Chain of Life" (Teacher)	Susan Osborn. See page 208.
*"I Am a Warrior" (Warrior/Leader)	Cynthia Crossen. See page 215.
"Keep Breathing" (Warrior/Leader)	Nina Wise, *Circle of Song*, 125.
*"Make Me Your Instrument"	Tom Walker. See page 219.
*"Mother and God"	Miriam Therese Winter. See page 222.
*"My Roots Go Down" (Healer)	Sarah Pirtle. See page 223.
"Reunion"	Susan Osborn, *ReUnion*, compact disc (Orcas, Wash.: Golden Throat Recordings, 1997). Copyright ©1997 SUSANSONGS ASCAP. See words on page 169.
*"They'll Know We Are God's Children by Our Love	Words: Claudia Walker. See page 231.
"Voices of the Future"	Lucienne de Naie, *Songs for Earthlings*, 364.
*"Woman, Let Your Voice Be Heard" (Visionary)	Cynthia Crossen. See page 234.
*"You Are a Rock"	Claudia Walker. See page 235.

SONGS TO GATHER OR END A SESSION

*"A Blessing for Life"	Bill Millford. See page 205.
*"Come Spirit"	Miriam Therese Winter. See page 210.

*"Let Your Beauty Sing"   Gaielle Fleming. See page 217.
*"Lifegiver" (A paraphrase   Words: Laurie Y. J. Aleona. See page 218.
    of the Lord's Prayer)

*"Mend and Weave"   Composer unknown. See page 221.
"O Grandmother, I Feel   Composer unknown. *Circle of Song*, 95.
    You Lift Me Up"

*"Sing of a Blessing"   Miriam Therese Winter. See page 224.
*"What You Hold"   Cathy Tisel Nelson. See page 233.

CAMPFIRE SONGS (FAMILIAR, OLD)

Begin with old-time songs familiar to your girls and women. A few we like
are: "Rocka My Soul," "Peace Like a River," "We Are Climbing Jacob's
Ladder," "Turn Around," "Make New Friends," "Gave My Love a
Cherry," "Bye'n Bye," "Kumbaya," "Vesper Hymn (jubilate) Mockingbird
Lullabye," and "All Through the Night."

*"And When I Rise"   Composer unknown. See page 205.
*"Child of God"   Tom Walker. See page 209.
*"Gathering Chant"   Phil Porter. See page 213.
"Keep Breathing"   Nina Wise, *Circle of Song*, 125.
*"Mother and God"   Miriam Therese Winter. See page 222.
*"They'll Know We Are God's   Words: Claudia Walker. See page 231.
    Children By Our Love"

*"We Take a Little Friendship"   Chet Earls. See page 232.
*"Wild Holy Power"   Elaine Kirkland. See page 233.
*"You Are a Rock"   Claudia Walker. See page 235.

MOVEMENT/ACTIVITY

"Dance for the Nations"   John Krumm, *Share the Music*, 150.
*"Mend and Weave"   Composer unknown. See page 221.
"O Grandmother, I Feel   Composer unknown, *Circle of Song*, 95.
    You Lift Me Up"

JOURNEY WALK

*"Come Spirit"   Miriam Therese Winter. See page 210.
*"Daughter Come Forth"   Joni Pohlig and Sara Rivers. See page 211.
*"Follow Your Heart"   Claudia Walker. See page 213.
*"Mother and God"   Miriam Therese Winter. See page 222.
*"Sister's Spiral"   Colleen Fulmer. See page 225.
*"The Tiptoe Song"   Composer unknown. See page 229.
*"You Are Not Alone"   Claudia Walker. See page 236.

TABLE GRACES

*"Blessed Be the Earth"	Jess Shoup Forest. See page 205.
"Dirt Made My Lunch"	Steve Van Zandt, *Songs for Earthlings*, 120.
"Johnny Appleseed"	American folksong.
*"Lifegiver" (paraphrase of the Lord's Prayer)	Words: Laurie Y. J. Aleona. See page 218.
"This Glorious Food"	Patricia McKernon, *Songs for Earthlings*, 120.

WORSHIP

*"Child of God"	Tom Walker. See page 209.
"Envia Tu Espiritu"	Bob Hurd, *Gather*, 2nd ed. (Chicago: GIA Publications, 1994), 324. Copyright © 1988 OCP Publications.
"Halle, Halle, Halle"	Caribbean traditional; origin unknown, arr. Mark Sedio. *With One Voice*, ed. Dick Jensen (Minneapolis: Augsburg Fortress Press, 1995). Copyright © 1995 Augsburg Fortress Press.
"Hymn of Promise"	Natalie Sleeth, *The United Methodist Hymnal*, 707.
*"I Was There to Hear Your Borning Cry"	John Ylvisaker. See page 216.
"Jesu Jesu"	Tom Colvin, *The United Methodist Hymnal*, 432. Copyright © 1989 United Methodist Publishing House.
"Lord You Have Come to the Lakeshore"	Cesareo Gabarain, *The United Methodist Hymnal*, 344. Copyright © 1989 United Methodist Publishing House.
*"Make Me Your Instrument"	Tom Walker. See page 219.
"On Eagle's Wings"	Michael Joncas, *Gather*, 2nd. ed. (Chicago: GIA Publications, 1994), 433. Copyright © 1979 New Dawn Music.
"Servant Song"	Richard Gillard, *Songs for a Gospel People*, 133.
"Shepherd Me O God"	Marty Haugen, *Gather*, 2nd. ed. (Chicago: GIA Publications, 1994), 29. Copyright © 1994 G.I.A. Publications.
*"Spirit of Gentleness"	Jim Manley. See page 226.
*"Take Off Your Shoes"	Jim Manley. See page 228.
"We Are God's Work of Art"	Marty Haugen, *Gather*, 2nd. ed. (Chicago: GIA Publications, 1994), 580. Copyright © 1994 G.I.A. Publications.

THE GIRLS' CEREMONY

*"Daughter Come Forth"	Joni Pohlig and Sara Rivers. See page 211.
*"Follow the Voice"	Sarah Pirtle. See page 212.
*"Follow Your Heart"	Claudia Walker. See page 213.
*"The Well"	Gaielle Fleming. See page 230.
*"Woman, Let Your Voice Be Heard"	Cynthia Crossen. See page 234.
*"You Are Not Alone"	Claudia Walker. See page 236.

And When I Rise: Call and Response

And when I rise   let me rise up   up   like a
And when I fall   let me fall up   down   like a

bird   with - out   re - gret   joy - ful - ly.
stone   with - out   re - gret   joy - ful - ly.

Chad Meyers, transcribed from memory by Claudia Walker of a song taught to her by Meyers at a Bortimeus Community Retreat on Whidby Island in 1996. Meyers said the words were inspired by a poem by Wendall Berry, author and theologian.

Blessed Be the Earth

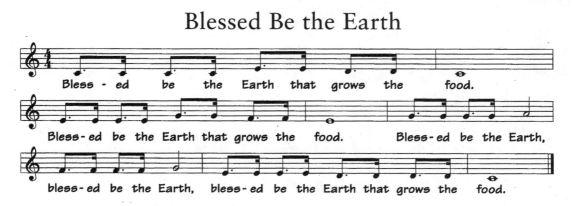

Bless - ed be the Earth that grows the food.

Bless-ed be the Earth that grows the food. Bless-ed be the Earth,

bless-ed be the Earth, bless-ed be the Earth that grows the food.

"Blessed be the hands that fixed the food." "Blessed be the rain that waters the crops," and so on.

Jess Shoup Forest, *Songs for Earthlings*, ed. Julie Forest Middleton (Philadelphia: Emerald Earth Publishing, 1998), 120. Copyright © 1992 Jess Shoup Forest. Used by permission of Emerald Earth Publishing.

A Blessing for Life

Bless us God_____ Bless these friends._____ Bless these

gifts you give that do not end._____ Make us

strong_____ and help us to grow to_ know the

peace of your Love_____ that's our home._____

Words and music attributed to Bill Millford, taught to Claudia Walker by Linnea Good at a women's retreat at Narmatata Center, British Columbia, in 1985. Claudia transcribed the words and music from memory.

Call to the Mother

Verse 1: Some-times I won-der___ why and whe-ther I've wait-ed much too long and when I wake-up___ from this dream I'll no long - er have a song.

Chorus: Mo-ther come to me Mo-ther hold___ me Mo-ther rock me in your arms Mo-ther come to me, Mo-ther hold___ me Mo-ther rock me in your arms

Verse 2: Some-times I won-der___ How I ev - er___ thought I could win this game, and when I'm sure I can go no fur - ther, my child calls out my name (Chorus)

Gaielle Fleming, *Held Together* (Langley, Wash.: personal cassette recording, 1995). Copyright © 1995 Gaielle Fleming; P.O. Box 792; Langley, Washington 98260. Used by permission.

Chain of Life

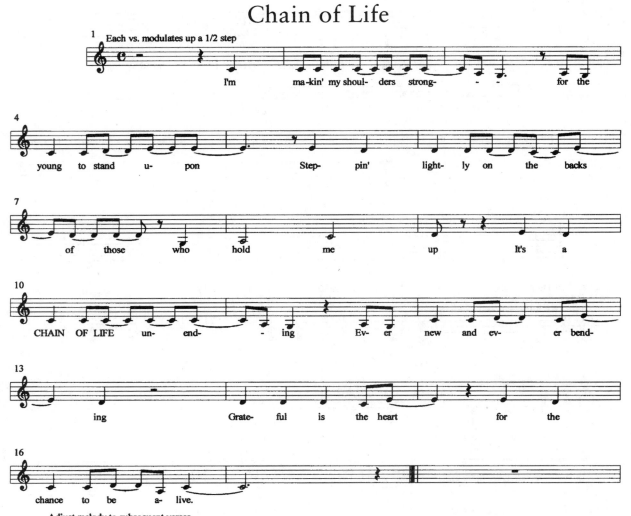

Each vs. modulates up a 1/2 step

I'm ma-kin' my shoul- ders strong- - - for the young to stand u- pon Step- pin' light- ly on the backs of those who hold me up It's a CHAIN OF LIFE un- end- - ing Ev- er new and ev- er bend- ing Grate- ful is the heart for the chance to be a- live.

Adjust melody to subsequent verses

Chant for Establishing the Breath

Sing several times before adding descant.

Voice

Ah la hoo, ee la la hoo, ah la hoo, ee la la hoo.

Descant

Oh_____ my love and my life.

Maureen Rowley taught this American Indian chant that she learned growing up in Minnesota to Claudia Walker, who transcribed words and music for the retreats.

Child of God

Tom Walker, *Pieces of Our Lives*, compact disc and songbook, arr. Jim Strathdee, ed. Jim Strathdee and Jean Strathdee (Carmichael, Calif.: Caliche Records, 1998). Words and music copyright © 1988 Front Room Music (360.579.2279). Chorus copyright © 1998 Tom Walker. Used by permission.

Come Spirit

♩ = 72

Sing, my soul, a Spir - it song,
Dance, my heart, at your re - birth,
When con - strained by thoughts or things,

call - ing all to sing a - long. Fill the world with
part - ner to the dance of earth. Thirst - ing spir - it,
hear the word the Spir - it brings: life is larg - er

joy - ful sounds: God is here and grace a - bounds.
drink your fill: love goes danc - ing where it will.
than it seems, hope is har - bin - ger of dreams.

Refrain

Come, Spir - it, come and be a new re - al - i - ty.___

___ Your touch is guar - an - tee of love a - live in me.

Daughter Come Forth

(Name)___ come forth. Let your life pour out of the rain-bow of Love at your core. Let your song grow, Let it ga-ther and burst out of your be-ing in pas-ions re-birth.

Words and music by Joni Pohlig and Sara Rivers. Copyright © 1986 Sara Rivers; Meeting Ground. Used by permission.

Follow the Voice

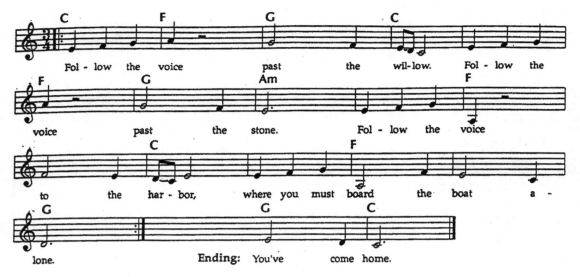

Fol - low the voice past the wil - low. Fol - low the
voice past the stone. Fol - low the voice
to the har - bor, where you must board the boat a -
lone. **Ending:** You've come home.

2
But if you set your hand to tiller
And if you steer her by the stars
And if you 'low the wind to fill her
That boat will take you where we are

3
There is a horse at the shoreline□
There is a horse you may ride.
Narrow the path through the canyon,
No turning back, no need to hide.

4
And if you ride her firm and gentle
And if you lean close to her mane
And if you 'low the wind of midnight
The wind will call you by your name.

5
Until you rise with the eagle
Until you rise to her nest
Where the soft wings will enfold you
Of all the ones who love you best.

6
And we will rock you long and steady
Until you feel you're not alone
And you will feel our hearts around you
And you will know that you've come home.
You've come home.

Sarah Pirtle, *Magical Earth,* recording (Albany, N.Y.: A Gentle Wind, 1993). Words and music copyright © 1993 Sarah Pirtle, Discovery Center Music; BMI. Used by permission.

Follow Your Heart

Fol - low Your Heart, fol - low un - seen,
What do you want? What do you know?
Come take your place, hon - or and blend

In - to the for - est of your dreams, And
What is the mis - sing gift of you can show? The
all of the my - ster - y Spi - rit can send through

there you'll find the sus - te - nance to grow.
world is long - ing to be whole in you.
all you do all you be - come for Life!

Words and music by Claudia Walker. Copyright
© 1992 Claudia Walker. Used by permission.

Gathering Chant

Ga - thered here in the mys - tery of this hour, ga - thered here in

one strong bo - dy, Ga - thered here in the strug - gle and the pow - er,

Spir - it draw near.

Words and music by Phil Porter, *The New Century Hymnal* (Cleveland: The Pilgrim
Press, 1995), 335. Copyright © 1990 Phil Porter. Used by permission.

Hallowed Ground

Verse 1
Truth is what we came for. Love is what we found.

Verse 2: Our hearts were o-pened u-pon this hal-lowed ground.

Love is what we looked at. Tears are what we found.

Verse 3: The ground was bro-ken. There was sing-ing all a-round.

Tears are what we stayed with. Truth is what we found.

Our bod-ies o-pened and be-came this hal-lowed ground.

I Am a Warrior

There are times in this world when we need to call on our warrior spirit
and to remind ourselves that we are always "standing in her light."

I Greet You

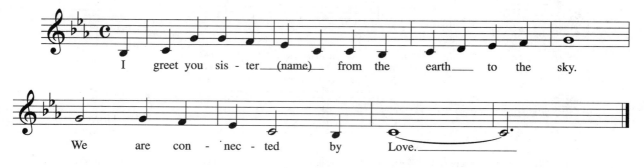

I Was There to Hear Your Borning Cry

John Ylvisaker. Alternate title: "Waterlife." Copyright © 1985 John C. Ylvisaker. Used by permission.

Let Your Beauty Sing

Gaielle Fleming, *Held Together*, (Langley, Wash.: personal cassette recording, 1995). Copyright
© 1995 Gaielle Fleming; P.O. Box 792; Langley, Washington 98260. Used by permission.

Life Giver, Lover of us all,
Upon your holy name we call;
Your new day come, Your will be done,
On earth as in all realms beyond.

We pray this day for bread to live;
Forgive our sins as we forgive;
And give us strength in time of test;
Grant us release from evil's death.

For all the cosmos
is your own,
Your power of love which
we have known,
The splendor, radiant,
without end.

To God be praise! Amen. Amen.

©1988 Laurie Y.J. Aleona
Marita McDonough,
scribe
1990

Words by Laurie Y. J. Aleona. Tune: any 88.88-meter tune. We use the "Tallis Canon." Used by permission.

Make Me Your Instrument

(continued)

Make Me Your Instrument (continued)

o - pen my eyes, _____ for _____ it is in giv - ing that_____ _____ we re - ceive; use me Lord _____ till I take my _____ leave, _____ make me your ins - tru - ment. Where there is sad - ness, _____ let me bring joy, where there's des - pair, _____ Lord, let me be there _____ use me in your em - ploy, _____ make me your ins - tru - ment, _____ make me your tool, _____ for, it is in dy - ing, _____ that we are born _____ to you. _____

Words and music by Tom Walker. Copyright © 1980 Tom Walker. Used by permission.

Mend and Weave

Mend and weave, mend and weave. Ga - ther the gol - den frag - ments of our sa - cred lives, oh sis - ters, mend and weave, mend and weave, sa - cred sis - ters, mend and weave.

Transcribed from memory by Claudia Walker from a song taught to her by Amy Windecker,
who does not know the source.

Mother and God

Moth - er and God, to You we sing:
wide - is Your womb, warm is Your wing.
In You we live, move, and are fed,
sweet, flow - ing milk, life - giv - ing bread.
Moth - er and God, to You we bring
all bro - ken hearts, all bro - ken wings.

My Roots Go Down: Zipper Song

Sarah Pirtle, *Song for Earthlings*, ed. Julie Forest Middleton (Philadelphia: Emerald Earth Publishing, 1998). Words and music copyright © 1989 Sarah Pirtle, Discovery Center Music; BMI. Used by permission of Sarah Pirtle and Emerald Earth Publishing.

Sing of a Blessing

Sing unaccompanied

Leader ... All

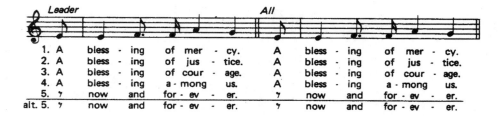

1. Sing, we sing of a bless - ing. Sing, we sing of a bless - ing.
2. Pray now, pray for a bless - ing. Pray now, pray for a bless - ing.
3. Share now, share in a bless - ing. Share now, share in a bless - ing.
*4. Live, live, live as a bless - ing. Live, live, live as a bless - ing.
**5. Rise up, rise for a bless - ing. Rise up, rise for a bless - ing.
alt. 5. Send forth, send forth a bless - ing. Send forth, send forth a bless - ing.

1. Sing, we sing of a bless - ing. Sing, we sing of a bless - ing.
2. Pray now, pray for a bless - ing. Pray now, pray for a bless - ing.
3. Share now, share in a bless - ing. Share now, share in a bless - ing.
4. Live, live, live as a bless - ing. Live, live, live as a bless - ing.
5. Rise up, rise for a bless - ing. Rise up, rise for a bless - ing.
alt. 5. Send forth, send forth a bless - ing. Send forth, send forth a bless - ing.

Leader ... All

1. A bless - ing of love. A bless - ing of love.
2. A bless - ing of joy. A bless - ing of joy.
3. A bless - ing of hope. A bless - ing of hope.
4. A bless - ing with - in. A bless - ing with - in.
5. A bless - ing be yours A bless - ing be yours
alt. 5. A bless - ing to all A bless - ing to all

Leader ... All

1. A bless - ing of mer - cy. A bless - ing of mer - cy.
2. A bless - ing of jus - tice. A bless - ing of jus - tice.
3. A bless - ing of cour - age. A bless - ing of cour - age.
4. A bless - ing a - mong us. A bless - ing a - mong us.
5. now and for - ev - er. now and for - ev - er.
alt. 5. now and for - ev - er. now and for - ev - er.

Leader ... All ... Leader

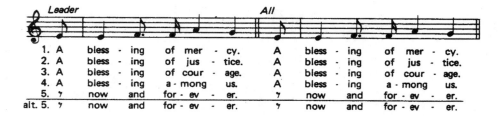

1.-5. Love will in - crease Love will in - crease a bless - ing of peace.
alt. 5. Love will re - lease Love will re - lease a bless - ing of peace.

All ... Leader ... All

1.-5. a bless - ing of peace. Love will in - crease Love will in - crease
alt. 5. a bless - ing of peace. Love will re - lease Love will re - lease

Leader ... All

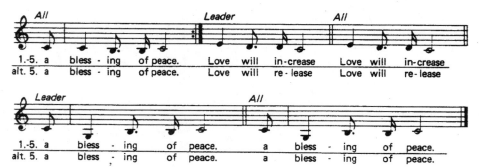

1.-5. a bless - ing of peace. a bless - ing of peace.
alt. 5. a bless - ing of peace. a bless - ing of peace.

* Transpose Verse 4 up one-half tone (D flat Major)
** Transpose Verse 5 up an additional half tone (D Major)

Sister's Spiral

Words and music by Colleen Fulmer. Copyright © 1993 Colleen Fulmer; Heartbeats; 20015
Detroit Rd; Cleveland, Ohio 44116; 800-808-1991. Used by permission.

Spirit of Gentleness

Spir- it, Spir- it of gen-tle-ness, blow thro' the wil-der-ness
call-ing and free, Spir- it, Spir-it of rest-less-ness,
stir me from plac-id-ness, Wind, Wind on the sea.

1. You moved on the wa- ters, you called to the deep,
2. You swept thro' the des- ert, you stung with the sand,
3. You sang in a sta- ble, you cried from a hill,

then you coaxed up the moun- tains from the val- leys of sleep;
and you goad- ed your peo- ple with a law and a land;
then you whis-pered in si- lence when the whole world was still;

and o- ver the ae- ons you called to each
and when they were blind- ed with their i- dols and
and down in the ci- ty you called once a-

thing: - - wake from your slum- bers
lies, then you spoke thro' your proph- ets
gain, when you blew thro' your peo- ple

and rise on your wings.
to o- pen their eyes.
on the rush of the wind.

4. You call from tomorrow, you break ancient schemes,
from the bondage of sorrow the captives dream dreams;
our women see visions, our men clear their eyes,
with bold new decisions your people arise.

James K. Manley, *Songs for a Gospel People* (Winfield, B.C.: WoodLake Books, 1987), 108.
Words and music copyright © 1978 James K. Manley; 690 Persian Dr. #67; Sunnyvale, California 94089. Used by permission.

Take Off Your Shoes

Take, take off your shoes, you're standing on holy ground. Take, take off your shoes, you're standing on holy ground.

The Earth is the Lord's and the fullness thereof, from the waters beneath to the heavens above. So take, take, take off your shoes, you're standing on my holy ground, you're standing on my holy ground.

1. On the eighth day of creation, well, the Lord looked around. At the power plants and freeways and the trash on the ground, plantations growing rubber where the grain should be high; you
2. You've heated up my rivers with your plants and your mills; and you're killing off my oceans with your wastes and your spills. You're fishing like there'll always be an endless supply, and

Jim Manley, *Everflowing Streams*, ed. Ruth Duck and Michael G. Bausch (New York: The Pilgrim Press, 1981). Words and music copyright © 1977 James K. Manley as New Wine Productions (ASCAP). Used by permission.

The Tiptoe Song

Composer unknown. Maureen Rowley learned this childhood song growing up in Minnesota.
She taught it to Claudia Walker who transcribed the words and music from memory.
Gaielle Fleming, "Call to the Mother," *Held Together*, trans. Claudia Walker (Langley, Wash.:

The Well

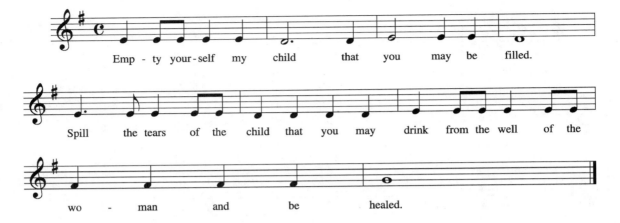

Emp - ty your-self my child that you may be filled.

Spill the tears of the child that you may drink from the well of the

wo - man and be healed.

personal cassette recording, 1995). Words and music copyright © 1998 Gaielle Fleming; P.O. Box 792; Langley, Washington 98260. Used by permission.

Gaielle says:

I was on a group-backpacking trip at Shi Shi Beach (on the Olympic Peninsula, Washington) with a twelve-year-old friend of mine. Grief over the loss of childhood and uncertainty about her emerging identity had settled in a serious respiratory illness. While meditating in a cave at the beach, I received this little song, a gift to her from White Buffalo Woman.

They'll Know We Are God's Children
by Our Love

We are one in the Circle; we are one in the Divine.
We are one in the Circle; we are one in the Divine.
And we pray dear God, that we will live in peace as wholly Thine.
And they'll know we're God's children by our love, by our love.
Yes, they'll know we're God's children by our love.

We will stand with each other; we will stand hand in hand.
We will listen to each other, being present on the land.
We will speak for justice, not afraid to take a stand.
And they'll know we are **warriors** by our action, presence, power.
Yes, they'll know we are warriors by our love.

We will walk with each other; we will walk side by side.
We will dream into the future for the sake of all our lives.
Without judging one another, in the truth we will abide.
And they'll know we're **visionaries** as we speak and do not blame.
Yes, they'll know we're visionaries by our love.

We will rest our weary bodies, in the arms of Mother Earth.
We will listen to Her heartbeat, and the feel of our own worth.
Singing to each gen-er-a—tion, the tales of death and birth.
And they'll know we are **healers** as we heed the heart's request.
Yes they'll know we are healers by our love.

We will call in the elders, and the love they have shown.
To the center of our Circle, where the sacred is known.
We will open to life's outcomes, letting love for fear atone.
And they'll know we are **teachers** by our laughter and our trust.
Yes they'll know we are teachers by our love.

Words by Claudia Walker, 1997; rev. Claudia Walker and Sally Windecker. Copyright ©
2000 Claudia Walker and Sally Windecker. Tune: Peter Scholtes, "They'll Know We Are
Christians by Our Love." Used by permission.

We Take a Little Friendship

Transcription by Chet Earls. Copyright © 1971, 1972 Chet Earls; 2211 NW Mulkey St.; Corvallis, Oregon 97330. Used by permission.

What You Hold

Text based on words of St. Clare trans.
by Regis Armstrong, OFM Cap.

Cathy Tisel Nelson

What you hold, may you al-ways hold. What you do, may you al-ways do and nev - er a-ban-don, nev-er a ban-don.

Wild Holy Power

Part 1

Part 2

Some-thing no-thing may-be ev-ery-thing wild ho-ly power

leap - ing laugh-ing dan - cing chan - cing fly a - way!

With a Love from Deep Within

With a love from deep with - in I greet you with my heart and hand.

Woman, Let Your Voice Be Heard

2. Woman let your feelings be cried,
For the world needs to hear
Your long-silenced heart.

We need your voice, we need your vision,
We need your passion rising into flame,
We need your truth, we need your caring,
We need your courage, lead the way.

We need your hope, we need your seeking,
We need your presence walking by our side,
We need your love, we need your laughter,
We need your wisdom, be our guide, be our guide.

3. Woman, let your hope shine forth,
For the world needs your wisdom
And love calls through you.

This song was a gift for a friend undergoing a painful divorce. It is very much inspired by Riane Eisler's *The Chalice and the Blade*, which reminds us that it takes women's voices and wisdom, in balance to men's, to heal our culture and the Earth.

Cynthia R. Crossen, *Songs for Earthlings*, ed. Julie Forest Middleton (Philadelphia: Emerald Earth Publishing, 1998), 97. Words and music copyright © 1989 Cynthia R. Crossen. Used by permission of Emerald Earth Publishing and Cynthia R. Crossen.

You Are a Rock

Chant-like

You are a rock and an an-chor for your-self and those you love.

— Know you are ves-sel smooth and broad from which life giv-ing wa-ters flow.

— You are a flame whose burn-ing pas-sion cleans-es soul and sets it free

— to soar and shim-mer as ma-jes-tic bird in flight.

— Ev-er-more, ev-er-more, ev-er-more, ev-er-more,

— to soar and shim-mer as ma-jes-tic bird in flight.

Words and music by Claudia Walker. Copyright © 1992 Claudia Walker. Used by permission.

You Are Not Alone

You are not a-lone You are not a-lone
I am not a-lone, I am not a-lone,
I am not a-fraid, I am not a-fraid,

We are here We are here you are not a-lone. You are not a-
You are here, You are here, I am not a-lone. I am not a-
You are here, You are here, I am not a-fraid. I am not a-

lone, You are not a-lone, We are here, We are here, and
lone, I am not a-lone, You are here, You are here, and
fraid, I am not a-fraid, You are here, You are here, and

you are not a-lone.
I am not a-lone.
I am not a-fraid.

Words and music by Claudia Walker. Copyright © 1999 Claudia Walker. Used by permission.

Notes

PREFACE

1. This, and the following quotations regarding COSROW, are taken from a pamphlet produced by the General Commission of the Status and Role of Women.

2. From a retreat evaluation by Maggie Shelton and Stephanie Weller.

3. Mary Pipher, *Reviving Ophelia: Saving the Selves of Adolescent Girls* (New York: Ballantine, 1995), 12.

4. Ibid., 19.

5. Rosemary Radford Ruether, *Women and Redemption: A Theological History* (Minneapolis, Minn.: Fortress Press, 1998), 1.

6. Pipher, *Reviving Ophelia*, 26.

USING THIS GUIDEBOOK

1. Harriet Kofalk, "Priorities," *Life Prayers from around the World: 365 Prayers, Blessings, and Affirmations to Celebrate the Human Journey*, ed. Elizabeth Roberts and Elias Amidon (San Francisco: HarperSanFrancisco, 1996), 16.

SECTION ONE

1. Bobby Freeman, *First Catch Your Peacock: Her Classic Guide to Welsh Food* (Talybant, Ceredigian: Y Lolfa, 1996), inside front cover.

2. George A. Buttrick, *The Parables of Jesus* (Grand Rapids, Mich.: Baker Book House, 1991), 8.

3. Angeles Arrien at a Women of Unity lecture, Seattle, Wash., February 1998.

4. Christina Baldwin, *Calling the Circle: The First and Future Culture* (New York: Bantam, 1998), 38.

5. Ibid., 26.

6. Ibid., 16–17.

7. Ibid., 65.

8. Ibid., 65–66.

9. Clarissa Pinkola Estés, ed., "The Ugly Duckling," *Women Who Run with the Wolves: Myths and Stories of the Wild Woman Archetype* (New York: Ballantine Books, 1992), 167–71.

10. Norma Kitson, ed., *Anthology/ Collected and Presented by Zimbabwe Women Writers*, no. 1 (Harare, Zimbabwe: The Writers, 1994).

11. Miriam Therese Winter, "Word Made Flesh," *WomanPrayer, WomanSong: Resources for Ritual* (New York: Crossroad, 1993), 76. Used by permission.

12. Richard Nelson, *The Island Within*, audio selections (Louisville, Co.: The Audio Press, 1991), transcribed from audio.

13. Thomas Acquinas (1225–1274), as qtd. in *Earth Letter* (Sept. 1998).

14. Martin Luther, as qtd. in *Living Quotations for Christians*, comp. and ed. Sherwood Eliot Wirt and Kersten Beckstrom (New York: Harper and Row, 1974), 95.

15. Julian of Norwich, as in *A Little Book of Women Mystics*, ed. Carol Lee Flinders (San Francisco: HarperSanFrancisco, 1995), citing *A Book of Showings to the Anchoress Julian of Norwich*, ed. Edmund Colledge and James Walsh (New York: Paulist Press, 1978), 183.

16. Angeles Arrien, *The Four-fold Way: Walking the Paths of the Warrior, Teacher, Healer, and Visionary* (San Francisco: HarperSanFrancisco, 1993). All subsequent ideas referred to in this book as having been taken from this text are used by the permission and encouragement of Angeles Arrien.

17. Ibid., 7.

18. Winter, "Mother and God," *WomanPrayer, WomanSong*, 207. Used by permission.

19. Tom Walker, "Child of God," *Pieces of Our Lives*, songbook and compact disc, arr. Jim Strathdee, ed. Jim Strathdee and Jean Strathdee (Carmichael, Calif.: Caliche Records, 1998). Used by permission.

20. Maureen Rowley taught this song to Claudia Walker who transcribed the words and music from memory.

21. Gaielle Fleming, "Call to the Mother," *Held Together* (Langley, Wash.: personal cassette recording, 1995). Used by permission.

22. Winter, "Mother and God," 207.

23. From an original composition by Claudia Walker, "You Are a Rock," in Donna Humphreys, Gloria Koll, and Sally Windecker, *The Daughters' Journey: A Celebration of Passage to Womanhood Rooted in the Love of Christ* (Clinton, Wash.: COSROW, 2000), 264. Composed 1992. Used by permission.

24. Fleming, "Let Your Beauty Sing," *Held Together*. Used by permission.

25. Marlena Fontenay, "Behold a Sacred Voice," *Circle of Song: Songs, Chants, and Dances for Ritual and Celebration*, comp. Kate Marks (Lenox, Mass: Full Circle Press, 1993), 14.

26. Heather Murray Elkins, *Worshiping Women: Reforming God's People for Praise* (Nashville, Tenn.: Abingdon, 1994), 15.

27. Estés, "Vasalisa the Wise," *Women Who Run with the Wolves*, 75–80.

28. Estés, "Sealskins, Soulskins," ibid., 258–62.

29. Estés, "Crescent Moon Bear," ibid., 347–50.

30. Estés, "The Ugly Duckling," ibid., 167–71.

31. C. S. Lewis, ed., *George MacDonald, an Anthology* (New York: MacMillan, 1978), 16–17.

32. As seen on a small poster in Pastor Rand O'Donnell's office, Simpson United Methodist Church, Pullman Washington.

33. From a printed sermon by Rev. David Vergin, preached in Langley, Washington, August 8, 1999.

34. Estés, *Women Who Run with the Wolves*, 85.

35. Ibid., 84–85.

36. The Stephens Ministries, "Confidentiality," folder II-H; and "Ministering to Suicidal Persons and Families and Friends," folder II-R, *The Stephens Ministries Manual* (St. Louis, Mo.: Stephens Ministries, 1993).

SECTION TWO

1. Hildegard of Bingen, "Antiphon for the Holy Spirit," *Symphonia*, trans. Barbara Newman (Ithaca, N.Y.: Cornell University Press, 1988). Qtd. in *A Little Book of Women Mystics*, 17.

2. African American spiritual, "My Lord, What a Morning." *With One Voice: A Lutheran Resource for Worship*, ed. Dick Jensen (Minneapolis, Minn.: Augsburg Fortress, 1995), 627.

3. Miriam Therese Winter, "Circle of Love—First Spiral," *WomanPrayer, WomanSong : Resources for Ritual.* Used by permission.

4. South African traditional melody, "Hallelujah, We Sing Your Praises," *With One Voice*, 722.

5. Taizé, "Eat this Bread," adapt. Robert J. Batastini, *With One Voice*, 709.

6. Winter, "Prayer," *WomanWord: A Feminist Lectionary and Psalter: Women of the New Testament* (New York: Crossroad, 1995), 68. Used by permission.

7. Winter, "An Anointing Psalm," ibid., 68.

8. Jean Shinoda Bolen, *Crossing to Avalon: A Woman's Midlife Pilgrimage* (San Francisco: HarperSanFrancisco, 1994), 150.

9. Mary Pipher, *Reviving Ophelia : Saving the Selves of Adolescent Girls*, 12, 27, and back cover.

10. Bolen, *Crossing to Avalon*, 172.

11. Peter Rutter, *Sex in the Forbidden Zone: When Men in Power—Therapists, Doctors, Clergy, Teachers, and Others—Betray Women's Trust* (New York: Fawcett Crest, 1991), 243.

12. Judith Duerk, "Know Your Self . . . Yourself," *I Sit Listening to the Wind* (San Diego, Calif.: LuraMedia, 1993), 102–03.

13. Pipher, *Reviving Ophelia*, 254–58.

14. Duerk, *Circle of Stones: Women's Journey to Herself* (Philadelphia, Innisfree Press, 1999), 14; 39.

15. Renita J. Weem, *Just a Sister Away: A Womanist Vision of Women's Relationships in the Bible* (San Diego, Calif.: LuraMedia, 1988), 88.

16. Susan Osborn, "Reunion," *ReUnion*, compact disc (Orcas, Wash.: Golden Throat Recording, 1997). Used by permission.

17. Arrien, *The Four-fold Way*, throughout.

18. Ralph Metzner, "Four Elements Medicine Wheel Prayer: Turtle Island West Coast," *Earth Prayers*, ed. Eliza-beth Roberts and Elias Amidon (San Francisco: HarperSanFrancisco, 1991), 134–36. This original and the following adaptation are used by permission.

19. Nigerian drummer Babarunde Olatunji, as qtd. in Arrien, *The Four-fold Way*, 57.

20. As qtd. in Arrien, *The Four-fold Way*, 117.

21. Walt Whitman, "Song of the Open Road," *Leaves of Grass*, deathbed ed. (New York: Modern Library, 1993), 184.

22. Chief Sitting Bull, *The Indigenous Voice*, vol. 1, ed. Roger Moody (London: Zed Press, 1988), as qtd. in Arrien, *The Four-fold Way*, 17.

23. Winter, *WomanWord*, 67.

24. Stephen Levine, *A Year to Live: How to Live This Year as if It Were Your Last* (New York: Bell Tower, 1997), 9.

25. Arrien, *The Four-fold Way*, 61.

26. Ibid.

27. Ibid., 58.

28. Adapted from ch. 2 of *The Four-fold Way*.

29. Marianne Williamson, *A Return to Love: Reflections on the Principles of a Course in Miracles* (New York: Harper Collins, 1992), 165.

30. 19. John L. Bell, "Be Still and Know that I Am God," *Gather*, 2nd ed. (Chicago: GIA Publications, 1994), 438.

31. Arrien, *The Four-fold Way*, 114.

32. Bell, "Be Still and Know that I Am God."

33. Clarissa Pinkola Estés, "Vasalisa the Wise," *Women Who Run with the Wolves : Myths and Stories of the Wild Woman Archetype*, 75–80.

34. Estés, *Women Who Run with the Wolves*, 80–114.

35. The primary resource for this presentation is Christiane Northrup, *Women's Bodies, Women's Wisdom: Creating Physical and Emotional Health and Healing* (New York: Bantam Books, 1994), 41–49; 50–60; 101–63.

36. Mihaly Csikszentmihalyi, Keynote Address at the Twelfth World Conference of the World Council for Gifted and Talented Children, July 29–August 2, 1997, Seattle, Wash.

37. Estés, *Women Who Run with the Wolves*, ch. 6 and 166–98.

38. Ibid., 166.

39. Ibid., 176.

40. Ibid., 177.

41. Alice Ann Rowe, *Where Have All the Smart Women Gone?* ed. Margaret D. Smith (Seattle, Wash.: HaraPub, 1996), 25.

42. Kathleen Noble, qtd. ibid., 27.

43. Rowe, *Where Have All the Smart Women Gone?*, 19.

44. Rosemary Radford Ruether, *Women and Redemption: A Theological History*, 1.

45. Pipher, *Reviving Ophelia*, 286.

46. Judith Viorst, *Necessary Losses* (New York: Simon & Schuster, 1986) 142–58.

47. Pipher, *Reviving Ophelia*, 284.

Annotated Bibliography

BIBLE RESOURCES

Coffey, Kathy. *Hidden Women of the Gospels*. New York: Crossroad, 1996. Nineteen scripture and midrash stories with discussion questions.

Jones, Alexander, ed. *The Jerusalem Bible*. Garden City, New York: Doubleday, 1966. Alternative wording to *New Revised Standard Version*. Uses "Yahweh" instead of "Lord" in translations of the Psalms.

Meeks, Wayne A., ed. *The HarperCollins Study Bible, New Revised Standard Version with the Apocryphal/Deuterocanonical Books*. New York: HarperCollins, 1993. *New Revised Standard Version* is more recent and inclusive in language than the older *Revised Standard Version*. This HarperCollins edition includes many helpful footnotes and historical context.

Metzger, Bruce M., and Roland E. Murphy, eds. *The New Oxford Annotated Bible with the Apocryphal/Deuterocanonical Books*. New York: Oxford University Press, 1991. Outstanding study Bible of the *New Revised Standard Version*.

Newsom, Carol A., and Sharon H. Ringe, eds. *The Women's Bible Commentary*. Louisville, Ky.: Westminster/John Knox Press, 1992. Women scholars comment on books in the Hebrew Bible and books in the New Testament. These writers provide new perspectives on the Bible, which has been used at times to control women and at other times to empower them.

Norris, Kathleen. *Amazing Grace: A Vocabulary of Faith*. New York: Riverhead Books, 1998. Norris writes of her personal faith journey as she redefines the vocabulary of Christianity.

CIRCLE AND CEREMONY

Arrien, Angeles. *The Four-fold Way: Walking the Paths of the Warrior, Teacher, Healer, and Visionary*. San Francisco: HarperSanFrancisco, 1993. Four archetypes, the Warrior/Leader, the Teacher, the Healer, and the Visionary give understanding and tools for living within ourselves and in the world.

Baldwin, Christina. *Calling the Circle: The First and Future Culture*. New York: Bantam Books, 1998. Baldwin's vision and guidelines for creating Circle and acknowledging spiritual energy as a guiding force.

ISSUES CONCERNING GIRLS AND WOMEN

Anderson, Sherry Ruth, and Patricia Hopkins. *The Feminine Face of God: The Unfolding of the Sacred in Women*. New York: Bantam Books, 1991. As the subtitle suggests, this book explores the variety and power of "the unfolding of the sacred in women ['s experience"].

Cunningham, Sarah, ed. *We Belong Together: Churches in Solidarity with Women*. New York: Friendship Press, 1992. A reader that serves as a checkpoint on the churches' journey to full justice for, and affirmation of, women. With study guide (see Horn-Ibler).

Duerk, Judith. *Circle of Stones: Woman's Journey to Herself*. Philadelphia: Innisfree Press, 1999.

——— *I Sit Listening to the Wind: Woman's Encounter within Herself*. San Diego: LuraMedia, 1993.

These two volumes deal with the discovery of one's own inner wisdom, and the quest for wholeness by exploring the inner masculine. We are particularly indebted to Judith Duerk for phrasing the question, "How might it have been different?"

Horn-Ibler, Barbara. *Study Guide to We Belong Together*. New York: Friendship Press, 1992. This study-guide companion to *We Belong Together* (see Cunningham) offers creative guidance and resources for a six-session course in the congregation or other setting. *Arise and Shine*, a thirty-minute video, captures the energy, struggles, and visions of women from churches across Africa, encouraging viewers to explore what women's roles mean in their own societies.

MacHaffie, Barbara J. *Her Story: Women in Christian Tradition*. Philadelphia: Fortress Press, 1986. An overview of the history of women's roles in Christian history from the Bible to recent times. A valuable, accessible resource.

Northrup, Christiane. *Women's Bodies, Women's Wisdom: Creating Physical and Emotional Health and Healing*. New York: Bantam Books, 1998. Dr. Northrup's practical, holistic-medical guide empowers women to take control of their physical and emotional health.

Pipher, Mary. *Reviving Ophelia: Saving the Selves of Adolescent Girls*. New York: Putnam, 1994. Life stories of girls derailed by today's sexual and psychological pressures, together with hopeful suggestions for helping girls find strength and direction.

Ruether, Rosemary Radford. *Women and Redemption: A Theological History*. Minneapolis: Fortress Press, 1998. Considers what Paul's assertion—"in Christ there is no male and female"—means in the Christian tradition.

Winter, Miriam Therese. *Defecting in Place: Women Claiming Responsibility for Their Own Spiritual Lives*. New York: Crossroad, 1994. Stories and ideas of women of faith, both within and outside the institutional church, describing "the growing grassroots nature of feminist spirituality."

WORSHIP, PRAYER, AND POETRY

Elkins, Heather Murray. *Worshiping Women: Reforming God's People for Praise*. Nashville, Tenn.: Abingdon Press, 1994.

Flinders, Carol Lee, ed. *A Little Book of Women Mystics*. San Francisco: HarperSanFrancisco, 1995. A tiny treasure of poetry and spiritual vision from Hildegard of Bingen, Julian of Norwich, Saint Teresa of Avila, and other early mystical writers.

Gilbert, Sandra M., Susan Gubar, and Diana O'Hehir, eds. *Mothersongs: Poems for, by, and about Mothers*. New York: W. W. Norton, 1995.

Martensen, Jean, ed. *Sing Out New Visions: Prayers, Poems, and Reflections by Women*. Minneapolis: Augsburg Fortress, 1998. An ecumenical collection of women's writing created for worship and meditation. Topics include "Birthing," "Naming," "Healing," and "Justice and Peace."

Roberts, Elizabeth, and Elias Amidon, ed. *Earth Prayers from around the World: 365 Prayers, Poems, and Invocations for Honoring the Earth*. San Francisco: HarperSanFrancisco, 1991. A collection of prayers and poems from around the world, grouped by topic: "Affirmations," "Kinship with All Life," "Dark Night of the Soul," and others.

Schug, Tricia, Mary Sellon, and Kelly Smith, eds. *Qumran Anthology*. Vol. 1. Seattle, Wash.: Pacific Northwest Conference of the United Methodist Church, 1998. A collection of writings and art created by members and friends of the Pacific Northwest Conference of the United Methodist Church.

Sewell, Marilyn, ed. *Cries of the Spirit: A Celebration of Women's Spirituality*. Boston: Beacon Press, 1991. A parish minister offers an anthology of women's words honoring female wisdom and faith. The works, largely of contemporary American poets and writers, embody earthy, relational female imagery and symbolism. The women's perspective is healing and life-giving, one, we can ill-afford to ignore.

The following books by Miriam Therese Winter, a Medical Mission Sister and professor of liturgy, worship, and spirituality at Hartford Seminary, are some of her inspiring and foundational works. These are helpful, particularly for worship and midrash:

WomanPrayer, WomanSong: Resources for Ritual. New York: Crossroad, 1993. Rituals and songs incorporating women's experience, recovering feminine biblical images of God.

WomanWisdom: A Feminist Lectionary and Psalter, Women of the Hebrew Scriptures, Part One. New York: Crossroad, 1991.

WomanWitness: A Feminist Lectionary and Psalter, Women of the Hebrew Scriptures, Part Two. New York: Crossroad, 1992.

WomanWord: A Feminist Lectionary and Psalter, Women of The New Testament. New York: Crossroad, 1995.

The Medical Mission Sisters are an international community of Catholic sisters called to be present to life in the spirit of Jesus the healer.

MYTH AND STORY

Dresser, Cynthia. *The Rainmaker's Dog: International Folktales to Build Communicative Skills*. New York: St. Martin's Press, 1994. A collection of tales from regions of Africa, Haiti, Australia, and Asia, with English skill-building questions.

Dübois, Ia, and Katherine Hanson. *ECHO: Scandinavian Stories About Girls*. Seattle: Women in Translation, 2000. Translated stories by twenty-eight authors, such as Astrid Lindgren and Sigrid Undset, marking big and small events in the lives of Scandinavian girls.

Estés, Clarissa Pinkola. *Women Who Run With the Wolves: Myths and Stories of the Wild Woman Archetype*. New York: Ballantine Books, 1992. Folktales and myths elicit discussion of what must happen for girls and women to embark on their life adventures.

Hamilton, Virginia. *Her Stories: African American Folktales, Fairy Tales, and True Tales*. New York: Blue Sky Press, 1995. Beautifully written and illustrated by Newbery and Caldecott medallists. African American stories told in a vibrant, immediate voice.

Kitson, Norma, ed. *Anthology/Zimbabwe Women Writers*. Harare, Zimbabwe: Zimbabwe Women Writers, 1994. Wonderful stories!

L'Engle, Madeleine. *The Rock that is Higher: Story as Truth*. Wheaton, Ill.: H. Shaw, 1993. L'Engle's faith is whole as she sees that story—not creeds, scholarship, or literalism—carries truth to our spirits.

Wood, Douglas. *Old Turtle*. Duluth, Minn.: Pfeifer-Hamilton, 1992. A tale, beautifully told, and equally, beautifully illustrated by Cheng-Khee Chee, about the restoration of right relationship among all of creation.

SONGBOOKS

Batastini, Robert J. and Michael A. Cymbala, eds. *Gather*. 2nd ed. Chicago: GIA Publications, 1994. A Roman Catholic publishing house collection of singable hymns and songs, most of them by living composers, including Marty Haugen. Also, Hispanic, African American songs, and meditative chants from the Taizé and Iona communities.

Blood-Patterson, Peter, ed. *Rise Up Singing: The Group-Singing Song Book* . Bethlehem, Penn.: Sing Out Corporation, 1988. The ultimate source for the words that you almost remember to camp, folk, and gospel songs. You have to know the tune though. Guitar chords provided.

Cherwien, Susan Palo. *O Blessed Spring*. Minneapolis: Augsburg Fortress, 1997. Contemporary hymns by Cherwien using inclusive language for God and humans. Beautiful words and melodies with piano accompaniment.

Haugen, Marty. *Holden Evening Prayer*. Chicago: GIA Publications, 1990. A melodic, peace-filled, sung liturgy for the closing of the day. Inclusive language. One song is based on Mary's "Magnificat" (Lk. 1:28).

Hobbs, R. Gerald, ed. *Songs for a Gospel People*. Winfield, B.C. Canada: Wood Lake Books, 1987. A supplement to the hymnbook of The United Church of Canada.

Jensen, Dick, ed. *With One Voice: A Lutheran Resource for Worship*. Minneapolis: Augsburg Fortress, 1995. This recent supplement to the decades old *Lutheran Book of Worship* contains a collection ranging from new hymns to lively old gospel songs. Overall, language is more inclusive and tunes are singable. Songs with a variety of singing styles and ethnic roots.

Makeever, Ray. *Dancing at the Harvest*. Minneapolis: Augsburg Fortress, 1995. Easy-to-learn songs about a loving God, longing for a world of peace and justice. Many can be used by a song leader in a call-and-response style of group singing.

Marks, Kate, comp. *Circle of Song: Songs, Chants, and Dances for Ritual and Celebration*. Lenox: Full Circle Press, 1993. A collection of songs, chants, and dances for ritual celebration.

Middleton, Julie Forest, ed. *Songs for Earthlings: A Green Spirituality Songbook*. Philadelphia: Emerald Earth, 1998. A collection of songs whose topics include: "The Elements, Prayers, and Praise," "Circles and Cycles of Life," "I and Thou," "Changing," and authors' biographies. A must for any song leader!

Stotd, Frank, and Lani Willis, eds. *Global Songs: Bread for the Journey: Songs of Faith, Hope, and Liberation from the Church and around the World*. Minneapolis: Augsburg Fortress, 1997. A collection of songs of faith from around the world. Songbook, tape, and compact disc.

Strathdee, Jim and Jean. *Pieces of Our Lives*. Carmichael, Calif.: Caliche Records, 1998. A collection of songs by the Strathdees and others.

The United Methodist Hymnal: Book of United Methodist Worship. Nashville, Tenn.: United Methodist Publishing House, 1989.

Witt, Tom, Mary Preus, and Bret Hesla, eds.. *Global Songs: Local Voices: Seventeen Songs of Faith and Liberation from around the World*. Minneapolis: Bread for the Journey, 1995.

GENERAL RESOURCES

Buechner, Frederick. *Peculiar Treasures: A Biblical Who's Who*. San Francisco: Harper & Row, 1979. A compendium of brief, deeply insightful, often humorous biographies of women and men of the Bible. The illustrations by Katherine A. Buechner (Buechner's daughter) add life and perspective.

Dillard, Annie. *Teaching a Stone to Talk: Expeditions and Encounters*. New York: Harper & Row, 1982. A treasured book of essays on the natural world and human experience of it. In exquisite prose, Dillard explores the mystery of nature and of faith.

*In loving memory of my Ojiisan, Motosuke Kajikawa, and with thanks
and acknowledgment to Lafcadio Hearn, who had a special gift of
getting to the kokoro (heart) of the people.*   —KK

*For Barbara McManus of Office Ink, whose constant support
fuels my work so much, and so often.*   —EY

Tsunami! is adapted from Lafcadio Hearn's story "A Living God" (*Gleanings in Buddha-Fields*, 1897).

Designed by Semadar Megged. The illustrations were rendered in gouache, pastel, and collage.

Text copyright © 2009 by Kimiko Kajikawa.
Illustrations copyright © 2009 by Ed Young.
All rights reserved. Published by Scholastic Inc., 557 Broadway, New York, NY 10012,
by arrangement with Philomel Books, a division of Penguin Young Readers Group.
Printed in the U.S.A.

ISBN-13: 978-0-545-27398-5 ISBN-10: 0-545-27398-6

4 5 6 7 8 9 10   40   19 18 17 16 15 14 13 12 11

Kimiko Kajikawa

illustrated by **Ed Young**

SCHOLASTIC INC.

New York Toronto London Auckland Sydney New Delhi Hong Kong

ong ago in Japan, there was a wise old rice farmer who lived near the sea.
The people in the village called him Ojiisan, which means "grandfather."
Even though Ojiisan was the wealthiest person in the village, he lived

a very simple life. His thatched cottage stood high on a mountain, overlooking the village and the sea. People often climbed the long zigzag road up the mountain to

One autumn day, Ojiisan's family prepared to walk down to the village to celebrate the rice harvest. To their surprise, Ojiisan did not want to go.

"Something does not feel right." Ojiisan wiped the sweat from his brow.
So he and his grandson, Tada, stayed home.
Ojiisan and Tada stood on the balcony to watch the celebration below.

Nobori banners and strings of paper lanterns decorated the houses. At the temple court, men and women in village costumes danced their thanks for the many golden rice fields waiting for harvest.

Ojiisan felt a rumbling underneath his feet. "An earthquake is coming," he said.

And presently an earthquake came—a long, slow, spongy motion. The house rocked gently several times. Then all was still.

This shock was not strong enough to frighten anyone. The people kept celebrating. But Ojiisan, who had felt hundreds of earthquakes in his time, thought this shock strange—

Ojiisan turned his keen old eyes anxiously toward the sea. It had darkened suddenly and was moving against the wind. *THE SEA WAS RUNNING AWAY FROM THE LAND!* The beach grew before Ojiisan's eyes. He had never seen anything like this, but he remembered what his grandfather had told him when he was a child. Ojiisan shivered.

Ojiisan knew he must get the villagers out of danger.
"Tada! Hurry!" he said. "Light me a torch."

Tada lit a *taimatsu* torch at once,

But Ojiisan had no time to answer. Four hundred people were in terrible danger.
He rushed to finish burning his fields.
Tada stared at the blazing rice and burst into tears.

Ojiisan's wealth was gone. Now all he could do was hope and wait.
He looked back out at the sea.
   The sun was going down, and still THE SEA WAS RUNNING
AWAY FROM THE LAND!

"HURRY! FLEE!" Ojiisan screamed to the villagers. But no one was close enough to hear him.

A priest saw the burning fields and boomed the temple bell. *KĀAN! KĀAN! KĀAN!*

Ojiisan watched the villagers hurry up from the beach, like a swarm of ants, to help put out the horrible fire.

A group of young men and women arrived first, beating the fire with their mats.

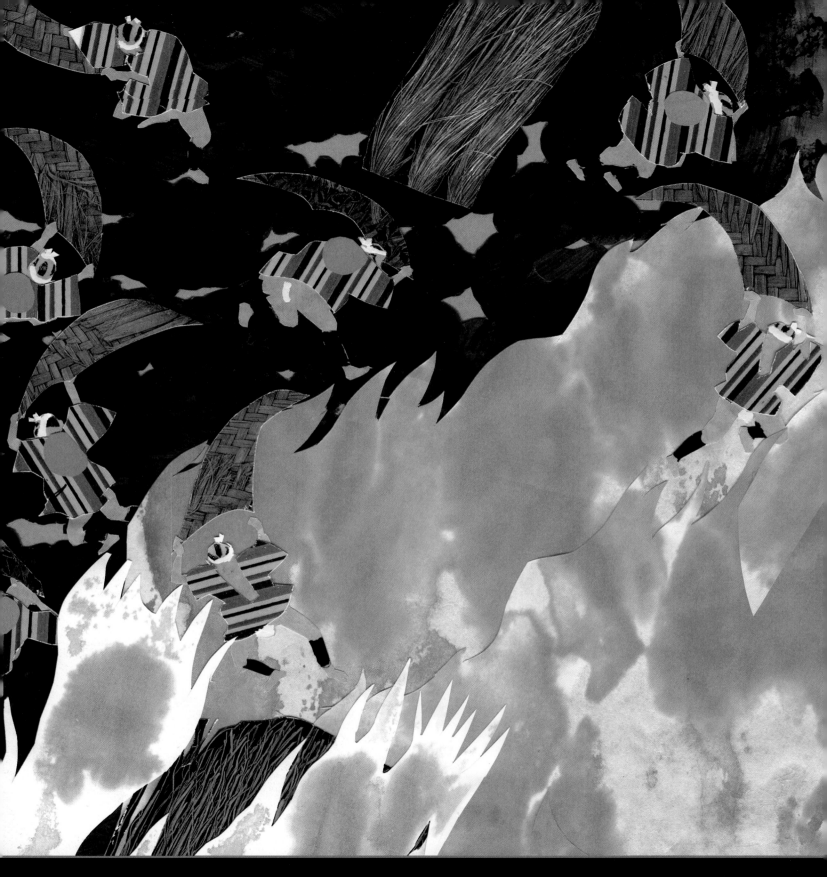

But Ojiisan held out his arms. "No! Let it burn! We need all the people here," he commanded. "There is a great danger—*taihen da*!" More young villagers arrived, followed by older adults, mothers with babies on their backs, children and, finally, elders.

All the people gazed sadly at the flaming rice fields and the still face of their Ojiisan. And the sun went down.

"I am afraid of Ojiisan!" Tada sobbed. "I saw him set fire to the rice on purpose."

"Tada tells the truth. I set fire to the rice," Ojiisan said. "Are all the villagers here?"

The people looked in wonder at one another. "All are here!" a woman cried.
"But we cannot understand. Why did you do this, Ojiisan?"
Suddenly, a thunderous BOOM shook the mountain. Then the sky ROARED.
"*Kita!*" Ojiisan shouted, pointing toward the sea.

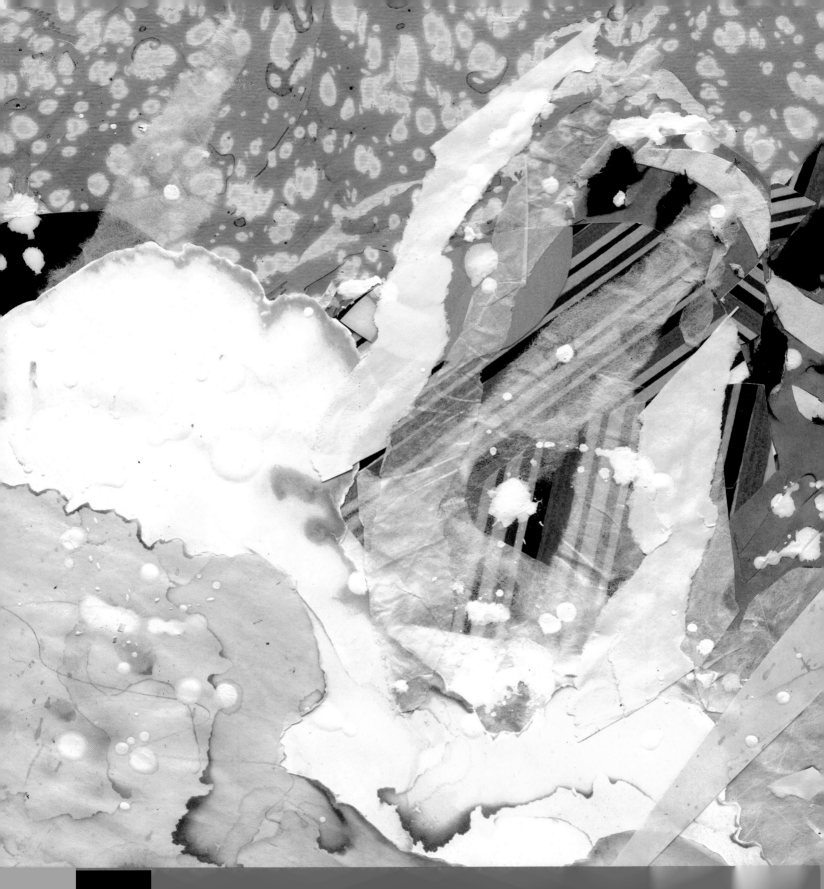

Throu
the coast.
as the sky
"TSU

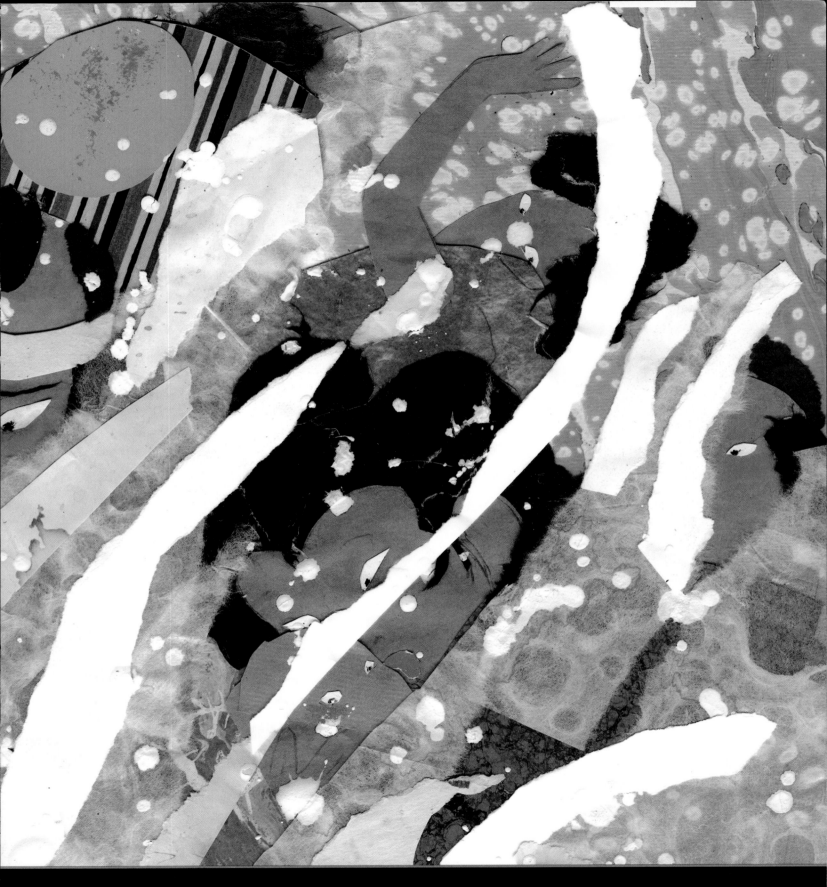

The monster wave struck with a jolt mightier than any thunder. The mountain shuddered. A storm of spray shot up the mountainside like a dark cloud.

Terrified, people ran farther up the mountain. When they looked down, they saw the angry white sea swallowing up the village.

Then the sea drew back, roaring, tearing out the land as it went.

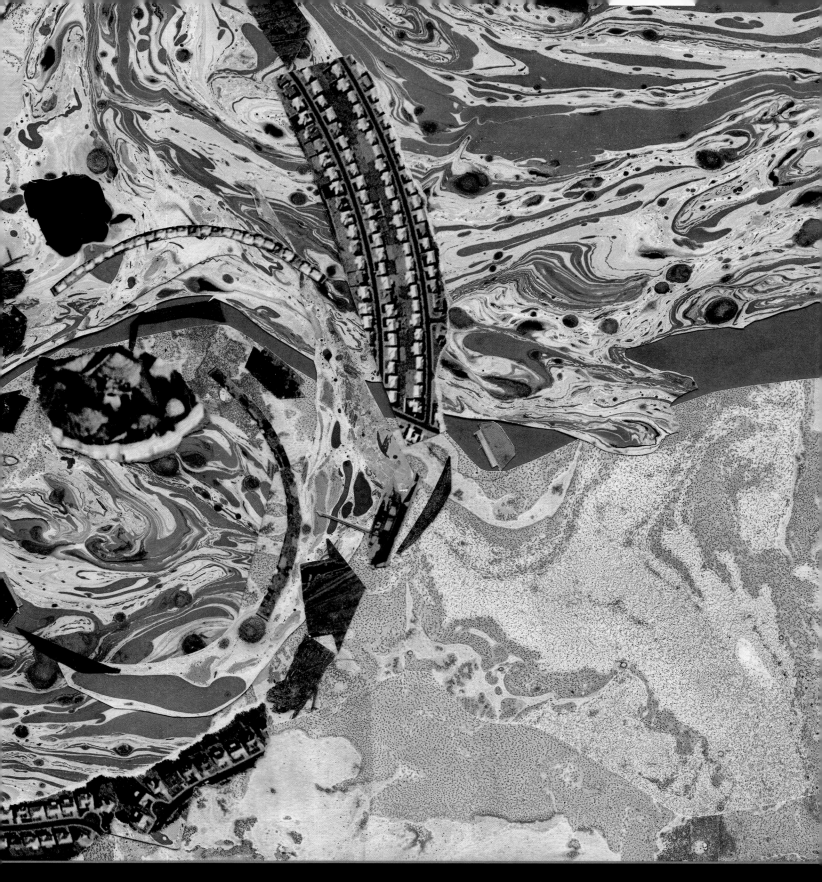

Twice, thrice, four times, the furious sea devoured the village.

Finall   n

The whole village bowed down before Ojiisan and thanked him.
Ojiisan smiled. "My house remains," he said. "And there is room for many." Then he led the way to his house.

The people never forgot their debt to Ojiisan. When better times came, they built a temple to honor him. On its front, they inscribed Ojiisan's name in gold.

One hundred years and more have passed, but Ojiisan's temple still stands. And the villagers still give thanks to the good farmer who burned his rice fields to save the people.